THE *Love* LANGUAGE OF GOD

Loving God, God's Way

JAMES "BUDDY" SHEETS

DESTINY IMAGE® PUBLISHERS, INC.

P.O. Box 310, Shippensburg, PA 17257-0310

"Speaking to the Purposes of God for This Generation and for the Generations to Come."

This book and all other Destiny Image, Revival Press, MercyPlace, Fresh Bread, Destiny Image Fiction, and Treasure House books are available at Christian bookstores and distributors worldwide.

For a U.S. bookstore nearest you, call 1-800-722-6774.

For more information on foreign distributors, call 717-532-3040.

Reach us on the Internet: www.destinyimage.com.

Trade Paper ISBN: 978-0-7684-3692-1

Hardcover ISBN: 978-0-7684-3693-8

Large Print ISBN: 978-0-7684-3694-5

E-book: ISBN: 978-0-7684-9023-7

For Worldwide Distribution, Printed in the U.S.A.

1 2 3 4 5 6 7 8 / 14 13 12 11

Dedication

With a grateful heart, I dedicate this book to my lovely wife, Kaye. Your passion for life and for our Glorious Bridegroom, Jesus, constantly amazes me, encourages me, and challenges me to press in ever deeper. I love you now and forever!

Acknowledgments

I thank Dr. Bryan Lee for modeling for me what it looks like to love God and still love His people as well—all of them.

I thank Dr. Bill Hamon, John Wimber, Mike Bickle, and countless others who gave me quality instruction over the years about how to love God with all of my heart, soul, mind, and strength.

I thank Eddie Smith for putting together his seminar on how to write. I gladly share all the accolades with you; and of course, I'll take all the criticisms as my own.

I express my appreciation to the leadership team of Atlanta South Metro House of Prayer (ASMHOP) for their endless encouragement and support while I was off in the corner slaving away at a computer keyboard. You guys are the best!

Thanks to all of the intercessors who were on their knees begging for bread from Heaven for this humble servant to have something that will bless the Bride—you truly are heroes of the faith!

I thank Virgil and Lori Simms, Linda Simmons, Bruce Lacombe, Richard and Virginia Frazier, and Scott Schade for sacrificially taking the time to read and reread the manuscript and for your highly insightful suggestions that helped make the book better than I could ever have on my own.

To Ronda Ranalli and the good folk at Destiny Image Publishers—you are an amazing group of people! Thanks for everything! I thank my lovely bride, Kaye. Thank you for not only understanding when I was off writing but for also demanding many times that I do so. No one could ever ask for a better companion, friend, and lover!

And last but not least, Jesus. Words can never convey what You mean to me. I once was lost, but now am found, was blind, but now I see. You are my hero. I want to be like You when I grow up. I love You!

Endorsements

The Love Language of God—Loving God, God's Way is the fullest treatise on the subject of love that I have ever observed. James has done a masterful job in this splendid volume of taking us on an exciting journey over the landscape of love from beginning to now amid an amazing mixture of powerful and pertinent Scriptures, great loves of literature, and personal observations. I believe this book will become a recognized resource on the subject.

Jack Taylor
Dimensions Ministries
Melbourne, FL

The first Bible verse I learned as a child was First John 4:8 (also verse 16), *"God is love."* However, memorizing and quoting the verse wasn't the same as experiencing it. My first experience of God's love was through my godly earthly father. The day my first child was born and placed in my arms, I began to understand the heavenly Father's love on a new, higher level. I too was a father. In this excellent book, my friend James identifies, examines, and expresses wondrous life-changing truths of God's love in fresh and revealing ways. Read it and be transformed!

Eddie Smith
Best-selling author and teacher

James, you have written on the favorite subject of Jesus Christ, His beloved Bride. Most Christians do not understand God's purpose for the human race. You reveal the love of God for humanity and the passionate love of Jesus for His Church. Your revelation and presentation of the Bride of Christ will enlighten and inspire the Body of Christ to be more than engaged to the Lord Jesus but to be one with Him in marriage. Being joined together with Christ Jesus makes us one spirit with Christ as husband and wife become one flesh. This makes us joint heirs with Christ to receive, be, and do all God the Father has purposed for Christ Jesus. Every Christian should read this book, for it will bring transformation to their lives. Bless you, James, for researching this truth, living and experiencing its reality, and taking the time to put it into a book for the Church to read and receive all the benefits of being the Bride of Christ.

Dr. Bill Hamon, Founder and Bishop
Christian International Ministries
Author of ten major books, including *The Eternal Church*

Jesus tells us that the marker of His disciples is their love for one another and that when we love we will automatically fulfill all the commandments and enjoy life. Paul tells us that without love nothing else matters; and John tells us that God is love. I don't know of one Bible school or seminary class on love, and I rarely hear a sermon or workshop on love at a pastors' conference. This book is needed because the love of most, both inside and outside the church, is growing cold. With an emphasis on integrity, excellence, and holiness, we left too many hearts loveless. If we as believers don't know anything about love, we'll teach our doctrine and do what the experts teach us, and wonder why those outside the church don't care about what we say and do. It could be that we're missing the point of the Gospel, which is love.

Ted Haggard, Senior Pastor
St. James Church, Colorado Springs, CO and
founding pastor of New Life Church
Colorado Springs, CO

God as a Bridegroom is one of the strongest and most consistent revelations in the Word of God. In this book, James takes us on a journey through the Old Testament and into the New, shedding light on this glorious face of God. When the Church awakens to the understanding that He is a passionate, fiery, and compassionate Bridegroom, our hearts will come out of complacency and respond in like manner. I know from experience that when God was revealed as a Bridegroom to me, the Word of God, and my whole Christian life for that matter, was dramatically changed. This book has the potential of doing the same for you.

Corey Russell, Senior Leadership Team
International House of Prayer, Kansas City

The truths found in this book will transform your Christian life. With the turn of each page, I grew more and more captivated by the profound revelations found here. What a wonderful, life-changing book!

Rhonda Calhoun
International Speaker and Author
Cofounder of Harvest Home

What a fantastic book! There is nothing more important in Heaven or on earth than to love God the way He wants to be loved. We must keep the first commandment as the central motivation of our hearts so that all we do in life is done primarily to "keep this commandment." Sadly, there are reams of material on how to do many things in the Kingdom, but comparatively little that focuses exclusively on this core objective of all of Scripture. How thankful I am that James has written this book to provoke us back to our first love.

Stacey Campbell
www.revivalnow.com
www.beahero.org

In his book, *The Love Language of God—Loving God, God's Way*, James unveils unique aspects of the Lord's love that are bound to create fresh passion for Jesus in the heart of the reader. Using bridal language that is woven throughout Scripture, James takes you on a journey into the Lord's heart and paints a portrait of the fiery affections the Bridegroom King has for His Bride. You will be fascinated and intrigued by the truths found in this book. I highly recommend it.

S.J. Hill
Bible teacher and author
of four books, including *Enjoying God*

A brilliant exposition of what loving God means. James takes you on a powerful journey that will expand your understanding of the affections of God, uncover your real identity, and reveal your eternal destiny.

Pablo Pérez
Publisher, *Spiritual Fuel*
Founder, Encounter God University

James has an amazing faith to press into God. He has wonderful insight into the moves of God throughout Church history and recently. His passion is for the Church to move into intimacy with God. Join him on the journey.

Kirk Bennett, Vice President
Justice Division IHOP-KC and
Director, 7Thunders.org

The Love Language of God—Loving God, God's Way is not only a book for our time but also a read for all times. In a day when the judgment of God is a major focus, it is refreshing to hear about a love relationship between God and humanity. James Sheets communicates with unbridled passion the desire of God and the responsibility of man. It is a love story unparalleled not only in history, but in all of eternity! I commend this writing highly as you set out to enjoy God and bring pleasure to His heart.

Randall E. Howard
Senior Leader, The Gate Church and
President, Gateway Strategies International

In a world that perceives the church as unloving, judgmental, and irrelevant, *The Love Language of God— Loving God, God's Way* challenges each of us to reach beyond religious stereotypes of what loving God is all about into the fullness of the Father's heart—for our lives, our churches, and our generation.

Matt Tommey
The Worship Studio
http://www.theworshipstudio.org

The Love Language of God—Loving God, God's Way gives each of us a challenging look into what it means biblically to love the Lord with all our heart, soul, strength, and mind. James challenges our "easygoing" love for the Lord and sets a higher standard, yet assures us that this kind of love for God is exactly what God has desired for us all along. This book will take you to new places in your love relationship with God through Jesus Christ. It is a reminder of the importance of the first and greatest commandment.

Rev. Steve Loopstra
Senior Community Consultant
Journey to Transformation, The Sentinel Group

As James's friend and pastor for many years, I know this book to be his heart. *Passion for Jesus* is not only the name of his ministry but it is James's life. The book is a theological expression of intimacy and a practical guide for those serious about entering into the intimate realities of God. Many people talk about loving God but don't know how to enter into intimacy. You "need" to read this book.

Eddie Mason, Senior Pastor
Southside Christian Fellowship

I have spent the last six hours immersed in *The Love Language of God—Loving God, God's Way*. James is a biblical scholar with powerful things to say to the Body of Christ about what it means to truly love God. I really appreciate his insights and love for Jesus. He makes people hungry for Jesus! I definitely recommend *The Love Language of God,* and I pray that the Body of Christ receives the blessing James intends for us in this book.

Melinda Fish
Internationally known teacher, author,
and editor of *Spread the Fire* magazine

The greatest thing in life is to love the Lord your God with all your heart and to turn around and exhibit that covenant grace to others. In fact, there is a new breed of bridal warriors arising in this hour who do exactly that. James Sheets, based out of the Atlanta South Metro House of Prayer, is one of those lovesick warriors God has His hand upon in this generation. Way to go, James! You have given a jewel to the Body of Christ to help us keep the main thing the main thing!

James W. Goll
Encounters Network
Author, *The Seer, Dream Language,* and many more

Table of Contents

Foreword

There is going to be a wedding! I have been preaching on the Bride of Christ for over 20 years, and I have discovered that the message of the Bride of Christ opens the human heart to experience the deepest place of intimacy with the heart of God.

> *...Eye has not seen, nor ear heard, nor have entered into the heart of man the things which God has prepared for those who love Him. But God has revealed them to us through His Spirit. For the Spirit searches all things, yes, the **deep things** of God* (1 Corinthians 2:9-10 NKJV).

The Holy Spirit desires to reveal these "deep things" to us. This reality about God's heart is beyond anything that we have ever imagined. The fullness of this has never entered the human heart. This is the way to live a fascinated life as a lovesick worshiper. Intimacy with God is not just an option—it is the very essence of true Christianity.

God has declared that He will change the understanding and expression of Christianity in one generation. There are a growing number of people throughout the Body of Christ worldwide, myself included, who believe that we are in the beginning of the beginning of that season now. Jesus' leadership over the Church is perfect. He in His wisdom knows how to best motivate His people to love Him with all of their heart, soul, mind, and strength. In Jeremiah 3:14, the Lord says, *"Return, O backsliding children, for I am married to you"* (NKJV). The bridal paradigm (or perspective) of the Kingdom of God is the highest and most effective motivator for calling God's people to position themselves in a life of abandonment to Him. The power of the bridal identity is a very powerful revelation in Scripture. This is not to negate other types of biblical motivation, for they are all valid and necessary, but to be motivated by love is the most superior motivation. This end-time emphasis of the Holy Spirit will be a very significant impulse toward transforming the Body of Christ in the final hours of natural history as the Lord raises up a Bride with a heart after God's.

God has reserved this revelation—the "best wine"—for the generation in which His Son returns. Though statements like, "I am married to you," were rare in the Old Testament, they were powerful and they set the stage for the proper understanding of God's end-time purposes as described by other prophetic passages. Hosea and Isaiah spoke about it, but still God was only giving them whispers. There have been hints of it here and there throughout church history. However, never in history has the whole Body of Christ fully understood and walked out the revelation that they are Jesus' cherished Bride.

But in the generation in which the Lord returns, the Holy Spirit will universally emphasize this revelation with great power, clarity, and intensity. The knowledge that Jesus is a Bridegroom filled with desire for His people and we are His cherished Bride will crescendo and become a worldwide cry in the Church as we move toward the moment when the Spirit and the Bride together will cry, "Come, Lord Jesus!"

As this prophetic message seizes the hearts of the hearers, the Body of Christ will change dramatically in the way it approaches God with a deep confidence based on His love. Church life, relationships, ministries, and outreaches will look different.

One of the greatest truths about our eternal destiny is that God has ordained that He will share His heart with human beings. This bridal identity, this privileged position of intimate nearness to God's heart, far surpasses positions given to the angelic order. Our position is one of unimaginable spiritual privilege. The heavenly hosts stand as servants at a distance from encountering the heart of God as compared to the Bride of Christ. Yet Jesus Himself beckons weak human beings to draw near to His heart. He freely gives to His Church what He has never offered to angels.

What does it mean to be married to the Lord? We must begin by recognizing that He is a passionate Bridegroom King. That leads us to understand that we are His prized Bride. Our spiritual identity flows out of this revelation. We cannot understand ourselves as a cherished Bride until we know what the heart of our Bridegroom King is like. If we perceive God as mostly angry or mostly sad, how can we enter into our identity? We'll have a distorted picture of ourselves as we stand before Him.

John the Baptist, the man Jesus identified as the greatest man who ever lived, grasped this reality of the Bride and Bridegroom. As Buddy points out in this book, when asked, "Who are you and what are you about?" John answered by declaring who he was in light of the Bridegroom God.

He who has the bride is the bridegroom; but the friend of the bridegroom who stands and hears him, rejoices greatly because of the bridegroom's voice. Therefore this joy of mine is fulfilled (John 3:29 NKJV).

John had discovered who he was! The secret to who we are lies in the heart of the Man we stand before. He is the Bridegroom God. Only by gazing in His eyes and understanding who He is will you know who you are.

Like John the Baptist, the greatest need in the Body of Christ is to discover who Jesus is as a Bridegroom and to feed our spirits on what His personality is like. When that knowledge begins to come alive in your mind and spirit, you will inevitably discover His affections, His desires, and His tender dealings with you in your weaknesses. You will see that you are indeed a cherished Bride. The real you will emerge and blossom in light of who He is.

I met Buddy 14 years ago at a Passion for Jesus conference in Atlanta. He spent a season in Kansas City in 2002. Buddy is a lover of God and a student of God's emotions. This book was written to help you position yourself before God as the Bride of Christ, that you may be more equipped to experience a deeper connection with His heart. *The Love Language of God—Loving God, God's Way* will challenge and inspire you!

Mike Bickle
International House of Prayer of Kansas City
www.IHOP.org

Introduction

"Preacher, I want you to marry us." I have heard that phrase many times over the years. Performing marriages is one of the common services people think of when they discover you are a minister; it sort of goes along with the territory. It truly is a joy and a privilege to be part of joining two lives into one. However, sometimes, you just have to say no.

While fully being committed to the institution of marriage, I have learned not to jump at every opportunity to perform a marriage when asked to do so. The longer I live, and the longer I serve those whom the Lord has granted me the privilege to do so, the more I have come to realize that while marriage is good, now is not always the time.

There is more involved in the making of a successful marriage than just "getting hitched," as my dad used to say. There is also the little issue of being adequately prepared to "stay hitched," and in today's socio-political environment, that is often much easier said than done.

My wife, Kaye, and I have many opportunities to counsel couples concerning many of life's dynamics, marital issues being one of them. One of the issues that often arises in discussions with couples is the issue of spiritual compatibility, or what the Bible refers to as "being equally yoked."[1]

The apostle Paul emphatically states the necessity for followers of Jesus not to be in close friendships or intimate relationships with people who do not share their commitment and love for Jesus

Christ. This is especially pertinent for Christians considering marriage, which is the deepest natural relationship.

You must understand that this is not a legalistic, "religious" law; it is just plain common sense. If you are going to spend the rest of your earthly existence with someone, it had better be someone who shares your core spiritual ideals. If you are a follower of Christ, and are single contemplating marriage, possibly the most important question you should be asking is, "Is the person I am thinking about spending the rest of my life with deeply seated in his or her commitment to Jesus?" You do not want to be unequally yoked with an unbeliever.

What does it mean to be unequally yoked? The illustration is one of two oxen "yoked" together at the neck by a wooden harness so they can pull a plow. Both of them have been trained to respond to the same commands in the same manner, at the same moment, so when they are joined together, they are a team.

May I share something with you? This might come as a surprise to you, but Jesus has never asked any of His followers to do something that He would not do, or has not already done Himself! How does that relate to our discussion? Jesus, though He is fully God, is also fully human. Sometimes we forget that part. He does not require of us, in our humanity, anything that He, in His humanity, has not already done. What is good for the goose *is* good for the gander. He can only ask us to be yoked with someone of like character, interest, and goals because that is what He does.

There are several analogies used in the Scriptures when describing the relationship between God and His covenant people: the family of God, the children of God, the army of God, the Body of Christ, and one of the least known and understood by many, the Bride of Christ.

The apostle Paul, under the inspiration of the Holy Spirit, or as I like to say, the Holy Spirit speaking through the apostle Paul, makes an astounding statement while discussing the marital responsibilities of a man and wife. The Holy Spirit instructs wives to submit to their husbands.[2] He then commands husbands to love and cherish their wives.[3] As Paul closes his discourse on the relational dynamics in a marriage, the Holy Spirit has the apostle make the most astounding statement. Paul declares that the mystery concerning marriage is profound because while what he has said relates to marriage, he was mainly talking about the relationship between Christ and the Church.[4]

Track with me here. Paul has laid down this detailed discourse on how to have a successful marriage, and then he ends it by saying that he hasn't been primarily talking about an earthly marriage between a man and a woman (though it certainly applies in that arena), but he was actually instructing us as believers on how to have a successful marriage relationship with Christ! Wow!

In theological circles, this is the foundation of what has been commonly called the bridal paradigm (paradigm simply means perspective) of the Kingdom of God. While every illustrative paradigm of the Kingdom is both important and profitable, the bridal paradigm is the closest to the heart of God. We will look at why that is in more detail later.

In these volatile times that we live in, it is imperative that we study to know how to have a successful marriage relationship with our earthly spouse. It is no longer a given that marriages will last. That would explain why when I did a Google search for books on how to have a successful marriage, it returned 78,200,000 listings. If you want a marriage relationship to last, you have to work at it.

However, as important as being knowledgeable on the dynamics necessary to have a successful natural relationship is, how much more important do you think it is that we study to know how to have a successful "marriage" relationship with our Savior and Bridegroom King! Just as in the natural marriage context, it is not a given that you can have a good relationship with the Lord without working at it.

This is not just a good idea, it is a necessity. I am convinced of that. Because I am convinced—that is the reason I am writing this book.

CHAPTER I

Do We Love God?

MY SICKNESS

I went to my doctor to try and see
if he possibly could prescribe for me
A potion or lotion or even a pill
that would improve or cure,
or alleviate my ills
The doctor sad, "Hi," and "How do you do,
(and at $40.00 a shot) what can I do for you?"
I said, "Doc, these are my symptoms,
I'll tell them to you,
I think that maybe I've contracted the flu.
My palms are sweaty, my pulse it'll race,
All the blood will suddenly rush to my face.
My temperature rises, my head starts to swim,
My knees get weak, my vision it dims.
My pupils dilate, my throat'll contract
My chest starts to heave and I lose all track
Of time or when or where I will be
And there's only one thing that I clearly can see.
It seems funny to me that these 'symptoms'
occur day or night
But only whenever 'she' enters my sight!

And all of these problems they don't make me sigh,
Ah..., contraire, Doc, they make me quite high!"
The doctor smiled and said,
"Friend, I can't help you I'm sorry to say,"
(Though he was still more than glad to take my
money away!)
"You have no disease that I've ever heard of,
To put it more simply, God's blessed you with love!"[1]

Does that poem remind you of your first love? Do you recall how you felt, how you acted, when you first "fell in love"?
I fondly recall how I felt when I first realized that I had fallen in
love with Kaye, who is now my wife. Everything changed. When I
awoke in the morning, she was my first thought. As I prepared to
meet the day, my thoughts frequently returned to her. Whatever
my duties or activities throughout the day, she was never far from
my thoughts. When planning my evenings, I always was thinking
how to include her.

Most everyone has had a time like that in his life when he
was "in love." Whether we were young or not so young, whether we ended up spending our lives with that special person or
we just remember back when, we never forget our first love, do
we? Wherever we go, whatever we do, we always remember
that first love. We always compare all other loves to that love,
don't we?

For those of us who are Christians, this same kind of devotion should be applicable to our love for God. For instance, do
you recall, when you first came to the Lord, how the grass was
greener and somehow the sky was a deeper shade of blue? Do you
remember when you thought about Jesus how giddy you would
become? Am I the only one who, when someone would just mention His name—Jesus—would melt inside?

In my early days of walking with Jesus, I would sneak away
to spend more time reading my Bible or to get in a little more

prayer time. And it was legal! Like the old Mary Hopkins song says, "Those were the days, my friend, we thought they'd never end..."[2]

A REVELATION FROM REVELATION

In the Book of Revelation, Jesus sent a message through the apostle John to the church at Ephesus. The city of Ephesus at one time was the revival epicenter, the "hotspot" for Holy Spirit activity. At the time John was delivering this message to the Ephesians, those days were long gone. All the people had settled down into the day-to-day activities of just doing what they do. While there is something to be said for consistency, in this particular instance, that is not necessarily a good thing.

First, Jesus acknowledges several positive dynamics concerning the Ephesian church. He says, *"I know your works, your toil and your patient endurance, and how you cannot bear with those who are evil, but have tested those who call themselves apostles and are not, and found them to be false. I know you are enduring patiently and bearing up for My name's sake, and you have not grown weary."*[3]

That is not all He has to say to the Ephesian believers, however. He goes on to say, *"But I have this against you, that you have abandoned the love you had at first. Remember therefore from where you have fallen; repent, and do the works you did at first. If not, I will come to you and remove your lamp stand from its place, unless you repent."*[4]

Jesus said, in essence, "All the positive activities that you have done in the past, and are still doing today, while good and admirable, aren't the things I am most interested in. I am more concerned about what is in your heart. I am more concerned about how you feel about Me than I am about what you do for Me. In all of your busyness and flurry of spiritual activities, your heart does not beat faster at the mention of My name like it used to.

When you think about Me, the things I have done, or am doing in your life, or in the life of those around you, you do not get the 'Holy Ghost goose bumps' like you used to do. And you know what? That's not OK with Me! That really needs to change."

Wow! If that doesn't stir your soup, then your spoon has fallen out of your bowl!

Jesus is saying to the church at Ephesus, and to the Church in the 21st century as well, that it is possible to be involved in even "supposedly" spiritual activity; to be consumed with doing "churchianity," involved in many various ministry opportunities to others, but if we aren't living with a burning heart, then the relationship we profess to have, and may even have the reputation of having in other people's estimations, is actually rejected by Jesus. Man!

Is It True Love?

Is it possible, that while we would say that we love Jesus, and that love for Him is what drives all the activities that keep us so busy and that we are so proud of, that Jesus might be discerning the motives of our hearts and saying, "What *you* call loving Me and what *I* call loving Me are two very different things altogether." Here is where we all either say a big amen or a hearty oh my!

So the bottom-line question is this, do we love God? Better yet, do we love God in the way that He desires and would approve of? Hard questions, I know. But these are the questions that we have to wrestle with if we really want to stand before Him on that day and hear the words, *"Well done, good and faithful servant."*[5] Before we can even begin to answer those questions, we first have to ask ourselves a couple of other questions. Like exactly what does God mean when He says that we should "love God"?

Three times in the Scriptures, we are told that no one seeks after God,[6] twice in the Psalms and once in the Book of Romans. If under both the Old and New Covenants, the Holy Spirit states that no one naturally seeks after God, then we must ask ourselves the question: do we love Him? As Saint Bernard of Clairvaux pointed out, it takes God to love God![7]

There is a foundational truth of the Kingdom of God that applies here: we can only love God in the way that we see that He loves us.[8] Of course, as Christians, we say it is a settled fact that God loves us.[9] Isn't that true? Good answer, but unfortunately it answers the wrong question. You see, the issue is not whether He loves us, but rather, what is the nature of His love for us? The Scriptures give us several insights into the various aspects of God's love. Let's look at a couple of them.

GOD ENJOYS HIS PEOPLE

The Scriptures are clear that God loves the world[10] and that He loves the saints.[11] However, is the love that He has for His people the same type of love He has for the world? Have you ever considered the fact that while God *loves* the world, He does not *enjoy* the world—He does not experience pleasure in His relationship with them while they are in their present state? He desires to see them come to salvation, but they are not His children—they are the sons of disobedience.[12] Believers, on the other hand, are called His beloved.[13]

God loves His children, but not in the same fashion He loves unbelievers. You see, God enjoys—receives pleasure in—His people. He actually likes us! Therefore, in what way does God relate, love, enjoy those who have said yes to His love and His Son?

As the beloved of God, we are depicted in the Word of God by various descriptive names: the Body of Christ, the children of God, the temple of God, the army of God, the people of God, the nation of God, etc. Each name illustrates important aspects of our relationship to the Lord. However, the description that possibly reveals the deepest and highest relationship of all is the Bride of Christ.

In Isaiah chapter 62, the prophet is prophesying the nearness of Zion's deliverance. In the midst of his prophecy, Holy Spirit has

Isaiah delve into the heart of God so that we can catch a glimpse of how God relates to us as His covenant people. Isaiah says, under the inspiration of the Holy Spirit, *"You shall no more be termed Forsaken, and your land shall no more be termed Desolate, but you shall be called My Delight Is in Her, and your land Married; for the Lord delights in you, and your land shall be married."*[14] Let's look at this a little more in depth, shall we?

God delights in, or enjoys, His people. Because this represents the heart of God, it is in the Word of God as a bona fide, legitimate, God-given revelation. Yet, to many this is still a new revelation, something they have never heard or thought of before. However, this revelation that God enjoys us is not unique, for the entirety of Scripture declares the fact that God enjoys His people.

WHAT MANNER OF LOVE IS THIS?

The fact that God loves His people is nothing new, but what Isaiah says next is unique. In fact, it is the only time in the entirety of divine revelation that this fact is so clearly stated. For while it is true that the whole of the counsel of God proclaims the fact that God loves us, what Isaiah says next is the only time in all of the Scriptures that declares the *nature* of that enjoyment.

Isaiah says, *"For as a young man marries a young woman, so shall your sons marry you, and as the Bridegroom rejoices over the Bride, so shall your God rejoice over you."*[15] Isaiah informs us not only that God delights in us, or enjoys us, but he also goes on to tell us the core nature of that enjoyment. Are you ready? Isaiah says that God rejoices over His people as, or in the same manner, a bridegroom rejoices over his bride.

To many believers, the concept of God delighting in, or enjoying, them is a far enough stretch in itself. But nothing compared to the concept that God actually delights in, or relates to us, as a bridegroom does to a bride. What does that look like?

When I was growing up, one of my heroes was George Washington Carver. Carver was one of America's greatest agriculturists and scientists, and he was the pioneer of the modern synthetics industry which revolutionized life in this country and around the world. One day an aged Carver was sharing with a group of students the story of his single most crucial undertaking—unlocking the mysteries of the peanut.

He told the students that he had asked God, "Oh, Mr. Creator, why did You make this universe?" "Then," he told the students who were listening intently, "the Creator answered me. 'You want to know too much for that little mind of yours.' He said, 'Ask Me something more your size.' So I said, 'Dear Mr. Creator, tell me what man was made for.' Again, He spoke to me, and He said, 'Little man, you are still asking for more than you can handle.' Cut down the extent of your request and improve the intent.' And then I asked my last question. 'Mr. Creator, why did You make the peanut?' 'That's better!' the Lord said, and He gave me a handful of peanuts and went with me back to the laboratory and together, we got down to work."[16]

WE NEED TO SET OUR MINDS

We, like George Washington Carver, when trying to wrap our minds around the deeper spiritual truths, sometimes would find it more profitable to start off by looking at the simpler natural things first. The apostle Paul said it this way: *It is not the spiritual that is first but the natural, and then the spiritual.*[17] As we examine commonly understood natural things, the Holy Spirit uses those natural things to reveal God's deeper spiritual truths to us.

In order for us to grasp what it looks like for God to relate to His people "as a bridegroom does to a bride," we might find it helpful to spend a few moments looking at how the Word of God says that natural bridegrooms should relate to their brides.

He who loves his wife loves himself.[18]

29

An excellent wife who can find? She is far more precious than jewels.[19]

Husbands, love your wives, as Christ loved the Church and gave Himself up for her, that He might sanctify her, having cleansed her by the washing of water with the Word, so that He might present the Church to Himself in splendor, without spot or wrinkle or any such thing, that she might be holy and without blemish. In the same way husbands should love their wives as their own bodies. He who loves his wife loves himself. For no one ever hated his own flesh, but nourishes and cherishes it, just as Christ does the Church, because we are members of His body.[20]

AS CHRIST LOVED THE CHURCH

How should husbands love their wives? In the same way that Christ loved His Church. That statement begs that we ask the question: how did Christ love the Church? "He gave Himself up for her." Why did He do that? "That He might sanctify and cleanse her." Why did He want to sanctify and cleanse her? "That He might present Her in splendor to Himself"!

Do you see it now? *"For the joy that was set before Him [He] endured the cross."[21]* What was the joy that was set before Him that was powerful enough to enable Jesus to endure the agony of the Cross? It was the joy of marriage to His Bride, the Church. That's you and me! It is like the words to the old Southern Gospel song, "When He was on the Cross (I was on His mind)"![22]

Beloved, Jesus was not desirous of having a worldly or unholy wife. Therefore, He was willing to endure the agonies of the Cross in order to "sanctify and cleanse" His betrothed so He could present her to Himself a Bride "in splendor." While He did it for His enjoyment first, it was for our benefit as well.

As the Church, isn't that our desire as well? Don't we all seek to be cleansed and sanctified, so that we can be presented to Christ as a glorious Bride? Therefore, Christ pursued not only our good, but also His own satisfaction, He just did not seek it selfishly, and He sought it by giving us—His Bride—our greatest desire! Isn't that the definition of true love: our joy is giving the one we love the things that bring him or her joy?

Let us look at something else Paul said, or as I like to say, what Holy Spirit said through the apostle Paul: *"For no one ever hated his own flesh, but nourishes and cherishes it, just as Christ does the Church, because we are members of His Body."*[23]

SANCTIFIED SELFISHNESS

In other words, the spiritual union between Christ and His Bride is so close (that "one flesh" thing) that the good and profitable things He does for Her (us) is, in His mind, a good and profitable thing done for Himself. Why? Because Christ is the eternal Bridegroom, desiring a holy and committed Bride. Therefore, He nourishes, cherishes, sanctifies, and cleanses His Bride, so that by giving her the deepest desire of her heart, He also gets the deepest desire of His heart. Wow!

Many psychologists and psychiatrists reject this train of thought based on the belief that love, in order to be "true" love, must be free of any self-interest. Even many "Christian" counselors prescribe with that philosophy. To be honest with you, for most of my Christian life, I espoused that point of view myself. As a counselor, I would question anyone who held a view of love that was devoted solely to what he desired as its main basis.

We cannot escape the fact that God the Spirit plainly states that what Christ has done, and is still doing, for His Bride is defined in the heart of God as the proper demonstration of love: *"Husbands, love your wives, as Christ loved the Church...."*

God's design is for us to pursue love in the pursuit of the joy of those we love. Contrary to the in-vogue philosophies that abound, we do not have to exclude self-interest from our pursuit of love because self-interest is not the same as selfishness. Selfishness seeks its happiness at the expense of others and to the exclusion of the other's desires, needs, and best interests. Godly love seeks its happiness in the happiness of one's beloved. In fact, the biblical lover will gladly suffer and, if need be, die for the one who is loved if in that suffering you are assured that the one you love will reap the benefit of life and purity.

EVERYONE DESIRES TO BE HAPPY

No one "hates his own flesh," if by that it is meant that one pursues what he is sure will only produce personal misery.

> All men seek happiness. This is without exception. Whatever different means they employ, they all tend to this end. The cause of some going to war, and of others avoiding it, is the same desire in both, attended with different views. The will never takes the least step but to this object. This is the motive of every action of every man, even of those who hang themselves.[24]

For a husband to fulfill his God-given responsibility, he must love his wife the way Christ loved the Church. That means he must find his own joy by doing what is best for his wife. In the same manner, husbands should love their wives as their own bodies. He who loves his wife actually loves himself.[25]

The apostle Paul paraphrases a quote from Jesus who was quoting Leviticus 19:18, *"You shall love your neighbor as yourself."*[26] The popular misconception is this teaches us to "esteem" ourselves so that we can love others. That is not what this command means. Jesus never commands us to love ourselves; rather, He just assumes that we do, and we will. He should know, for after all, He created us. What Jesus is saying is, "In the same manner that you love yourself, love others."

Paul then takes this truth as it applies to natural, physical marriage and uses it to illustrate Christ's relationship to His Bride. He sees it as an illustration of how husbands and wives become "one flesh." Husbands should love their wives as their own bodies for he who loves his wife loves himself. Husbands should devote the same energy in making their wives happy as they would naturally give to making themselves happy. The result? They will be happy, for he who loves his wife loves himself.

Remember, we are looking at how a bridegroom relates to his bride. Paul is showing us what love looks like between a husband and wife. Then he quotes Genesis 2:24, *"Therefore a man shall leave his father and his mother and hold fast to his wife, and they shall become one flesh."*[27] Then he adds a statement that is not in the Genesis account. *"This mystery is profound, and I am saying that it refers to Christ and the church."*[28] Why is Paul calling Genesis 2:24 a "profound mystery"?

To answer that question, we will have to go back to the Old Testament context and see more clearly what Genesis 2:24 meant.

CHAPTER 2

The Genesis Context

THE OLD TESTAMENT CONTEXT

In the Genesis account of creation, God spoke and created the world out of nothing.[1] Seven times God spoke,[2] resulting in the creation of light, the second heaven (the atmosphere around the earth); dry land; vegetation; the sun, moon, and stars; the birds and fish; and the animal kingdom.

After having spoken all the wonders of creation into existence, God breaks His creative pattern. For then we read, *"then the Lord God formed the man of dust from the ground and breathed into his nostrils the breath of life, and the man became a living creature."*[3] Notice, God did not speak man into existence, as He did with everything else so far; instead, He lovingly formed him with His hand and then breathed part of Himself into man, causing him to be a living soul.

You know, I had always heard it taught that after God formed man and breathed into him the breath of life, He placed man in the Garden of Eden. That is not what the Scripture says. What it says is, *"And the Lord God planted a garden in Eden, in the east, and there He put the man whom He had formed."*[4] After His crowning act of creation—man—God then took the time to plant a special place to be the home of His special creation. Whoa! Think of that. What must that "special garden" have looked like?

ADAM'S OCCUPATION

The Lord then placed man in the garden alone and commissioned him to *"work it and keep it."*[5] Have you ever stopped to think about what this commission entailed? What does it look like to work and keep a garden that has no weeds? Remember, weeds did not come until after man had sinned. And he didn't have to water the garden, for the Scripture says, *"a mist was going up from the land and was watering the whole face of the ground."*[6] No weeds, and the garden did not need to be watered. I wouldn't mind having a gardening job like that, would you?

Many commentators state that God created the garden so that man would have a job to do, a task to perform ("Adam, go move that rock…"). They have missed an important aspect of what is actually occurring here. The Scripture describes the garden this way: *"And out of the ground the Lord God made to spring up every tree that is pleasant to the sight and good for food. The tree of life was in the midst of the garden and the tree of the knowledge of good and evil."*[7]

God spoke all of creation into existence, but He personally hand-planted this "special" garden as a delight for man—with trees that were *"pleasant to the sight and good for food."* Beloved, this was not a job; God planned this garden to be a place of daily encounter for Himself and His man!

Let us read on: *"The Lord God took the man and put him in the Garden of Eden to work it and keep it. The Lord God commanded the man, saying, 'You may surely eat of every tree of the garden, but of the tree of the knowledge of good and evil you shall not eat, for in the day that you eat of it you shall surely die.'"*[8]

The Garden became the place of pleasure for man, the "secret place" of encounter and spiritual delight, where his heart was refreshed and where love was exchanged in the cool of the shade. Man's primary task wasn't to tend the garden by the sweat of his brow—man wasn't even capable of sweating until after the fall.[9] Gardening was not man's occupation—his job description was to tend the place of spiritual pleasure, the place of divine encounter. Spiritual delight was, and is, humanity's main calling and occupation. Adam was to nurture the place of encounter in order to feed the place of passion and to aid its seasons of beauty.

In the garden of encounter, Adam enjoyed freedom and God offered him the joy of obedience. The cultivation of this garden of delight was a voluntary enterprise—an act of love. Man's free will was accompanied by "safe" boundaries for the enjoyment of beauty. That was why the Lord said, *"Of the tree of the knowledge of good and evil you shall not eat."*[10]

The foundational "occupation" of man was to nurture the place of encounter with His Creator—and it still is. The means of this nurturing was to come through the cultivation of inner beauty through an encounter with life, with the living God who is life.[11]

What About the Trees?

God did not desire that Adam's communion with Himself be limited to the boundaries of human wisdom. Why not? Because *"it is written, 'What no eye has seen, nor ear heard, nor the heart of man imagined, what God has prepared for those who love him.'"*[12] As the Image-bearer of God, Adam's life was to be wrapped up in God's life.[13] God never intended humanity to function outside of the context of a life of intimate communion with His Creator.

Knowledge of spiritual principles, rules, and laws will never be able to sustain the inner life requirements of humanity. Head knowledge outside of intimate heart communion with God will always lead to independence and self-exertion. Man was made for God to reflect God in. The two trees in Eden presented man a choice, a love test: what would man choose to be the source of his life?

THE CULTIVATION OF LONGING

Then the Lord God said, "It is not good that the man should be alone; I will make him a helper fit for him." Now out of the ground the Lord God had formed every beast of the field and every bird of the heavens and brought them to the man to see what he would call them. Whatever the man called every living creature that was its name. The man gave names to all livestock and to the birds of the heavens and to every beast of the field. However, for Adam there was not found a helper fit for him.[14]

From the beginning, before the foundations of the world, God desired a companion for Adam. Why? Because the first Adam was a prophetic foreshadowing of the last Adam who was to come. God's plan was to use Adam's loneliness or his desire for a like-companion, to birth and cultivate something God-like in the heart of Adam. Remember, this longing, this ache, was in Adam's heart before the fall, before sin. Do you see it? God created a longing in Adam's heart and then set him up to endure a rigorous process of recognizing the something he lacked.

Loneliness became the birthplace for a righteous longing and a God-like desire. Aloneness presupposes desire and longing. Without the longing for something else, loneliness is impossible. While Adam occupied himself with the task of naming all of the animals, he began to notice something was missing and that something was being kindled in him. Desire for a companion was growing.

God was using the naming of the animals as an object lesson for Adam to understand something deep within himself. What was that? He was a creature of desire and intimacy, made in the image of His Creator. God had stamped His own longing for communion into the very DNA of human beings.

God used the naming of the animals to create longing and passion in the heart of Adam. Beloved, understand, we are designed by God to feel the longing of love, the relentless pursuit of the heart for another person like no other creature. We were created to share the God-like experience of longing for love.

Many commentaries state that Adam's naming of the animals was a symbol of his authority. While there is an element of truth in that statement, it is not the whole truth. You see, there was never a moment when Adam's God-given authority was ever in question. God had a much higher plan than just demonstrating the fact that He had given man dominion over the animal kingdom.

He was using the naming of the animals to help Adam discover the higher God-given attributes of love and desire. God has dominion, He utilizes power, but He is love.[15] Can you imagine the heart pain Adam experienced as he named the animals, two of each kind, all the while recognizing his own lack of a companion and in the process, as painful as it was, discovering the power of a new emotion?

Two dogs, two cats, two birds, two fish—one Adam! No suitable helper, no acceptable life companion was anywhere to be found for Adam. All the while, the desire, the inner ache was growing, intensifying, growing stronger and stronger. Desire was reaching its climax, but wait—hold on! A wedding is coming!

THERE'S GOING TO BE A WEDDING

"The Lord God caused a deep sleep to fall upon the man, and while he slept took one of his ribs and closed up its place with flesh. And the rib that the Lord God had taken from the man he made into a woman and brought her to the man."[16] This is a prophetic foreshadowing of the Cross: the Bride of both the first and second Adam will come forth through the suffering love of the Groom. Oh my goodness, the wise God sets forth the story of His Son and His Bride from the very first.

Adam longed for a companion, for someone like himself with whom to fellowship. In his longing, the heavenly Father provided the only thing that could righteously satisfy the aching in his heart.

He put him to sleep, and from Adam's broken side God fashioned another human from man's own flesh and bone to be like him—and yet very much unlike him. He did not create another male. He created a female, an equally yoked spouse for His beautiful son and then presented her to him. Talk about a romance!

It is the story, the romance of the ages. Can you see it? The wedding of the ages, the wedding to top all weddings, and it is established from the very beginning in the very DNA of humanity. *"Then the man said, 'This at last is bone of my bones and flesh of my flesh; she shall be called Woman, because she was taken out of Man.'"*[17] God created a person like Adam, yet unlike Adam as well. Unity through diversity.

"Then the man said, 'This at last is bone of my bones and flesh of my flesh; she shall be called Woman, because she was taken out of Man.' Therefore a man shall leave his father and his mother and hold fast to his wife, and they shall become one flesh."[18] Notice the connection between verses 23 and 24, signaled by the word *therefore*. Whenever you find the word *therefore* in the Bible, you need to stop and see what it is "there for."

Because the woman is part of man's flesh and bone, Adam experiences great joy and his longing is satisfied. Therefore, or because of the facts just mentioned, *"a man shall leave his father and his mother and hold fast to his wife, and they shall become one flesh."* In other words, in the beginning, as a type of Christ and His Bride, God took woman out of man as bone of his bone and flesh of his flesh, and presented her back to the man so he could discover what it means to be one flesh.

A bridegroom, who now experiences the joy of the fellowship that comes from being with his bride, one who is like him, yet unlike him, because of this, he leaves his father and mother and holds fast to this companion alone and to no other.

THE GREAT MYSTERY OF MARRIAGE

Now back to our question, why does Paul call the text in Ephesians 5:22-31 a "profound mystery"?

Paul by divine revelation had learned from Jesus Himself that the Church is Christ's Body.[19] By faith, a person is joined to Jesus Christ. Thus, a person becomes one with all believers so that we *"are all one in Christ Jesus."*[20] Believers in Christ are the Body of Christ. We are the organism through which He manifests His life and in which His Spirit dwells.

Realizing this relationship between Christ and His Church, Paul sees a parallel with marriage. He sees that a husband and his wife become one flesh in the same manner that Christ and His Church become one Body. So Paul writes to the believers in Corinth and says, *"I feel a divine jealousy for you, since I betrothed you to one husband, to present you as a pure virgin to Christ."*[21] He pictures Christ as the Husband, the Church as the Bride, and conversion as the act of betrothal that Paul had helped to bring about.

The apostle uses the natural relationship of human marriage, as presented in Genesis 2, to teach us about the spiritual relationship between Christ and the Church. Remember the premise we started with: first the natural, then the spiritual!

If we stopped there, marriage would not be a mystery as Paul described it in Ephesians 5:32; it would be an obviously clear thing that simply explains the mystery of Christ and the Church. However, Paul said it was a mystery. What is it that is so mysterious about marriage and its spiritual dynamics that is not obvious to the naked eye?

The mystery, so profound yet so amazingly simple, is this: human marriage is not a natural example to understand the mystical union of Christ and the Church. Instead, Paul states that it is only because of the eternal reality that exists between the heavenly

Bridegroom and His redeemed Bride that we can understand the significance of the natural, human institution of marriage.

The mystery is that God designed human marriage based on the pattern of Christ's Bridegroom-Bride relationship to the Church. The creation account in Genesis is a type or a symbol of Jesus' relationship to His people. A surface reading of the Genesis account does not always result in a proper understanding of what was actually transpiring.

The natural human relationship of marriage was designed by God as a pattern, an on-ramp, to the understanding of the relationship He desires every human being to have with His Son. Therefore, marriage is a mystery—because it contains a hidden, concealed meaning and relevance that has eternal ramifications. With that understanding in mind, in the next chapter we will look more at what the Bible says concerning God as our Husband.

CHAPTER 3

God as Our Husband

If we were to stop the average person on the street and ask the question, "Tell me what God is like?" we could possibly get any number of opinions concerning the nature of God: Creator, Father, Judge, Master, or Savior, just to name a few. If we were given any of these answers, they would be valid, wouldn't they? However, the one answer that you could almost bet on *not* getting might just be the most important one of all! It certainly would be the most important related to our quest to define and have the kind of love for God that He desires us to have—God is like a Husband to His Bride.

THE LAW OF GENESIS

The law of Genesis comes from Genesis chapter 1 where we read, *"And God said, 'Let the earth sprout vegetation, plants yielding seed, and fruit trees bearing fruit in which is their seed, each according to its kind, on the earth.' And it was so. The earth brought forth vegetation, plants yielding seed according to their own kinds, and trees bearing fruit in which is their seed, each according to its kind. And God saw that it was good."*[1]

God designed everything so that it reproduces *"according to its kind."* Dogs reproduce dogs, cats reproduce cats, duck-billed platypuses produce duck-billed platypuses, and you get the picture.

That does not just apply to natural things, but that principle is valid related to spiritual things as well. *"We love because He first loved us."*[2] Another way to say that is we love God in the way we see that He loves us! Another way we could say it is, before we can love God the way He desires us to love Him, we have to understand the way that He loves us.

I am the director of Passion for Jesus Ministries. Because of the ministry's name, many people over the years have asked the question, "Buddy, how can I love God more?" My answer, while simple, is profound. I tell them that in order to love God more, you have to have a greater understanding *and experience* of the nature of how God loves you. The law of Genesis, get it?

I mean really, most of us know that God loved us first; with most believers that is not even an issue. I have found that the question in most people's experience is not, "Did God love me first?" The real question is, "What does He think about me today?" We all know that He demonstrated the fact that He loved us at the Cross. Because, after all, that is what a God of love does, right? He dies for us on a cross! But after I said yes to Him, how does He feel about me right now? The question isn't: did He love me first? The lingering question is: will He love me at the last?

> *He has no need, like those high priests, to offer sacrifices daily, first for His own sins and then for those of the people, since He did this once for all when He offered up Himself.*[3]

Jesus died a vicarious death; He did not deserve to die. He died in my place, for my sin, because I deserved to die! This was not just a once and never to be repeated again sacrifice—although it was that, once and for all, and it is good forever—but what motivated Him to die for you and me remains His motivation forever! The Scripture says that He is the same yesterday and today and forever![4]

HOSEA—THE PROPHET OF THE KING'S RELENTLESS LOVE

Throughout all of redemptive history, whenever God desired to communicate to humankind, the Image-bearers, He almost always would raise up a spokesperson, an emissary, a prophet to communicate His desire and His message. But prophets were not just "messengers," they were also human ambassadors who not only presented God's message, they *represented* God's message—or as Pastor Bill Johnson says, they "re-presented Him."[5] They were people who shared the burden of God's heart concerning His people. They loved what He loved and they hated what He hated. The New Testament term for someone like that is a Friend of the Bridegroom.[6] John the Baptist, the forerunner of the Lord Jesus, is the clearest example of that reality.[7]

> The prophet is not a mouthpiece, but a person; not an instrument, but a partner, an associate of God.... An analysis of prophetic utterances shows that the fundamental experience of the prophet is a fellowship with the feelings of God, a sympathy with the divine pathos, a communion with the divine the consciousness which comes about through the prophet's reflection of, or participation in, the divine pathos.[8]

One of the Old Testament prophets who gives us the clearest picture of how God loves us and how He wants us to love Him is the prophet Hosea. To give you a little of the context of what we are about to look at, Hosea's name means *salvation,* as do the names Joshua[9] and Jesus.[10]

Hosea was a contemporary of Isaiah and Amos—he ministered during 775–715 b.c.—and ministered primarily to the ten Northern tribes of Israel. Hosea is the first of what are commonly called the 12 minor prophets. The designation minor prophet is not a reference to their importance; instead, it refers to the length of their prophecies, as compared to some of the major prophets like Isaiah or Jeremiah.

Although Hosea ministered in the same period as Isaiah and Amos, what makes his ministry significant is that he is considered by many scholars as possibly being the first "written" prophet, the first prophet to have his messages recorded in written form. We know that there were other prophets before him (Elijah and Elisha, for instance), but as far as written letters recorded in the Old Testament, Hosea is one of the first, along with Isaiah and Amos.

THE LAW OF FIRST OCCURRENCE

One of the rules of biblical exegesis (*exegesis* is a theological term meaning rules of interpretation) is called the Law of First Occurrence or the Law of First Mention. Whenever something is mentioned for the first time in Scripture, it lays the foundational framework of understanding for that thing or idea in the rest of Scripture. The Law of First Occurrence is important in regard to what we are about to look at.

Whenever the first written prophecy is recorded for posterity, we need to sit up and pay attention to what that prophet is saying. The first recorded prophet or prophetic revelation lays a foundation for the proper understanding of all the rest of recorded prophetic revelation about God that follows.

Hosea was the son of Beeri.[11] Often, under the Old Covenant, when individuals recognized that they had a prophetic gift and call from God, they would join a school of the prophets (sometimes referred to in various translations as "groups of the prophets," "sons of the prophets," or "bands of the prophets").[12] These specialized schools were for the training of those called to prophetic ministry. Undoubtedly, Hosea followed this precedent and probably joined a prophetic training school.

We are not sure, so this is hypothetical, but it could have happened something like this:

Hosea is sitting in a school of the prophets class where he is being instructed in how to be a man of God, a man of integrity, and how to develop and minister in his prophetic gifting and calling, when "suddenly" the Word of the Lord comes to him.[13] If you have had the experience of having a bona fide prophetic word come to you, then you can empathize with what Hosea is experiencing. The excitement of the realization that the living God is actually speaking to you is almost overwhelming.

SURPRISE, SURPRISE

Often when the Lord speaks a prophetic word, the recipient just "knows," is sure, that this word from the Lord will change the world! Hosea could have had a sense of something like, "Hosea, I want to give you a word, a revelation that no one has ever had before. Hosea, I want to give you an insight into who I am that no one has ever seen in all of prophetic history. How about it, Hosea, are you with Me?"

Oh the thrill that must have charged through Hosea's heart! Just think about it! A revelation of God's character and heart that no one else has ever seen before. Hosea might have thought, *Oh, the other prophets are going to be so jealous! Yes, Lord, of course I'm onboard!*

Then the Lord says to Hosea, *"Go, take to yourself a wife of whoredom and have children of whoredom, for the land commits great whoredom by forsaking the Lord."*[14]

Can you imagine the look on Hosea's face? "Uh, excuse me, Lord, would You mind repeating that? It sounded almost like You said that You wanted me to marry a wife of whoredom?"

God could have answered him, "Yes, Hosea, you heard Me right! Isn't this exciting, I am sharing with you the deepest part of My heart, a part that I have never shared with any other prophet before! I want you to go, Hosea, and take to yourself a wife of whoredom! Go quickly. This is My heart, this is who I am! And oh, Hosea, this is your lucky day. You don't even have to go and search for her, I have already picked her out especially for you! Her name is Gomer, the daughter of Diblaim."[15]

I am making it humorous, but you do understand that this was not an allegory or a parable. This was a very real flesh-and-blood girl, the daughter of a real father, whom God had chosen for Hosea, "the man of God," to marry because God wanted to show Hosea, and the nation of Israel—and we who are alive to-day—something about His heart that we had never seen before! Something we *desperately* need to see.

God is saying, "I want you to understand the motivations of My heart, the deepest emotions in My heart, so I am about to pull back the veil and let you see who I am and what I am all about!"

Hosea might have responded, "Uh, marry a wife of whoredom? But that sounds like it might be kinda hard. I mean, that would really disrupt my life, cause me such pain. Lord, don't You think that maybe it would show Your heart better if I went out and, like, called down fire from Heaven and destroyed a group of false prophets or something like Elijah did? What do You think?"

A HIGHER CALLING

God could have answered something like, "No, Hosea, this is a much higher call, a much grander assignment. In fact, this will demonstrate to everyone throughout all of redemptive history, like nothing else you could do, what is in My heart toward Israel, My people! I want you to go and marry Gomer and then walk out in front of everybody what it means to be wed to an unfaithful wife. Hosea, you have prayed over and over saying that you wanted the high call, the deepest revelation of who I am, the picture of what I feel about My people. This is it, Hosea! I have chosen you above all other prophets! Trust Me, you might not like it now, but oh, you will! Because in the end, it is good news for you and good news for My people! Because she is you, Hosea."

And so, Hosea starts his prophetic journey and ministry by marrying a wife of whoredom. Hosea, as a prophet and as a friend of the Bridegroom, was to walk out before Israel the Di-vine drama of what it was like for a righteous person to love and be married to someone who was unfaithful. Hosea really loved Gomer! Moreover, when she proved to be unfaithful, and she left

Hosea for her other lovers, it really hurt! Hosea, the friend of God, felt the sting of betrayal, like God feels when His people do not return His love.

The Law was clear: Hosea could have had Gomer put to death for her unfaithfulness,[16] just as God justly could cut off all humankind because of their sin. But then there is the matter of love, isn't there?

However, it does not stop there. Then the Lord says, "Hosea, let's take it up a notch, what do you say? Now not only are you going to marry a wife of whoredom, but I am going to allow you to bear children of whoredom as well."[17] Can you just sense Hosea's exuberance?

Then the Lord might have said something like, "Hosea, not only are you going to have children of whoredom, as prophetic symbols before everyone, but they are going to have bizarre and strange names, because, Hosea, it is so bizarre and it is so strange that My children would live lives of whoredom before Me!"

THE OFFSPRING

So Hosea and Gomer get married and soon they have a son and God has them name him Jezreel, which means "God Scatters" or "God Sows." Jezreel was the name of the place where Jehu had killed the 70 sons of Ahab.[18] God tells Hosea to tell Israel that as Jehu brought an end to the line of Ahab, so now God's will is about to bring an end to the dynasty of Israel. And that happened, not long afterward: the Northern kingdom and its capitol, Samaria, fell in 722 B.C.

It does not end there. Hosea and Gomer then have a daughter and God has them name her Lo-ruhama,[19] which means "no mercy." God tells Hosea, "Tell Israel that I will no more have mercy on the house of Israel." Imagine having to name your little girl No Mercy.

Then they have another son who God tells them to name Lo-ammi,[20] which means "not my people." God says, "Tell Israel, Hosea, that because of their sin, they will not be My people and I will not be their God. In this hour, in this season, I do not want this woman or her children."

It does not end there. Just when you think that all is dark and all is lost, then we turn a corner toward restoration.

Now Hosea might have responded in his humanity, "God, You told me to marry a wife of whoredom. Then when we have children, You have us name them all these strange names that represent the judgments You are about to pour out on Israel. Did You just have me do all of this just so You could proclaim Your judgments? Is this what You called me into the prophetic ministry for?"

God could have responded, "No, I am setting you up, Hosea! I am about to turn the tide. All of this was necessary so you could see, so all of Israel could see, the darkness of their situation. Hosea, unless you, and Israel, see how dark is the way you have treated Me, you would never understand what I am about to show you. Israel and her children brought all of this upon themselves. They deserve this, Hosea. I am holy, and I loved them and I called them and yet they loved the world and they loved their sin and they turned away from Me and from all My ways."

The Lord does say, *"Yet the number of the children of Israel shall be like the sand of the sea, which cannot be measured or numbered. And in the place where it was said to them, 'You are not My people,' it shall be said to them, 'Children of the living God.' And the children of Judah and the children of Israel shall be gathered together, and they shall appoint for themselves one head. And they shall go up from the land, for great shall be the day of Jezreel."*[21] Remember one of the meanings of Jezreel was "God Sows."

There's Always Hope

God could have responded, "Hosea, you thought I had you go through all of this just so that I could judge Israel. But there is more! There is good news, great news! Before it is over, I will turn it all around, Hosea! The objects of My judgment are about to become the objects of My affection! I make all things right, Hosea!"

In fact, He says, *"Say to your brothers, 'You are My people,' and to your sisters, 'You have received mercy.'"*[22] He is telling Hosea to tell his little girl who grew up with the name No Mercy that mercy will be shown!

So here we see the prophetic promise come forth: it will all turn around. The people who should have been pure and loyal to the Lord, but instead lived lives of whoredom and compromise, will receive mercy in the end and walk in the blessings of the Lord. The question is: Lord, how? How will You turn a whoring, compromising people to the degree that they are positioned before You not to receive a just judgment but instead to receive Your great mercy—how?

God says, *"I will allow her to run after her other lovers, I will allow her to receive the consequences of her spiritual adultery. I will allow her life to be a wilderness, a parched land, where she thirsts for more than what the pleasures of her sin can ever give her.... I will hedge her way with thorns and I will build a wall against her so that she cannot find the peace she yearns for in her ways of sin and compromise."*[23]

Oh, but Beloved, He does not leave her there. He goes on to say, *"...behold, I will allure her, and bring her into the wilderness, and speak tenderly to her."*[24]

The way of forgiveness, the way of restoration, the way for fallen and frail human beings to be delivered from their own ways and the just and deserved judgment of God, is for Israel to hear Him speak tenderly to her.

MERCY TRIUMPHS OVER JUDGMENT

Have you ever noticed that even though many in the Church have loudly and boldly proclaimed the surety of the judgments of God, very few have seemed to respond to that message? How many times have we seen the few who did respond to the message of judgment eventually return to a life of sin? You see, people will only respond for so long to being held over hell on a rotten stick!

God could have said to Hosea, and to us as well, "You know Me as the Holy God, the Creator, your Master and your Righteous Judge; you have known Me as all of these things. But what you haven't known, what you haven't seen, what you haven't experienced is who I am at the core of My being—I am the Romantic, I am the Lover!" God said, "I will court her, I will woo her, I will win her, and it will be through speaking tenderly to her heart as a Lover!"

Why do we court the one we love? Why do we chase after and pursue him or her until we win the person's heart and the pursued succumbs to our love and says, "Yes"? It is not just because of hormones, sensuality, or sexuality; it is much more than that. We court the one we love because we are the Image-bearers; we are the ones who were created in the image of God, the Eternal Lover. We are lovers because He is a Lover; God is Love![25]

God was saying, "Do you want to know how I am going to win the hearts of My people? Do you want to know how I am going to draw them out of their lives of compromise and sin? Do you want to know how I am going to present the Church to Myself in splendor, without spot or wrinkle or any such thing, that she might be holy and without blemish?[26] It's through My divine courtship, through the divine romance—the romance of the Gospel, that's how!"

The Lord says, "*...behold, I will allure her, and bring her into the wilderness, and speak tenderly to her. There I will give her her*

vineyards and make the Valley of Achor [Achor means trouble]
*a door of hope. And there she shall answer as in the days of her
youth, as at the time when she came out of the land of Egypt."*[27]

God speaks tenderly to our hearts, even in the times when we
are wandering far away from Him. Yes, He warns us of the errors
of our ways; yes, He calls us to turn away from sin and the world
and to return to Him. However, He does not say it in a vacuum.
There is a context in which He speaks to His people. He speaks to
us out of His love for us. When He speaks to us out of His love,
He reveals to us His identity and ours as well.

I Am Your Husband

*"And in that day, declares the Lord, you will call Me 'My Hus-
band,' and no longer will you call Me 'My Baal.'"*[28]

In the original Hebrew text of Hosea 2:16 there is a wordplay
going on that we miss in our English translations. The Hebrew
word translated Husband, *ishi,* and the Hebrew word for Baal,
ba'li, both can mean husband. However, the term *ishi* is a title of
affection while the term *ba'li* emphasizes the husband's legal position. God desires that our relationship with Him not be based on
an outward legal commitment but instead on an inward bond of
mutual affection and love.[29]

God goes on to say, *"And I will betroth you to Me forever. I
will betroth you to Me in righteousness and in justice, in steadfast
love and in mercy."*[30]

Beloved, Froggy is not the only one that went a-courtin'! Jesus is a Lover, He is a Bridegroom. He is courting His people,
romancing His people, speaking tenderly the words of love that
She was created to hear and to respond too. And respond She
will! You can put all of your eggs in that basket; it is a sure thing,
a done deal!

In the last days before the Lord returns, God's people, the
Church, will respond, not out of fear, but out of a revelation of

how much She is loved by God. This understanding will not just be of love in a general sense, and not just the love of a parent to a child (as true and valid as that is), but She will respond to the love of a Bride to a Bridegroom!

Earlier we looked at the Law of First Occurrence and saw how when something is mentioned for the first time, it lays the foundational understanding for future references to that subject. God chose Hosea, one of the first written prophets, to lay down the foundational truth of who He is and how He relates to His people. He is a Bridegroom. If we miss this foundational understanding, we run the risk of misunderstanding all the dealings of God.

We must grasp what God has revealed through Hosea, the first of the written prophets, for all of the other prophets to make sense. The message of the prophets, and in fact, the entire message of redemption, has to be viewed through the lens of the bridal paradigm to make any sense.

Earlier we looked at how God used the creation of man and the subsequent creation of woman to prophetically foreshadow the glorious day to come when the last Adam—Jesus—would be put to sleep and a beautiful Bride would come forth out of His side. From the beginning, God defined reality for man so that he would pursue a companion. This was the prophetic foreshadowing of the nature of things for the second Adam to come. Just as God desired to create in His image and join humanity unto Himself in the person of His Son, so God desired that the first Adam be joined to a companion.

We looked at how God used loneliness to cultivate longing and desire in Adam's heart. Loneliness presupposes desire and longing. Without loneliness, longing for something else is impossible. Adam bore the weight of naming all that is created so that his heart would notice something was missing, so that something else could be kindled—desire for a companion. God was setting forth the ultimate object lesson for Adam, and us, to understand something of Himself.

We are creatures of desire and intimacy because we were made in the image of God—we are the Image-bearers. The longing in God's heart for communion, for intimacy, is stamped on the very nature of all human beings so that as we walk out that reality in the natural realm, it will open up the way for us to understand that reality in the spiritual realm.[31] This was the design of God: to create longing and passion in the heart of humankind so we would feel the longing of love and the relentless pursuit of the heart for another person, so we would share in the experience of God and understand God's pursuit of us.

THE BRIDAL PARADIGM—THE SEED PLOT FOR ALL OF REDEMPTION

Israel, the chosen race, had been entrusted with the revelation that Yahweh is the Creator and the King. They carry the message and represent Him to all of the nations of the earth. However, in the process they stumbled and fell, and they lost the intimacy that they should have been walking in.

So God uses the prophetic ministry of Hosea to pull the veil back a little further, past Creator, past Master, past Law-giver, to reveal the heretofore unknown, and yet foundational truth that the heart of the King is that of a Bridegroom. Mind-boggling. However, is that revelation in itself sufficient?

For even though they now have a deeper insight into God's passion for humanity, and a clearer understanding of how God desires to win the heart of His people through His speaking tenderly to their hearts, there is still something else that is necessary.

God says:

"And I will betroth you to Me forever. I will betroth you to Me in righteousness and in justice, in steadfast love and in mercy. I will betroth you to Me in faithfulness. You shall know the Lord. And in that day I will answer," declares the Lord, "I will answer the heavens, and they

shall answer the earth, and the earth shall answer the grain, the wine, and the oil, and they shall answer Jezreel, and I will sow her for Myself in the land. I will have mercy on No Mercy, and I will say to Not My People, 'You are My people'; and he shall say, 'You are my God.'"[32]

God has revealed His heart as the heart of a Bridegroom. He has told of His willingness to bless His people, represented by Gomer and her three children. Here He declares His willingness to reverse the prophetic declarations against Jezreel, No Mercy, and Not My People. However, even after baring His heart and His love for the Image-bearers, all is not well in the Kingdom.

The Lord had shown prophetically through Hosea His heart as a Bridegroom and a Husband. He had spoken tenderly to the heart of Gomer and her children. He had shown His mercy and grace to them—mercy is when we do not get what we deserve; grace is when we do get what we do not deserve. After having experienced the goodness of God to herself and her children, you would think that she would have committed herself to being a good wife to Hosea, wouldn't you? Although we do not know the specifics, for the Scriptures do not give us the full details, we are told that after all that has happened, Gomer turned away again.

And the Lord said to me, "Go again, love a woman who is loved by another man and is an adulteress, even as the Lord loves the children of Israel, though they turn to other gods and love cakes of raisins."[33]

Commentators offer different opinions about what actually transpired. The Hebrew phrase translated here in the English Standard Version of the Bible as *"who is loved by another man"* is debated as it has a broad range of possible meanings: "friend," "lover," "companion," "neighbor," and "another." The Hebrew lexicons (theological term meaning dictionary) favor the nuance of "lover" or "paramour."

Most scholars agree with the lexical definitions; however, a few suggest that the phrase does not refer to another man, but to Hosea. Both approaches are reflected in English Bible translations:

New American Standard Bible—*a woman who is loved by her husband.*

New International Version—*though she is loved by another.*

New American Bible—*a woman loved of a paramour.*

King James Version—*a woman beloved of her friend.*

New Jewish Publications Society—*a woman who, while befriended by a companion.*

Good News Bible—*a woman who is committing adultery with a lover.*

Contemporary English Version—*an unfaithful woman who has a lover.*[34]

However, regardless of whether she was physically with Hosea or with another, whether she loved another or was loved by another, one thing is clear: she was an adulteress, her heart was not where it should have been. Hosea loved Gomer and he was true to her, but her heart was elsewhere, and thus she was a clear representation of the people of Israel. God loved Israel; and while they claimed to be His, their hearts were caught up in the pursuit of other gods demonstrated by their loving cakes of raisins.

The fact that we are told that the children of Israel loved "cakes of raisins" reminds us of Song of Solomon 2:5, where the maiden said to her Beloved, *"Sustain me with raisins; refresh me with apples, for I am sick with love."*[35] The similarity is that the maiden in the Song is crying out for more of what she craves for in her relationship with her Beloved, who in the Song represents the Lord Jesus. Here in Hosea, however, the children of Israel are crying out for what they enjoy as well, but instead of it coming from a relationship with the true God, they desire the forbidden fruit that comes from a relationship with false gods.

So how would you react to a wife you had opened your heart to, showing her nothing but unconditional love by giving her not what she deserved but mercy and grace, and then she responds to your love by being unfaithful and following after other lovers? How would you react? In the next chapter, we look at how God told Hosea to react.

CHAPTER 4

Go Again, Hosea!

I love a great adventure story, don't you?

There are two types of stories that people never seem to tire of. The first is the theme of a king who loves his people, humbles himself, and fights for and wins the people's freedom. The movie *Braveheart* is a classic example of this type of story. We all love the thought of a king who has great wealth and power and yet does not sell out, but humbly serves the people, even to the point of death.

There is an axiom that states, "absolute power corrupts absolutely." If we are honest, we have to admit that more often than not, the saying has proven to be true. The proof is not always secondhand, is it? Yet we are still hopeful to find that "special" man or woman who is the exception to the rule. Therefore, we continue to purchase the novels, buy the movie tickets, rent the videos, and turn on the television, anything to "experience" someone who lives right and does not sell out.

The second theme that never seems to fail to catch our attention is that of a man who fights for the heart and honor of his bride, even to the peril of his own life. Two movie examples of that genre that immediately come to mind are *Les Misérables* and *Man from LaMancha.*

To lay a foundation to help you understand Hosea's reaction to what the Lord told him to do next, allow me to recap the three adventures portrayed in these three movie and theater classics.

While reading, keep in mind the following statements: 1. Women want to be rescued. 2. God has an adventure in store for you. 3. Jesus was a Warrior.

BRAVEHEART

In the year A.D. 1280, Edward I of England, also known as "Long-shanks," had occupied much of Scotland. Under his regime, William Wallace's father and brother were killed. Wallace is then raised under the tutelage of his uncle outside of Scotland. During this period, the Scots continue to live under Longshanks' cruel reign.

After he is grown, Wallace returns with the intent of living as a farmer and avoiding any involvement in the ongoing problems around him. Wallace runs into his childhood sweetheart, Murron, and rekindles their romance. They are married in secret to avoid the "prima nocte" decree the king had set forth.

Wallace gets into a scrap with a group of English soldiers who are attempting to rape Murron. In the process, the village sheriff kills her before Wallace is able to save her. Wallace, with the assistance of his fellow townsmen, slaughter the English soldiers, and kill the sheriff. He then orders that the local English fort be burned, and in the process of doing that unintentionally kindles a Scottish rebellion.

News of the rebellion spreads quickly, and hundreds of Scots from the surrounding clans show up to volunteer to join Wallace's militia. Wallace leads his new army through a series of successful battles against the English. However, he is eventually betrayed by the Scottish nobility and defeated at the Battle of Falkirk. He then goes into hiding, continuing his attacks against the English in a guerrilla war.

Meanwhile, a neglected Princess Isabelle, who is married to Longshanks' son and heir, meets with Wallace as the English king's emissary. She and Wallace share a tryst, during which she conceives Wallace's child. Still believing there is some good in the nobility of his country, Wallace agrees to meet with Robert the Bruce, son of the Scottish nobleman Robert the Bruce, who is the chief contender for the Scottish Crown. Wallace is caught in a trap set by the elder Bruce and the other nobles, beaten unconscious, and handed over to the English Crown.

In London, Wallace is brought before the English court and tried for high treason. He denies the charges, announcing that he had never accepted Edward as his king. The court responds by sentencing him to be "purified by pain." Later, in a London square, Wallace is tortured to death, being alternately hanged, racked, castrated, and finally disemboweled alive.

Before he dies, he signals to the magistrate that he wishes to speak. Using the last ounce of strength, he cries out, "FREE-DOM!" He turns his head and sees Murron in the crowd smiling at him, and smiles lovingly back at her as he is finally beheaded.

Braveheart is the story of a leader, who refuses to compromise, even if it costs him his life, who stays true to his convictions to the end, and from the beginning to the end, has his bride in sight. While I certainly can't condone everything that occurs in the movie, the big picture is an inspiring one of Jesus and what He has done for us.

LES MISÉRABLES

Les Misérables is the story of a peasant named Jean Valjean. Having been recently released from prison—he had been locked up for stealing bread for his starving sister and his family—the law required that he carry a yellow passport that identified him as a convict, even though he had already paid his debt to society. As a convict, he had no place to sleep, so he ends up sleeping on the street. This makes him even more angry and bitter.

A benevolent priest takes him in and gives him shelter. In the middle of the night, he steals the bishop's silverware and runs away. He is caught, but the bishop rescues him by telling the authorities that the silverware was a gift, and at that point gives him his two silver candlesticks as well. He chastises him in front of the police for leaving in such a rush that he forgot these valuable pieces. The bishop then "reminds" him of the promise, which Valjean has no recollection of making, to use the silver to make an honest man of himself.

Later, as Valjean broods over these words, he steals a child's silver coin. He chases the boy away but soon repents, and decides to follow the bishop's advice and turn over a new leaf. Six years pass by and Valjean has assumed a new identity, Monsieur Madeleine, and is now a successful factory owner who is appointed mayor of his adopted town.

He meets a woman named Fantine, who is a worker at his factory. She falls into hard times, ends up losing her job at the factory, and has to resort to prostitution to pay for her daughter's board and expenses. Then we find out that she is also dying from tuberculosis. Valjean tries his best to help her as she is dying, and we are left with the impression that he would marry her if he could.

We hear, read, or watch stories like this and we cry, "Yes!" We love it, don't we? We love a good man who risks everything to try to help a fallen woman improve herself and live a better life!

Man From LaMancha

Man from LaMancha is based on the classic novel *Don Quixote de la Mancha* by Miquel de Cervantes. In this story, a retired Spanish nobleman named Alonso Quijano spends most of his time reading about knights and chivalry. He goes mad and develops delusions that he is a famous knight—Don Quixote de la Mancha.

Quixote and his sidekick, Sancho Panza, travel around looking for adventure and desiring to do good and "save the day." Along the way, they meet a servant girl named Aldonza, who sells herself for money at night. However, when Don sees Aldonza, he does not see a prostitute; he sees a lady, a princess named Dulcinea.

At first Aldonza is put off by Quixote, but at the same time, she likes the fact that Don, unlike the other men in the town, treats her with respect. Several days later, Quixote, about to start another adventure, sends Sancho with a letter to Aldonza, asking her for a token that he can wear in battle, something like a silk scarf. She scoffs at the request but is intrigued as well. She finally gives Sancho a dirty floor rag. Sancho returns and gives the rag to Don, who kisses it and holds it as if it were a beautiful and treasured silk scarf.

Later, Don and Sancho run into Aldonza on the roadside. She is bitter and upset. Quixote starts telling her again that she is Dulcinea, his queen. Aldonza starts mocking him, and shocked by her rejection, he collapses.

Next, we see Don Quixote lying in bed in a comatose state. Aldonza has come to see him. He opens his eyes and says he is Alonso Quijano, and only has a vague memory of Don Quixote. He asks a priest to write down his last will, as he knows he is dying. Aldonza, who has found she cannot live without being Dulcinea, begs him to remember. Weeping she asks him repeatedly, "Say my name again, say it one more time! Please!"

He finally says it, "Dulcinea, you're a queen!" Beloved, that is her story. Later, after Quixote has died, Sancho, speaking with her, calls her Aldonza. She responds by telling him that her name is Dulcinea!

Hollywood has taken advantage of the universal appeal of these types of stories. Have you ever sat down and thought about why this is so? It is because it is our story! In addition, it is Hosea's story as well!

BACK TO HOSEA

In the last chapter we learned that God loves His people, not in a generic way, but in an intimate "Husbandly" way. God told the prophet Hosea to marry Gomer, a wife of whoredom, and to bear children of whoredom, as a prophetic expression representing how God married a people—then Israel, now the Church—who are often unfaithful. He revealed to Hosea that though His wife was unfaithful, and though His children deserved His judgment, He would eventually draw them to Himself and pour out His mercy upon them.

After God has expressed His love for His people and poured out His mercy and grace upon them, even after those expressions of the divine love, Gomer, like the people of God, would turn away and return to her adulteress ways. After Hosea had loved, married, and forgiven Gomer, she still was not faithful in her heart to him. Likewise, the people of God, the redeemed, often turn away from loving Him, from following His ways, and turn to following other gods, enjoying the forbidden fruit of the pleasures of sin.

If you were Hosea, how would you react to those circumstances? Would you write Gomer off as a lost cause, a bad deal? Common sense would tell us yes, give up, walk off, and hope for a better day, right? And what about God? How should He have reacted? He loved a rebellious people; He spoke to their hearts tenderly, letting them know the error of their ways, the just consequences of their choices and lifestyles. That is not all He did, is it? He also told them of His love for them and how He desired to forgive and restore them.

What does a holy God do with a people who, after having received the revelation and the fruit of His goodness, choose to return to a lifestyle of wickedness, sin, and following after other gods? How should He respond? With wrath? Judgment? What else can a holy God do? He has to judge sin, doesn't He? Sure He does. The price has to be paid—in full! So what does God do?

He tells Hosea, "Go again, Hosea! Don't give up. Love her and win her heart!" How does Hosea respond to that? Hang on now, this is where it really gets good! Gomer had turned away, she had gone back out into a life of whoredom, and she had sold herself back into bondage.

Commentators are not exactly sure what may have happened here. One school of thought is that Hosea had legally divorced Gomer because of her unfaithfulness, and that she had become a temple prostitute or possibly had become the legal property of another man who had hired her as a concubine or a prostitute.[1] Either way, she was a slave and had to be bought back out of her slavery. Imagine the love Hosea must have had for Gomer to subject himself to such public humiliation in buying back his unfaithful wife out of slavery.

THE BRIDE-PRICE IS PAID

There are a couple of important things we should consider about this scenario. The first is the price Hosea paid for Gomer.[2] The price Hosea paid to redeem Gomer was 15 shekels of silver and 1½ homers of barley, which many scholars believe may have been equivalent to 30 pieces of silver, which was the price paid for a common slave.[3] Gomer, like Israel, had subjected herself as a slave to sin.[4] Barley was the offering used for one accused of adultery.[5]

The other important thing about this is that the price Hosea paid to redeem Gomer, as one who had sold herself into slavery and bondage, is the same price that was paid by the chief priests to put to death the One who redeemed us who had sold ourselves into slavery and bondage as well.[6]

This prophetic act by Hosea foretold the demonstration of God's love when Jesus paid the price for us. Then Hosea prophesied that from that point on Gomer would be true to him in the same manner that he was true to her.[7] Wow! The prophet Hosea makes a prophetic declaration that because of his paying the legal price for Gomer from her slavery, she would not return to her whoredom. He goes on to say that she would never again belong to another but from that point on she would be his and his alone. Wow! Double wow!

This is reminiscent of the reality expressed by the maiden in the Song of Solomon, where she exclaims her newfound commitment to her Beloved three different times: "*My Beloved is mine, and I am His*"; "*I am my Beloved's and my Beloved is mine*"; and, "*I am my Beloved's and His desire is for me.*"[8]

Isn't that our story as well? We had all rebelled against God, our Creator.[9] But as our intimate Husband, He kept speaking to our hearts reminding us the path we were on was leading us to where we really didn't want to go.[10] However, He was not content to just tell us of His love; He demonstrated that love by paying the price for our sins.[11] Now, because of the price He paid, on our behalf and in our place, our lives are no longer our own, we have been bought with a price,[12] and we are His for all of eternity and He is ours![13] No wonder the saints from throughout all the ages love and worship Him!

A GREAT PROPHETIC CLOUD OF WITNESSES

Hosea is not the only prophet who used this bridal language to express God's love for His people; he was just the first of many. All of prophetic revelation is birthed out of the bridal paradigm and must be viewed from that perspective if we are to make any sense of God's dealing with His people.

GOD'S PEOPLE ARE BETROTHED TO THE LORD

"*Go and proclaim in the hearing of Jerusalem, Thus says the Lord, 'I remember the devotion of your youth, your love as a bride, how you followed Me in the wilderness, in a land not sown.'"*[14] This is a clear reference back to the giving of the law at Mount Sinai. First, let us look at how that came to be.

In the Beginning

We looked earlier at how God revealed from the beginning that He wanted a bridal relationship with His people. He demonstrated that with the creation of Adam and Eve. They lived in union with each other and with their God in Eden, the Garden of Encounter. Two innocent people, in love with each other and with God. A perfect environment. Or was it?

Adam said, "This at last is bone of my bones and flesh of my flesh; she shall be called Woman, because she was taken out of Man." Therefore, a man shall leave his father and his mother and hold fast to his wife, and they shall become one flesh. The man and his wife were both naked and were not ashamed. Now the serpent was craftier than any other beast of the field that the Lord God had made. He said to the woman, "Did God actually say, 'You shall not eat of any tree in the garden'?"[15]

The serpent approached Eve with the intent to deceive her and to destroy her fellowship with God. What should have happened here? Earlier I made reference to the movie *Braveheart*. It was about a man of valor who fought for his people. We looked at *Les Misérables* where Jean Valjean came to the rescue of Fantine in her distress. Then we considered how Alonso Quijano, as Don Quixote de la Mancha, saw Aldonza as the beautiful princess Dulcinea and sought to win her love and fight for her honor.

When the serpent approached Eve, Adam should have stood up and rushed to his bride's aid, taken his place as Eve's defender and knight in white armor, and defended her from the enemy's attack. Adam had authority to "re-present" God in the Garden, and he should have exercised it.

Eve said to the serpent, *"We may eat of the fruit of the trees in the garden, but God said, 'You shall not eat of the fruit of the tree that is in the midst of the garden, **neither shall you touch it,** lest you die.' The serpent said to Eve, 'You will not surely die. God knows that when you eat of it your eyes will be opened, and you will be like God, knowing good and evil.'"*[16]

WHAT DID HE SAY?

Just as a sidebar: God never said that they could not touch the tree or its fruit; He only said they were not allowed to eat the fruit. We must pay close attention to what God has actually said, and be careful not to add to what He said, or the results can be disastrous. Anyway, back to our story...

For years when reading the account of Eve's temptation, I pictured her being off somewhere by herself, away from Adam, and thus easy prey to the serpent's attack. That is not the scenario at all. *"When the woman saw that the tree was good for food, and that it was a delight to the eyes, and that the tree was to be desired to make one wise, she took of its fruit and ate, and she also gave some to her husband **who was with her,** and he ate."*[17]

The buck stopped with Adam. He was formed first; he was there when God said not to eat of the tree of the knowledge of good and evil. Scripture tells us Eve was deceived, Adam was not.[18] Some erroneously claim that he ate of the forbidden fruit which she offered him out of love for her. No one ever sins out of love, so the reason Adam sinned was even worse than Eve's. She was deceived, but the Scripture plainly says Adam was not deceived.

Adam spiritually dropped the ball, turned away from the two great loves of his life—God and Eve, and in so doing, sold all of his descendents down the proverbial river. Because of his decision, Adam, Eve, and all of their descendents were cut off from God's glorious Presence. Total disaster. Thank God, the story does not stop there!

God came to the Garden of Encounter, knowing what had just transpired. He called out to Adam, who along with Eve, had hidden because of their sin.[19] By the way, when Adam told God what happened is not when He found out about it. And it is the same with us. We often feel down when we confess our sins to God, as though now we have just given Him a piece of information that suddenly "changes everything." But God calls the end from the beginning, and nothing we do catches Him off guard or by surprise.[20] God called out to Adam, "Where are you?"[21]

Always remember, an omniscient, all-knowing God does not ask questions to get information! When He asks us questions, He is asking them for our benefit.

Adam answered God, *"I heard the sound of You in the garden, and I was afraid, because I was naked, and I hid myself."* That statement was a result of Adam and Eve's having lost that enswathing light of purity that previously had covered their physical bodies.[22]

God replied to Adam, *"Who told you that you were naked? Have you eaten of the tree of which I commanded you not to eat?"*[23]

THE BLAME SHIFT GAME

Adam replied, *"The woman whom You gave to be with me, she gave me fruit of the tree, and I ate."*[24] Adam first of all blamed God, and then blamed Eve; he recapitulates the history, as if he wasn't to blame for what had happened due to the actions of others; humankind has been doing this ever since.

God said to Eve, *"What is this that you have done?"* The woman said, *"The serpent deceived me, and I ate."*[25] The two questions, "Where are you?" and "What is this that you have done?" are representative of the ongoing human dilemma. Eve blamed the serpent; in a sense, she was blaming God as well, simply because God had made the serpent.

The Lord said to the serpent, "Because you have done this, cursed are you...on your belly you shall go, and dust you shall eat all the days of your life. I will put enmity between you and the woman, and between your offspring and her offspring; He shall bruise your head, and you shall bruise His heel."[26]

God is saying to satan, "You used the woman to bring down the human race, and I will use the woman as an instrument to bring the Redeemer into the world, who will save the human race."

This is one of the greatest promises in the Word of God. Notice the phrase *"her offspring."* The Hebrew word translated here "offspring" is actually the word for "seed," and is given as such in most translations. The problem? A woman does not have a seed; the seed comes from the man. This is actually a prophetic promise referring to the birth of Jesus, who while having an earthly mother, Mary, had no earthly father—His Father was God!

The latter part of the verse is also a prophetic foreshadowing of the fact that Jesus, the seed of the woman, the first bride in the Bible, would by His vicarious death pay the ultimate price to purchase a Bride for Himself!

What to Do, What to Do?

Now, man is in a predicament. Adam and Eve had been given dominion over the Garden and the earth,[27] and had just committed high treason and given that authority to God's enemy. We can see this was an actual, legal transaction because in Jesus' wilderness temptation, the enemy attempted to use this as his trump card to seduce Jesus into worshiping him.[28] Now, God the Creator, the Eternal Lover, has had to turn away His beloved Image-bearers because of the sinful choices they have made.

However, God, being the eternal, omniscient One, had already predetermined that His Son, Jesus, would take on the form of flesh, become a man, and pour out His own blood on the Cross as the all-sufficient Bride-price to win the hearts of His beloved ones and make them His eternal Bride and Queen!

What path could get fallen man from the position of a rebellious, sinful, and demonized traitor to the position of an equally yoked Bride of the Lamb? God promised that there would be an offspring from the woman who would bruise the serpent's head. The Holy Spirit, through the apostle Paul, echoes that promise in his epistle to the Galatians, *"Now the promises were made to Abraham and to his offspring. It does not say, 'And to offsprings,' referring to many, but referring to one, 'And to your offspring,' who is Christ."*[29]

God appeared to a man named Abram and offered him a deal he could not refuse, a covenant of love! God told Abram to leave his home country and that He would lead him to a new land that He was going to give to him and his descendents. God promised that He would make his descendents into a great nation, that He would bless him, make his name great, and through him, bless all the nations of the earth.[30] Abram accepted God's offer and left Ur.[31] When Abram arrived in what we know now to be the land of Canaan, God appears to him again and offers to enter into a covenant with him.[32]

As the first stipulation of the covenant, God promises Abram that He would be his shield. This promise includes being Abram's glory, the lifter of his head, his fortress, deliverer, his God, his rock, stronghold, hiding place; He also promises to give him supernatural favor and honor.[33] Amazing, isn't it? But not that amazing if you understand the importance of covenant, and the great lengths that God will go to demonstrate His love.

Steve "S.J." Hill says in his book *Burning Desire*:

A covenant was a binding agreement between two parties. But, in reality, it was so much more than just a mere contract. The Old Testament Hebrew word for covenant literally means "to cut" or "to cut in pieces."[34]

The phrase "cutting the covenant" was a reference to the cutting or dividing of animals into two parts, with the contracting parties passing between them, in making a covenant.[35] The corresponding word in the New Testament Greek has the same meaning. The word is used with reference to God's revelation of Himself in the way of promise or of favor to men.[36]

In ancient cultures, as well as in many cultures even until today, a blood covenant was the strongest bond and agreement that could be entered into between two parties. When one entered into a covenant with another, they were committing to give their life, love, and everything that was part of them. Stanley and Livingston, two of the most famous missionaries to Africa, reported that they had never heard of a blood covenant that had been broken.

In the light of this, you can see the staggering significance of what God was offering to Abram. It is almost unfathomable to think that the uncreated God would enter into this type of covenant with a human being. One of the commitments that the Lord made to Abram was that his descendents would be as many as the stars in Heaven.[37] Abram chose to believe what God offered him.[38] Abram had only one question, *"O Lord God, how am I to know that I shall possess it?"*[39]

In the next chapter, we will see how significant that question, and God's answer was—to Abram, to the people of God throughout all of redemptive history, and to our study on the way God loves us!

CHAPTER 5

I Promise—The Covenant

In the last chapter, we looked at how God told Hosea to go again after Gomer, his wife, who had broken her covenant with him and run after other lovers. We saw that what Hosea did was a prophetic foreshadowing of how God passionately pursues the ones He loves when they turn away from Him.

Next we looked at how Adam failed as Eve's protector, and how even after the first couple had been separated from God by their sin, God promised to redeem them and to bring forth an Ultimate Redeemer through the Person of His Son Jesus. We then looked at how, in order to prepare a people from which His promised Redeemer could come forth from, God approached a man named Abram with a covenant proposition.

God offered a covenant relationship to Abram in which He promised to be everything to Abram. Even though the promises were mind-staggering, Abram believed the Lord.[1] But Abram did ask one question of the Lord, *"O Lord God, how am I to know that I shall possess it?"*[2] There are two ways to ask questions when it comes to things of the Spirit—the right way and the wrong way. First, let's look at the wrong way.

WRONG WAY

In Luke's Gospel, we read about a priest named Zechariah. Zechariah was married to a descendent of Aaron named Elizabeth.

They were both elderly and had no children, for Elizabeth was barren. Zechariah in his duty as a priest was chosen to enter the temple of the Lord and burn incense. While he was carrying out that duty at the hour of incense, there was a multitude of people praying outside.[3]

What a privilege it was to be selected to enter into the inner court of the temple in order to minister to the Lord of Hosts. Zechariah was indeed a blessed man! And was he ever in for a surprise! While the rest of the people waited outside of the Holy Place separated by several feet of solid stone walls and the thick veil, still he could have heard the chants, moans, and cries of the people.

Picture with me this scene. Zechariah stepped up to the ancient altar of incense in Herod's temple behind the curtain, carrying finely ground bits of freshly mixed incense. No doubt, he was reciting the ancient intercessory prayers from the Torah dating back to the time of Moses.

Imagine with me, here is Zechariah, one of the faithful who served in the House of the Lord, keeping the fire on the altar burning as was commanded in the law.[4] And while he was ministering to the Lord, an angel of the Lord appeared on the right side of the altar of incense.[5] Not just another day at the office today, Zechariah. When the angel appeared, Zechariah was troubled and afraid.[6]

> *The angel said to him, "Do not be afraid, Zechariah, for your prayer has been heard, your wife Elizabeth will bear you a son, and you shall call his name John. You will have joy and gladness, and many will rejoice at his birth, for he will be great before the Lord. He must not drink wine or strong drink, and he will be filled with the Holy Spirit, even from his mother's womb. He will turn many to the Lord, and he will operate in the spirit and power of Elijah, to turn the hearts of the fathers to the children, and the disobedient to the wisdom of the just, to make ready for the Lord a people prepared."*[7]

Zechariah's response? A question. *"How shall I know this? For I am an old man, and my wife is advanced in years."*[8] Was that a good response? We get a hint at the answer from the angel's response to Zechariah's query. The angel answered him, *"I am Gabriel. I stand in the Presence of God. I was sent to speak to you and to bring you this good news. And behold, you will be silent and unable to speak until the day that these things take place, because you did not believe my words, which will be fulfilled in their time."*[9]

There is an old saying my mother used to say: "If you can't say anything good, then don't say anything at all." Our friend Zechariah got the opportunity to walk that one out. That was the wrong way to question the Lord and His ways. Now let us look for a moment at the right way.

RIGHT WAY

In the sixth month the angel Gabriel was sent from God to a city of Galilee named Nazareth, to a virgin betrothed to a man whose name was Joseph, of the house of David. The virgin's name was Mary. And he came to her and said, "Greetings, O favored one, the Lord is with you!"[10]

Here is a similar situation to the one we just looked at. Here is a young teenager, a God-fearing young woman who is engaged to be married. An angel appears to her. Like our friend Zechariah, she is caught off guard by this experience.

But she was greatly troubled at the saying, and tried to discern what sort of greeting this might be. The angel said to her, "Do not be afraid, Mary, for you have found favor with God. Behold, you will conceive in your womb and bear a son, and you shall call His Name Jesus. He will be great and will be called the Son of the Most High. And the Lord God will give to Him the throne of His father David, and He will reign over the house of Jacob forever, and of His kingdom there will be no end."[11]

Similar situation, but as we will see, Mary responded quite differently from Zechariah. Mary asks the angel, *"How will this be, since I am a virgin?"*[12] Like Zechariah, Mary responded with a question, but it was not a doubting question, it was an inquiring question. That makes all the difference in the world, as we will see by the angel's response to her inquiry.

"And the angel answered her, 'The Holy Spirit will come upon you, and the power of the Most High will overshadow you; therefore the child to be born will be called holy—the Son of God.'"[13] The angel was not bothered by Mary's question; he simply explained to her the "how" of what he had announced would happen. The lesson to be learned: it is acceptable to ask how, but it is unacceptable to doubt the things revealed by the Lord. Now back to Abram.

LET'S MAKE A DEAL

God was not upset by Abram's inquiry—evidently old Abe wasn't doubting, just asking. Instead, He responded by giving Abram the specific details, so that Abram would see the depth of the agreement and would believe and put his confidence in the enormity of the promise.

God told Abram, *"Bring Me a heifer three years old, a female goat three years old, a ram three years old, a turtledove, and a young pigeon."*[14] Abram brought the animals as he was told and then cut them in half, and laid each half over against the other.[15] Then God had him cut the animals in half. Abram would have known that God was preparing to cut a covenant with him. This in itself would have answered Abram's question, for he would have known that when you cut a covenant you did not have to worry about the provisions being fulfilled.

The animals were laid out with just enough space for someone to walk down the middle between the halves. Normally, both parties walked a figure eight between the cut pieces.[16] As the parties made "the walk of death," they would each proclaim the conditions of the covenant, the blessings if the covenant was kept, and the curses if it was broken.[17]

Not only did "cutting the covenant" involve the person(s) making it, it also included all of their assets and liabilities. If you were in covenant with someone and broke it, your family or tribe would carry out the curse of the covenant on you. If you had enemies, they would become the enemies of your covenant partner. If you had friends, they would become the friends of your covenant partner as well. Covenant was serious stuff!

This was what God was offering Abram. Everything that was Abram's would become God's, and in turn, everything that was God's would become Abram's! They would both now share all their assets, liabilities, friends, and enemies. However, there was a cost—they both had to keep the provisions of the covenant.

This scenario should make us stop and ask ourselves the question—how does a mere man enter into a life-and-death covenant like this with the Almighty God? How could a man keep the provisions of a covenant made with God? What did God hope to gain from such a covenant with a man?

THE HEART OF THE MATTER

As we have already seen, the custom was for both parties in the covenant to walk down the middle of the sacrificed animals. In this covenant, that was not how it happened. The Scripture tells us that as the sun was going down, God caused a deep sleep to fall on Abram.[18] The Hebrew word here is the same word used when God put Adam to sleep back in the Garden of Encounter.[19] Even though he appeared to be in a trance-like state, apparently Abram was still aware of events around him.

The Greek Septuagint was the earliest Greek translation of the Hebrew Scriptures. It was translated by 72 translators (thus its abbreviation LXX) in Alexandria under Pharaoh Ptolemy II (285–247 B.C.). It was the very first translation of Scripture. The Septuagint was widely used among early Christians. Eighty percent of the Old Testament quotations in the New Testament come from the Septuagint.[20]

Our text says, *"As the sun was going down, a deep sleep fell on Abram."* The Septuagint translates the word *sleep* as ecstasy, or trance. The Greek word here means to remove out of its place or state; a putting away, removal of anything out of a place; a trance, sacred ecstasy or rapture of the mind beyond itself when the use of the external senses are suspended and God reveals something in a peculiar manner.[21] There are a number of people throughout the Word of God who experienced this type of encounter with God.[22]

John Wesley, the founder of the Methodist and Wesleyan churches, in his commentary on the Bible, wrote that this was "not a common sleep through weariness or carelessness, but a divine ecstasy, that being wholly taken off from things sensible; he might be wholly taken up with the contemplation of things spiritual. The doors of the body were locked up, that the soul might be private and retired, and might act the more freely."[23]

We are told that a dreadful and great darkness fell upon him. The Hebrew here can mean "an overwhelmingly dark horror." Again, this appears to be a prophetic trance, resulting from being exposed to the indescribable holiness of the Lord.[24] Abram was about to experience the Presence of the Almighty. This was a moment of profound dread and holy awe.[25] Is it possible that this is what Jesus was referring to when He said that Abraham (Abram) saw His day and was glad?[26]

COVENANT IS IMPORTANT

The reason I am going into so much detail concerning the covenant that was cut with Abram is, in the Western church we have almost no understanding of covenant, especially covenant of this type and this magnitude. Remember when we looked at God's instructions to Hosea concerning his wayward wife—"Go again, Hosea!" We, as believers and followers of the Lord Jesus Christ, are told to be *"doers of the word, and not hearers only...."*[27]

Have you ever stopped to think about the fact that God never asks us to do something that He Himself is not doing first? That is why we can trust Him! He tells us to love,[28] but He loves first. He tells us to be merciful, but He is merciful first.[29] He tells us to forgive those who wrong us, but He modeled that for us first.[30]

He tells Hosea to go again after Gomer, to not quit, to do whatever it takes, but the reason He can "rightly" tell Hosea to do that is because that is what He always does for His people. The covenant God made with Abram is part of the overwhelming extent that God is willing to go in order to "go again" after us. Wow!

Let's examine it a little further.

God has instructed Abram to prepare to "cut the covenant" with the Almighty. Then when everything is ready, God's Spirit falls upon Abram, causing him to fall into an ecstatic prophetic trance. While he is in that receptive "spiritually enhanced state of receptivity," God informs him that his descendents will live in servitude in a land that is not theirs for 400 years.[31] He also promises that at the end of that 400-year period, He would judge their captors and bring them out with great wealth.[32]

Then we read, *"When the sun had gone down and it was dark, behold, a smoking fire pot and a flaming torch passed between these pieces."*[33] Abram, because he was in a prophetic trance, could not pass between the pieces of the dead animals as was required to fulfill the requirements of the covenant. So who fulfilled the covenant requirements?

The flaming torch that passed down the middle was Jesus in a pre-incarnate theophany—pre-incarnate referring to the fact that this was before Jesus took on the form of man and was birthed as a human being; a theophany means a God appearance.

WALK A MILE IN MY SHOES

Jesus walked the walk of death for Abram and all his children of faith.[34] Although God offered the covenant to Abram, it was ultimately between God and Christ. The sacrificial death of the animals by Abram was a prophetic symbol of the sacrifice that Christ would make Himself as the Lamb of God to take away the sin of the world.[35]

Now back to one of our earlier premises: we cannot love God until we understand how, or in what manner God loves us.[36] So what was the motivation behind Jesus going to such extreme lengths to ransom a people for Himself? Why would He do such a thing?

Remember what we learned from Paul's teaching in Ephesians 5. From the beginning, God ordained that His Son would have a Bride. Any good husband would lay down his life for the good of his companion.[37] Just as God had chosen the "perfect" bride for Hosea, He has chosen the "perfect" Bride for His Son, Jesus—the offspring of Abram.

To fully appreciate this, you have to understand that in the Jewish culture, marriages were arranged and brides were purchased. A dowry or a down payment was paid to the father of the prospective bride-to-be. In today's Western culture, some take offense at this and say that this would be demeaning to the woman. Not so. In fact, it was just the opposite—it proved the value and worth of the bride.

The bridegroom paid the required price to show how highly he esteemed and valued his future wife; no price was too great to win her love. The apostle Peter, under the inspiration of the Holy Spirit, expressed it this way:

Knowing that you were ransomed from the futile ways inherited from your forefathers, not with perishable things such as silver or gold, but with the precious blood of Christ, like that of a lamb without blemish or spot.[38]

Looking to Jesus, the founder and perfecter of our faith, who for the joy that was set before Him endured the cross...[39]

We were that joy!

Jesus walked "the walk of death" to win the Bride that the Father promised Him. God made a covenant with Abram and his descendents that was ratified by His own Son, so that the ones who believe and receive would be His Son's corporate Bride. Abram said yes, and his name was changed to Abraham,[40] because by cutting the covenant, he inherited the promise of an offspring without number, and from that offspring would come *the* Offspring, Jesus.

THE MARRIAGE PROPOSAL

From the descendents of Abraham, as the Lord had prophesied, was birthed a mighty nation—Israel. As the Lord had foretold, they went into Egypt for 400 years. At the appointed time, as the Word of the Lord had said, God raised up a deliverer, Moses. Moses, in the name of Yahweh, confronted Pharaoh, and brought the children of Israel out of their bondage and into the desert. The desert was not their end—it was their beginning!

Moreover, I have heard the groaning of the people of Israel whom the Egyptians hold as slaves, and I have remembered My covenant. Say therefore to the people of Israel, "I am the Lord, I will bring you out from under the burdens of the Egyptians, I will deliver you from slavery to them, and I will redeem you with an outstretched arm and with great acts of judgment. I will take you to be My people, and I will be your God, and you shall know that I am the Lord your

God, who has brought you out from under the burdens of the Egyptians. I will bring you into the land that I swore to give to Abraham, to Isaac, and to Jacob. I will give it to you for a possession. I am the Lord."[41]

Abraham's offspring are enslaved, feeling abandoned and rejected, living their lives as slaves to the Egyptian king and people. However, God had made a promise!

The prophet Ezekiel describes the same event many years later from the Lord's point of view:

And when I passed by you and saw you wallowing in your blood, I said to you in your blood, "Live!" I said to you in your blood, "Live!" I made you flourish like a plant of the field. You grew up, became tall, and arrived at full adornment. Your breasts were formed, and your hair had grown; yet you were naked and bare.[42]

In Exodus, the Lord records for us what is happening, and in Ezekiel, He reveals to us why it happened! God loves His people as a father loves his children. You can feel the passion when He says to His people:

And when I passed by you and saw you wallowing in your blood, I said to you in your blood, "Live!" I said to you in your blood, "Live!" [43]

God delivered the offspring of Abraham because He had made a covenant to purchase His Son a Bride. He wanted Israel to understand His heart, His motives, and His love! He desired that as they watched Him utterly defeat Pharaoh and his armies, they would realize the love He had for them. Think about it, Israel watched the utter destruction of the mightiest nation and army on the face of the earth at that time.

The wrath of God was awesome to behold, His judgments fearful to see. It was meant to encourage and comfort the people so they would recognize how deeply the Father loved them. His desire was to show Himself as Judge to Egypt but as Father to His people. So He told Moses to tell His people, *"Say this to the people of Israel, 'I AM has sent me to you.'"*[44] I AM your Father, I AM your deliverer, I AM the One who loves you with an everlasting love—I AM! Israel rejoiced, but they did not understand.

They did not understand that God was saying to them, "I want to be everything to you because you are everything to Me." Almost from the day they left Egypt, they murmured, complained, and constantly misinterpreted God's desires and intentions. Therefore, when we see them coming up on the wilderness of Sinai, they had completely forgotten where He had brought them from and where He had promised to take them. They had lost the vision of their destiny.

It is much the same today, isn't it? We can see the awesome power of God demonstrated, we can firsthand see lives changed by the glorious Gospel of our Lord Jesus Christ, we can see signs and wonders done in the name of Jesus; yet in just a moment—if the past couple of weeks haven't gone exactly the way we wanted them to—we forget where we've been, where we are going, and we start complaining. We like to think that we've come a long way, but we are all still much like humankind has always been, aren't we?

Therefore, God has to reintroduce Himself and His motives to His people all over again. "Go again, Hosea…"

WILL YOU MARRY ME?

God initially revealed Himself to the children of Israel as the sovereign Creator, national Deliverer, and loving Father. His intent was that they would recognize the depths of His love toward them and respond with wholehearted love and devotion to Him. However, that desired response was not supposed to be the end of their journey—it was but the beginning. His desire was that from that place of security, His fatherly love would prepare them for their ultimate and highest destiny—Bridehood!

Israel witnessed God's power and His mighty judgments as He delivered them from their Egyptian bondage. Yet, even though they saw it with their eyes, they did not comprehend it with their hearts. This turned out to be an ongoing issue with Israel throughout their history.

Yet God said of them years later, *"For forty years I loathed that generation and said, 'They are a people who go astray in their heart, and they have not known My ways.'"*[45]

It took years for me to understand that statement. I mean, they were in the desert, they packed up when He said move and they stopped when He said stop. They ate when He rained manna on them and they drank when He brought water out of a rock. They lived and traveled in formations that He commanded. They followed the cloud by day and the fire by night. Moses, who had received direct revelation and instructions from God Himself, led them. And they never knew His ways?

However, over the years I have begun to catch a glimpse of what God was referring to. You see, God is not concerned with us learning the letter of the law; He wants us to receive from the Spirit in which the law was given. God is all about relationship.

The law is not just a list of commandments, not at all. The Torah, the first five books of the Bible, was mistakenly translated in the Septuagint by the word *Law.* This misunderstanding of the meaning of the Torah is actually what helped foster the false concept many believe concerning the Old Testament. The Torah is not about Law, it is about covenant. It's about relationship.

God did not want Israel to only know His laws; He wanted them to know His heart! When they misunderstood what happened during the exodus, He came back and re-presented His love for them. However, this time He repackaged it in the form of a wedding proposal.

*You yourselves have seen what I did to the Egyptians, and how I bore you on eagles' wings and **brought you*** *to Myself. If you will obey My voice and keep My covenant, you shall be My treasured possession among all peoples....*[46]

The phrase *"and brought you to Myself"* is the language of a bridegroom bringing the bride to the chamber.[47] Jewish rabbis to this day believe that the Jewish wedding ceremony is a constant re-enactment of the covenant God cut with Israel at Mount Sinai.

The rabbis' understanding of the covenant is revealed by the Lord through Ezekiel, *"When I passed by you again and saw you, behold, you were at the age for love, and I spread the corner of My garment over you and covered your nakedness; I made My vow to you and entered into a covenant with you,"* declares the Lord God, *"and you became Mine."*[48]

You see, the Word of God only makes sense when viewed through the bridal paradigm. The prophetic Scriptures are full of the revelation of how God relates to His people. *"'For your Maker is your Husband, the Lord of hosts is His name; and the Holy One of Israel is your Redeemer, the God of the whole earth He is called. For the Lord has called you like a wife deserted and grieved in spirit, like a wife of youth when she is cast off,' says your God."*[49] God is not a legalistic God who is angry because we do not keep a set of religious rules. Instead, He is a jealous Husband who is fighting to win back the heart of an unfaithful Bride! Get it?

We are told throughout the Bible of the fact that God loves us. Yet, in only one place does God define the manner in which He loves us. *"For as a young man marries a young woman, so shall your sons marry you, and as the bridegroom rejoices over the bride, so shall your God rejoice over you."*[50]

In Jeremiah we read, *"'Behold, the days are coming,' declares the Lord, 'when I will make a new covenant with the house of Israel and the house of Judah, not like the covenant that I made with their fathers on the day when I took them by the hand to bring them out of the land of Egypt, My covenant that they broke, though I was their husband,' declares the Lord."*[51]

The whole of biblical revelation, in both the Old Testament as well as the New, is filled with bridal language and imagery that demonstrates the burning passion that God has for His people. He wants us to know that His heart toward us is as a bridegroom toward his bride.

In the next chapter, we will examine God's offer of marriage to Israel.

CHAPTER 6

The Ceremony

In the last chapter we looked at how the covenant God offered to cut with His people was not just a legal contract, but also a marriage proposal. In this chapter, let us look at this a little further and see the significance of His proposal.

THE BETROTHAL

According to Jewish rabbis, the ancient Jewish wedding consisted of two stages. The first stage is the betrothal. The Jewish wedding contract, called a *ketubah*, listed the terms of the agreement. The bride-to-be first read the contract before she agreed to commit herself to the prospective bridegroom. God's marital contract with Israel was the Torah—the first five books of the Bible.

The Lord spoke to Moses and said, *"Now therefore, if you will indeed obey My voice and keep My covenant, you shall be My treasured possession among all peoples, for all the earth is Mine; and you shall be to Me a kingdom of priests and a holy nation. These are the words that you shall speak to the people of Israel."*[1]

Moses then took the Lord's "proposal" and, *"...called the elders of the people and set before them all these words that the Lord had commanded him."*[2] The Lord had announced the terms of the *ketubah*, the marriage contract to His prospective bride-to-be, so that she could think about it, count the cost, as it were, and decide if she would accept or not.

THE CLEANSING

The next part of the Jewish marriage ceremony was the actual betrothal or the engagement. The Hebrew/Aramaic word for betrothal is *kiddushin*, which signifies "sanctification or separation."[3] A Jewish bride then entered the *mikveh*, ritual bath, in order to be purified prior to the marriage ceremony, as part of the *kiddushin*—literally "being set apart for God."[4]

That is what the Lord required of Israel when He had Moses tell the people, *"Go to the people and consecrate them today and tomorrow, and let them wash their garments."*[5] They were to *"...be to Me a kingdom of priests and a holy nation..."* which is reiterated by the apostle Peter:

> *But you are a chosen race, a royal priesthood, **a holy nation**, a people for His own possession, that you may proclaim the excellencies of Him who called you out of darkness into His marvelous light.*[6]

Years later, this is why John the Baptist came preaching to Israel the message of repentance—the changing of their mind and lifestyles—baptizing them in water.[7] Paul uses this analogy when he describes Jesus as sanctifying and cleansing His Bride. The apostle says, *"that He might sanctify Her, having cleansed Her by the washing of water with the Word, so that He might present the Church to Himself in splendor, without spot or wrinkle or any such thing...."*[8]

He states the same thought in his epistle[9] to Titus when he says, *"He saved us, not because of works done by us in righteousness, but according to His own mercy, by the washing of regeneration and renewal of the Holy Spirit."*[10] The Greek word translated "washing" both here and in the text in Ephesians is not the word for "baptism," but the word *loutron*, which means ceremonial washing—a reference to the *mikveh*, the ritual bath taken by the bride before her wedding.

Since the Jews saw natural marriage as a type of the covenant between God and His people, it was sacred, and therefore to be a lifelong commitment, just as their commitment to God was. Jewish weddings were never hasty events. They were soberly thought out and not rashly entered into, which helped ensure that they were not easily broken. They were well thought out and entered into only after prayerful consideration. Thus, Israel was given time by the Lord to consider and think about what they were giving themselves to.

> *And you shall set limits for the people all around, saying, "Take care not to go up into the mountain or touch the edge of it. Whoever touches the mountain shall be put to death. No hand shall touch him, but he shall be stoned or shot; whether beast or man, he shall not live. When the trumpet sounds a long blast, they shall come up to the mountain." So Moses went down from the mountain to the people and consecrated the people; and they washed their garments. And he said to the people, "Be ready for the third day; do not go near a woman."*[11]

The Lord warned the people not to approach the mountain or even to touch it until they were spiritually prepared to do so. These limitations were not because the Lord did not want them to approach Him, for He did. He gave these instructions because He desired that they would not only enter into His Presence, but also that they would be able to abide in His Presence. Entering into the Presence of the Holy One is a serious thing.

Do You? ...I Do

Jewish belief is that a person is only as good as his word; if a person's word is no good, then he is no good! Before one enters into a sacred covenant like marriage, you have to stop and "count the cost." God proposed and desired that Israel would think about it, and prepare for it, so when the marriage proposal was accepted and entered into, it would be forever.

So what was Israel's answer?

All the people answered together and said, "All that the Lord has spoken we will do." And Moses reported the words of the people to the Lord.[12]

Israel said, "I do"! She made a promise to accept the Lord's covenantal proposal and to commit to keeping her end of the bargain, remaining faithful forever to her Husband God.

HERE COMES THE BRIDE

This brings us to the second stage of the wedding—the consummation. In Jewish culture, once the proposal is offered, considered, and accepted, the bridegroom would then approach the bridal canopy called the *huppah.* There he would stand and wait for the coming of his bride-to-be. The groom usually has one or two attendants who stand with him as he waits. Once the bride joins the groom under the *huppah,* they remain there for the rest of the ceremony. The reason that they do this is because when the Lord descended on Mount Sinai in fire, He waited there for the people, His Bride-to-be, to come out of the camp to meet with Him.

"On the morning of the third day there were thunders and lightnings and a thick cloud on the mountain and a very loud trumpet blast, so that all the people in the camp trembled. Then Moses brought the people out of the camp to meet God, and they took their stand at the foot of the mountain. As the Lord descended upon Mount Sinai in fire, it was wrapped in smoke. The smoke of it went up like the smoke of a kiln, and the whole mountain trembled greatly."[13] The Lord's two attendants, according to the Jewish rabbis, were the two stone tablets containing the Ten Commandments.[14]

Next in Jewish weddings, the bridegroom and his bride, with the bridegroom's two attendants, make their way to the bridal canopy carrying candles. Again, this is modeled after what occurred at Sinai when, after the people joined God on the mountain, all of the people heard the thunder and lightning and saw the thick cloud.

On the morning of the third day there were thunders and lightnings and a thick cloud on the mountain and a very loud trumpet blast, so that all the people in the camp trembled...Now when all the people saw the thunder and the flashes of lightning and the sound of the trumpet and the mountain smoking, the people were afraid and trembled, and they stood far off.[15]

Many Jewish scholars consider the cloud that was on the mountain as the Hoopa, because the Hoopa is to be considered a canopy where the bride and groom would meet in public for the announcement of their union and the beginning of their ceremony. The Hebrew word in these verses for lightning means flaming torch.[16] Just as the Jewish groom and his bride are accompanied by fire, whether it is candles, lamps, or torches, Jehovah and His Bride were escorted by fire as well!

In summary, the Lord approached Abram because He desired to have a corporate Bride. He cut the covenant with Abram, and as part of that covenant promised to raise up a people from his offspring. Then, 430 years later, He keeps His promise to Abraham and delivers the people from their bondage to the Egyptians. What a time of rejoicing that should have been. However, instead of rejoicing in their deliverance, the people were fearful and desired to return to Egypt.

Like Hosea, however, the Lord goes after His wayward Bride yet again. He makes them a corporate proposal—a wedding covenant. He puts on a light show like no one has ever seen, not even on the grandest Fourth of July celebration! The people see and respond with a resounding yes. You would think, after all of that, the people would finally understand and see the Lord for who He is, the God who loves them with an everlasting love. Alas, it was not to be.

STOP IT—YOU'RE SCARING ME

The Lord revealed His glory, the thunderings, the flashes of lightning, the clouds of smoke, the shaking of the mountain under the weighty Presence of God—all intended by God to exhilarate and fascinate them, to cause them to love and worship Him. Yet again, as during the exodus, they misinterpret who the Lord is and what He is doing. Instead of being drawn to Him, they pull back from Him.

> Now when all the people saw the thunder and the flashes of lightning and the sound of the trumpet and the mountain smoking, the people were afraid and trembled, and they stood far off and said to Moses, "You speak to us, and we will listen; but do not let God speak to us, lest we die."[17]

Moses is appalled by the people's reaction. He says to them, "Do not fear, for God has come to test you, that the fear of Him may be before you, that you may not sin."[18] Notice, Moses heard the same thunderings, he saw the same flashes of lightning, and he experienced the same weighty cloud of the Lord's Presence as they did. Yet instead of being afraid, he responded appropriately, he wanted more. Therefore, he tries to reason with the people to get them to reconsider what they have chosen.

Moses recognized what all of Israel should have discerned as well, that God was not trying to frighten the people or harm them. God doesn't want a fearful Bride; He desires a wholehearted, loving Bride. God desired that Israel be so enraptured with Him that they would give their hearts fully to Him to such a degree that they would never be tempted to follow other lovers or other gods.

God has always wanted His people to be fascinated with Him. The Scriptures admonish us to have a healthy fear of the Lord,[19] but that doesn't mean that we are to "be afraid" of the Lord; rather that we should have a reverential respect and awe of Him. God's desire was that they see how big, how powerful, and how holy He was and respond in awe, in fascination, in worship, and in bridal love.

Solomon tells us the fear of the Lord is instruction in wisdom.[20] The Hebrew word for "fear" means reverence, fear, i.e., a state of piety and respect toward a superior; worship, i.e., the act, or speech of showing profound reverence toward a superior, which may include ritual action; awesomeness, i.e., that which causes wonder and astonishment.[21]

God's desire was to win the hearts of His people. That has always been His desire. The question is: how does an infinite God reveal Himself to finite humankind without either overwhelming them, which causes them to back away, or not showing them how holy He really is, which would encourage them to come before Him presumptuously, resulting in them being destroyed?

And the Lord said to Moses, "Go down and warn the people, lest they break through to the Lord to look and many of them perish. Also let the priests who come near to the Lord consecrate themselves, lest the Lord break out against them."[22]

If we rightly recognize the Lord for who He is, we are marked for Him alone; we are ruined for anything less; and as a result, we start to live for another age.

THE HEART'S LONGING FOR FASCINATION

Beloved, one of the greatest needs and desires we have is the need to be fascinated, to be in awe of something bigger than we are. God had offered Israel what every human being wants and needs, something bigger, something grander, and something that transcends the ordinary and draws us up into a higher realm. In our spiritual DNA, we have a need to be in awe, to be fascinated, to be spiritually "entertained" by something bigger and better than life in this world. In other words, we need God.

In several places, the Bible tells us about some of the heaven-ly beings that dwell in God's Presence. One group of these beings are called the living creatures, or seraphim, which literally means "burning ones." These burning ones gaze upon the throne of God night and day with holy fascination that results in them constantly expressing extravagant worship.[23] They constantly gaze at the Person of God and are repeatedly overwhelmed by the brilliance of His glory.

> *In the year that King Uzziah died I saw the Lord sitting upon a throne, high and lifted up; and the train of His robe filled the temple. Above Him stood the seraphim. Each had six wings: with two he covered his face, and with two he covered his feet, and with two he flew. One called to another: "Holy, holy, holy is the Lord of hosts; the whole earth is full of His glory!"*[24]

We see a similar scene thousands of years later.

> *...And around the throne, on each side of the throne, are four living creatures, full of eyes in front and be-hind: the first living creature like a lion, the second living creature like an ox, the third living creature with the face of a man, and the fourth living creature like an eagle in flight. And the four living creatures, each of them with six wings, are full of eyes all around and within, and day and night they never cease to say, "Holy, holy, holy, is the Lord God Almighty, who was and is and is to come!" Whenever the living creatures give glory and honor and thanks to Him who is seated on the throne, who lives forever and ever, the twenty-four elders fall down before Him who is seated on the throne and worship Him who lives forever and ever. They cast their crowns before the throne, saying, "Worthy are You, our Lord and God, to receive glory and honor and power, for You created all things, and by Your will they existed and were created."*[25]

Notice what the heavenly host say about the Lord. They declare that He is holy. In many Christian circles, when the word *holy* is used, the meaning conveyed is usually that of separation from what is unclean and a consecration to what is pure. This is a valid and necessary definition.

However, moral purity is not the primary definition of holy—at least not when used in referring to the Person of God. Now do not get me wrong, God *is* separated from what is unclean and He *is* pure to the nth degree! However, that is not the primary definition of *God's* holiness. The primary definition of *holy* is His transcendence over creation *and* the moral perfection of His character. God is holy in that He is utterly distinct from His creation and exercises sovereign majesty and power over it.

The *burning ones,* the beings nearest to God's throne, are constantly seen bowing and covering their eyes in response to the awesomeness of God's beauty. They bow and rise up, bow and rise, again and again, crying, *"Holy, holy, holy,"* which literally means, *"Transcendent in beauty, transcendent in beauty, transcendent in beauty!"*[26]

They testify that those who gaze upon the beauty of the Lord will never grow bored with such a gaze. It is no wonder then that Jesus' name is often called Wonderful because He alone can satisfy the hearts of His people with wonderment. The unceasing declaration of the ransomed will forever be, *"He is Wonderful."*[27]

We as the Image-bearers were created to experience the depths of God's glory and we can experience it to a measure in this life, and in a fuller measure throughout all of eternity. At the core of every human heart there is a yearning to be filled with perpetual wonder—as I said previously, it is in our DNA.

ENTERTAINMENT = FALSE FASCINATION

Hollywood and the entertainment industry discovered this longing and they have targeted it commercially. Even at its pinnacle, however, worldly entertainment is no match for encountering the fascinating God.[28] I hear it all the time, "I don't like to pray, to worship, to read the Bible. God is boring." The problem, however, isn't that God is boring; the problem is *we* are boring. Whenever we are not fascinated with Him, we live bored, spiritually dull, and spiritually passive. To a heart not regularly experiencing fascination with God, the inferior substitutes of money, drugs, alcohol, and immorality are far more enticing, though in the end they are entirely unsatisfying.

In the United States, our entertainment industry controls a major share of our economic system and an even larger portion of our time. It is the age-old economics of supply and demand on an emotional level; only in this instance, the product does not even begin to meet the demand. Today's blockbuster movies are ancient history, sometimes within a week.

We take turns between being fascinated by and subsequently bored with our hobbies. That which we believed we could not do without becomes abruptly unsatisfying to us. We do the same thing with all types of entertainment, sports, and hobbies. Once it has been experienced, it is too often finished. And we feel even more discontent for it.

I am certainly not against wholesome, healthy entertainment, but I am concerned about the primacy of its place in our society, especially its place in the Church. As believers increase their consumption of earthly amusements, they also deaden their ability to be fascinated by God—spiritual death on the installment plan. It is not that we do not want to experience God; it is just that we cannot find Him amidst the bombardment of data to which we are constantly exposing ourselves.

It is spiritually imperative we recognize the segments of entertainment that are more than just unsatisfying, they are also overtly harmful. As we endeavor to fulfill our inherent desires through books, films, music, and other forms of entertainment, we are moved in profoundly personal places. We expose ourselves to destructive messages, only to find ourselves disappointed, fractured, and abused by these forms of entertainment. By exposing our hearts to some forms of so-called entertainment, we feed our souls with attitudes about people and relationships that can take years to undo. And it is the enemy's plan for it to be that way.

The strategy of the enemy of our soul is to twist the God-given desire we have for fascination and to use it to lure us into activities that result in the numbing of our spiritual perception of the fascinating beauty of God. We find ourselves worn out with our pursuance of everything except the face of God. The push for position or entertainment will drop by the wayside only as we intentionally set out to behold the beauty of Jesus of Nazareth.

I have said a lot about entertainment. I truly do not want to discount the validity of some of these things. It is not that they all are illegitimate or bad; they are simply inferior to the superior pleasures of God. God's strategy is to free people from believing the lie that their earthly assignments are all that there is in life. Beloved, we are called to something bigger than that.

Most people live their lives with the fear of missing out on something. They cannot stand the thought of hearing their friends talk about the latest movie they have not seen or a new song they have not heard. They hunger for experience and expend a huge amount of energy to remain current on the temporal, inferior pleasures of life, while in the process they are missing the superior pleasures of God. They never have time to be fascinated by the beauty of God because they are consumed with the potential of what they can achieve on their own.

Fascination Is Only Satisfied in God

I have news for you—the devil did not invent the concept of pleasure. He does not create; he counterfeits and uses his counterfeits to ruin the hearts of humankind. God created us with the capacity to experience physical, emotional, and mental pleasures.

The highest and most intense of the God-given pleasures is found in the realm of spiritual pleasure. When God the Spirit reveals God the Son to those created in God's own image, the Image-bearers, our spirit resonates within us. This is the most outstanding experience of pleasure available to us. This revealing of God, by God, allows us to know "spiritual entertainments."[29]

As a young man, King David, *"the man after God's own heart,"*[30] encountered God's beauty, and it charted the course for the rest of his life. He writes:

> *One thing have I asked of the Lord, that will I seek after: that I may dwell in the house of the Lord all the days of my life, to gaze upon the beauty of the Lord and to inquire in His temple.*[31]

David was the man with the whole kingdom of Israel under his leadership, one of the most influential men on the planet at the peak of his reign, yet encountering God was the most important focus of his life. All the palaces, wives, horses, and armies paled compared to that one thing, and he established it as his life's ambition to acquire one more glance, one more...and one more....

MASTERING SPIRITUAL BOREDOM

One of the major issues in the Body of Christ today is that of spiritual boredom. Many churches are full of people who have been overwhelmed with entertainment and recreation. Pastors feel obligated to compete with the things that wrestle for the attention of their flocks. Listening to the Lord becomes secondary to working out how they are going to gain the atrophied attention of people who require an instantaneous shot of stimulation. An evening out at the latest Hollywood smash-hit movie moves us to tears, but the early morning worship service does nothing for us, numbed as we are into requiring drive-thru fulfillment and stimulation, instead of giving ourselves to eternal fascination. It is sad how we invest what limited passion we have in things that can never fulfill or satisfy us.

The apostle Paul tells us that the Holy Spirit searches, or discerns, the deep and hidden things of God's being in order that He may reveal and impart them to us.[32] Invited by the Spirit, directed by the glory of God, manifested through His creation and His Word, we have the privilege of searching out and observing an infinite God.[33]

We have a beautiful God, One who invites us to daily encounter His beauty, but there is one catch—it takes time and energy to plumb out the depths of God. It takes time and energy to worship, pray, fast, and meditate on the Word of God. Those who expend their energies in the pursuit of lesser forms of entertainment rapidly discover themselves exhausted and burnt out.

As I minister on the importance of prayer and moving into the deeper realms of a prayer life with Jesus, people often say to me, "I just don't have the time for a devotional life in prayer and the Word of God." The reason they "don't have time" is that they do not have a vision of what God has in store for them as they wait before Him.

A "devotional life" is not a bargaining chip to get God to pay attention to us. It is the doorway into the highest pleasure knowable to a human being. It is the fast track into God's power and into having an enthralled heart! In revealing His Son, God fascinates His people beyond anything they have ever known or even conceived of. This fascination serves as a "holy protection mechanism" from all the deceptions of the enemy, and it strengthens believers with a godly motivation to always reach toward the beauty that will remain when all else fades away.

Many of God's people, well-meaning people, find themselves without the time or vitality to worship, pray, or read the Bible. Beloved, we cannot give ourselves to a hundred pursuits at the expense of seeking out and encountering the fascinating God. We cannot over-saturate our souls with dead-end activity. If we do, it will only result in a dull spirit. A dull spirit is the breeding ground for a thousand forms of sin and evil.

That is why so many people have reduced their lives to rubble. Men and women who were made to wonder at the glory of God, instead live bored and directionless lives. They have no revelation of God. They graduate from high school full of hope and promise, and 15 years later find themselves spiritually bored, unconnected, and apart from God's people—addicted to porn, alcohol, drugs, or the pursuit of making money, and in the ruins of a second or third marriage. Sure, they have a myriad of excuses for their many addictions, boredom, and unsuccessful family relationships...but they typically all center on unmet expectations.

But I have good news for you! God is masterminding a glorious reformation that will unveil Himself to this generation as the One who truly satisfies. At the end of the age, God's people will be more fascinated with Jesus than at any other time in history.[34] They will be ravished by what they behold in Jesus. It will transform their very beings as the beauty of God on His throne stirs them.

THE ANSWER? GAZING ON THE BEAUTY OF GOD

There just are not enough hours in the day. If we are really going to satisfy the longing of our heart for fascination, we must make the same decision that David did, "to pursue one thing... to behold the beauty of God." Pleasure is the only thing that will motivate us to abandon the lesser things and commit ourselves to Jesus. God revealing God to the human spirit is the most exhilarating experience in the universe. This "spiritual entertainment" causes worldly entertainment and human achievement to fade away in obvious inferiority. As we increasingly see Him in all His glory and brilliance, boredom ceases to be an issue.

A satisfied, fascinated believer is spiritually secure with a heightened measure of protection from satan's strategies. Opportunities for sin are easier to pass up when we are occupied with the beauty of God. The deceptions of the enemy are more easily seen for what they are: unsatisfactory, and undesirable, distractions from that which is genuinely fulfilling.

The beauty of God achieves its high point in the revealing of Jesus as our Bridegroom King. The irresistible beauty of the Bridegroom King will ravish the end-time Church, enabling Her to overcome persecution and tribulation, while remaining impassioned in love.[35] Even in death, believers will set their eyes only upon the One who will soon split the sky with His appearing and demolish the enemy with His brightness.[36]

Jesus will be the focus of the saints, and they will burn with a holy fascination as they gaze upon His unsurpassed beauty. This is one of the primary themes in the bridal paradigm of the Kingdom of God—the Lord's promise to reveal the beauty of Jesus in an unequaled way to the generation that will see His return.

Within the bridal paradigm of the Kingdom, God is revealing the beauty of Jesus as the Bridegroom God, making the inferior pleasures obsolete, and communicating His own transcendent beauty in order to fascinate His end-time Church. Pornography, riches, or self-promotion do not appeal to a person fascinated with Christ Jesus.

Jesus Himself will win the heart of His Church as the Holy Spirit unlocks the treasure of His beauty and splendor. The Church will fall hopelessly in love—in a bridal manner—with the Man Jesus, considering it their glory to give up everything to and for Him.

Because, as we have seen, the bridal paradigm has been central to the Gospel message from the beginning, why do we hear so little about it? It is because of the faulty Western worldview. In the next chapter, we will look at worldviews.

CHAPTER 7

Worldviews

"For the life of me, I just can't see how in the world you can believe that."

Have you ever spoken those words to someone? On the other hand, maybe someone spoke those words to you about something you believe? Me too. More than once, I have to admit! Why would someone say those words to another person? Why would someone not be able to see or agree with what someone else sees or believes? The answer, or one of the possible answers, is the person's worldview.[1]

The worldview to which one ascribes determines the way in which one theologizes and the way one applies the teachings of the Bible to how one lives day-to-day life. Everyone has a worldview and operates from within the worldview he holds, but very few operating within a worldview are conscious that they even have one. We all assume that the way we view life is the way everybody sees life. Our assumption is that what we see is reality; while in fact, our worldview determines what we see and interpret as "reality." A person's worldview is his or her "control box."[2]

I am an American, and so like most Americans, I was raised with a Western/European worldview. For the most part, we in the Western church hold a worldview that has a blind spot that keeps us from dealing with or understanding problems related to God, the Bible, spirits, or anything supernatural. Dr. Paul Hiebert calls this "The Flaw of the Excluded Middle."

This Flaw of the Excluded Middle worldview often hinders us from fully engaging in a biblical lifestyle by making us blind to what is all around us—it's there but we can't see it. To understand or live in a biblical lifestyle requires a paradigm shift for most people because their worldview prohibits God from continuing to act or be the same in each era of history.

WHAT IS IN A WORLDVIEW?

Have you ever stopped to think that it is possible that your worldview, paradigm (same thing), or the way you have been taught to think, act, and react to the Bible might actually be preventing you from experiencing what God desires to give you as a Christian? Another way to ask it is: do we, as the Body of Christ in the Western world, and do I personally, have a worldview? If I have one, is it a valid one? Is my worldview working for me or against me? If my worldview is faulty, am I trapped in the worldview that I have, or can I change?

WORLDVIEW DEFINITIONS

James Sire, a Christian author, speaker, and former editor for InterVarsity Press, wrote the book *The Universe Next Door*, a textbook on worldviews that has been used at over 100 colleges and universities in courses ranging from apologetics and world religions to history and English literature. He defines a worldview:

> A worldview is a set of presuppositions (or assumptions) which we hold (consciously or subconsciously) about the basic makeup of our world.[3]

Dr. Charles Kraft, an American anthropologist and linguist, whose work since the early 1980s has focused on inner healing and spiritual warfare, is the Sun-Hee Kwak Professor of Anthropology and Intercultural Communication in the School of Intercultural Studies at Fuller Theological Seminary in Pasadena, California, teaching primarily in the school's spiritual dynamics concentration. Dr. Kraft says, concerning worldviews:

> Cultures pattern perceptions of reality into conceptu- alizations of what reality can or should be; what is to be regarded as actual, probable, possible or impossi- ble. These conceptualizations form what is termed the 'worldview' of our culture. The worldview is the central systematization of conceptions of reality to which the members of its culture assent (largely unconsciously) and from which stems their value system. The world- view lies at the very heart of the culture, touching, in- teracting with, and strongly influencing every aspect of the culture.[4]

Is that a mouthful or what? What Dr. Kraft is saying is every- one has a set of assumptions that serves as a starting point for his or her perceptions of reality. These assumptions are empirically, or experientially, learned realities. Therefore, people from differ- ent worldviews can use the same reasoning process to arrive at very different conclusions about a matter.

WORLDVIEW EXAMPLES

Suppose I were to hand a gas can to people who had never been taught anything concerning the laws of physics, and asked them to empty the can by pouring out all of the gas. They do as I ask and pour out all of the gas.

Then I ask them the following question, "What was in the can?" They would respond, "Gasoline." I then follow up with the inquiry, "What is in the can now?" They would probably come back with something like, "Nothing, the can is empty." Ah, but is the "empty" can actually empty? No. Because we know that as the gas was being poured out of the can, at the same time, and at the same ratio, the space in the can was being filled up by air that was displacing the gas. So is the gas can full or is it empty? All depends on your worldview.

FIRST THE NATURAL, THEN THE SPIRITUAL

Another example, this one from the Bible, occurred in Acts chapter 14. There was a lame man who had been crippled from birth and had never walked. Paul and Barnabas' apostolic team was ministering in Lystra; Paul received a word of knowledge[5] that God was going to heal the lame man. He publicly called him out and ministered healing to him in the name of Jesus.

The locals observed the healing of the cripple by Paul—supposedly, because of their worldview, only the Greek gods had power to heal—and recognized that Paul and Barnabas must be Zeus and Hermes come down to visit them. They proceeded to offer sacrifices to the "gods" of Paul and Barnabas. When Paul and Barnabas realize what the people believe and are about to do, they attempt to explain to them the facts. However, because of their worldview, what Paul tells them doesn't make sense, and therefore can't be true. Even after it was explained to them, they *"scarcely restrained the people from offering sacrifice to them."*[6] Illogical? Depends on your worldview.

DIFFERENT ASSUMPTIONS—DIFFERENT CONCLUSIONS

In our Western culture, we have been trained to hold a scientific worldview that says the world operates with predictable realities, cause and effect in a closed system. Therefore, we can usually find reasons why things happen—weather, sickness or health, misfortune or success—and we can predict what is going to happen.

For example, airplanes have a "black box" that is in actuality an onboard computer with a data storage device that collects and keeps data concerning the operation of the plane, both mechanically and of the personnel. If the plane has an accident, the investigators work to recover the black box because, in their worldview, everything has a cause, so if they can just find the data, they will then know the reason why the accident occurred. Case closed.

Therefore, we in the West have a worldview that our personal perceptions are founded on rational thought processes, even if they are not. That is why often when someone we know does something out of character or harmful to us or to someone else, most Westerners want to know why they did it. They want the offending person to explain why. There has to be a logical reason. Why? Because that is their worldview.

EASTERN CULTURE—THE EXPERIENTIAL WORLDVIEW

The Western worldview, as we have seen, believes everything has a simple cause and effect. In contrast, the Eastern worldview operates on a much more capricious note: people who hold it have been trained that there are powers beyond control or predictability. Because of that worldview, personal perceptions are more likely to be formed by experience than by theory or rational thought.

For instance, if we ask someone with an Eastern worldview who lives near the equator and has never seen or experienced snow, if they can grow food in snow-covered soil, their reply would be something like, "I don't know, I have never been there." To someone from the West, we would say, all we have to do is look up the information and we would know the answer. To someone with an Eastern worldview, that is a ridiculous answer, you *cannot* know that because you have not been there. The Western worldview depends upon rationale; the Eastern worldview depends upon experience.

HOW ASSUMPTIONS AND CONCLUSIONS WORK IN A CULTURE		
CULTURAL FEATURE	ASSUMPTIONS	CONCLUSION
Clothing	• Immodest to be naked (USA). • One covers one's body only if hiding something (Gava people, Nigeria). • For ornamentation only (Higi people, Nigeria).	• Must wear clothes, even to bed. • Go naked to prove yourself innocent. • Wear on occasion only. Rearrange or change in public.
Buying	• Impersonal, economic transaction (USA). • Social, person-to-person (Africa, Asia, Latin America).	• Fixed prices. No interest in seller as a person. Get it over quickly. • Dicker over price. Establish personal relationship. Take time.
Youthfulness	• Desirable (USA). • Tolerated, to be overcome (Africa).	• Look young, act young. Cosmetics. • Prove yourself mature. Act older.
Aged	• Undesirable (USA). • Desirable (Africa).	• Dreaded. Old people unwanted. • Old people revered.
Education	• Primarily formal, outside home, teacher-centered (USA). • Primarily informal, in the home, learner-centered (Africa).	• Formal schools. Hired specialists. • Learn by doing. Discipleship. Proverbs and folktales.

HOW ASSUMPTIONS AND CONCLUSIONS WORK IN A CULTURE		
CULTURAL FEATURE	ASSUMPTIONS	CONCLUSION
Family	• Centered around spouses (USA). • For the children (Africa).	• Compatibility of spouses is key. • Mother/child relationship is key.
Rapid change	• Good, change = progress (USA). • Threat to security (Africa).	• Encourage change/innovation. • Conservatism/stability valued.

Want to hear a shocker? You do not believe the Bible. Don't get upset, neither do I. Most people don't. We do not believe the Bible, we believe what "we" believe about the Bible. In other words, we are at the mercy of our worldview—good or bad. Let me give you an example.

A THEOLOGICAL EXAMPLE

In his book *The Charismatics*, well-known Bible teacher John MacArthur writes:

As we study the Scripture, we find three categories of spiritual gifts. In Ephesians 4 there is the category of gifted men: apostles, prophets, evangelists, teaching pastors and teachers. These gifted men are called to be leaders in the church. Secondly, there are the permanent edifying gifts, which would include knowledge, wisdom, prophecy, teaching, exhortation, faith (or prayer), discernment, showing mercy, giving, administration, and helps (see Rom. 12:3-8; 1 Cor. 12:8-10, 28).

Thirdly, there were the temporary sign gifts. These were certain enablements given to certain believers for the purpose of authenticating or confirming God's Word when it was proclaimed in the early church before the Scriptures were penned. These sign gifts were temporary. Their purpose was not primarily to edify, although sometimes edification did occur. The four temporary sign gifts were miracles, healings, tongues, and interpretation of tongues.

These four sign gifts had a unique purpose—to give the apostles credentials, to let the people know that these men all spoke the truth of God. But once the Word of God was inscripturated, the sign gifts were no longer needed and they ceased.

The gift of miracles and...the gift of healing were miraculous sign gifts that were given to help the apostolic community to confirm their preaching of the Gospel message in the early years of the Church. Once the Word of God was completed, the signs ceased. Miraculous signs were no longer needed.[7]

What Pastor MacArthur is articulating in these paragraphs reflects what Sire has called "worldview confusion," which "occurs whenever a reader of Scripture fails to interpret the Bible within the intellectual and broadly cultural framework of the Bible itself and uses instead *a foreign frame of reference.*"[8]

MacArthur's "worldview confusion" comes at a point of forcing a system of interpretation on the Scriptures known as Dispensationalism, a framework that comes with a set of presuppositions that the miraculous works of the Scripture are no longer for today's Church. Therefore, they do not exist, and any evidence of signs and wonders is therefore false.

How does that affect Christians in the West who share MacArthur's worldview? Approximately 75 percent of Jesus' earthly ministry as recorded in the four Gospels was focused on healing, casting out devils and miracles; 25 percent was focused on teaching. Those who share Pastor MacArthur's worldview put all of their emphasis on the 25 percent focused on teaching and relate to the other 75 percent mainly as unique to the earthly ministry of Jesus and the generation of the original apostolic company.

Healing, casting out devils, and miracles, since they were unique to that timeframe, has little or no practical bearing on modern believers. If they are taught on at all, it is usually within the context of proving the Messianic mission of Jesus, demonstrating the apostolic calling of the 12 apostles of the Lamb—in preparation for their part in the writing of the biblical canon—or as illustrative examples to be used in teaching. For instance, Jesus calmed the literal raging sea to show us that He can calm the emotional sea that we find ourselves in today. Get it?

So if a 21st century believer prays for the sick based on the teachings of Scripture, the dispensational, cessationist worldview cannot see or accept the validity of that scriptural practice due to his or her worldview that maintains that the Bible cannot mean what it says in those areas. Therefore, a Christian who practices praying for the sick either is deceived or is a deceiver. In addition, the person who has received healing is deceived because the person mistakenly believes that God healed him; but since that is not for today, he was actually either healed by the devil or it was just a psychosomatic illness—he was never really sick in the first place.

THE FLAW OF THE EXCLUDED MIDDLE

Dr. Paul Hiebert, former professor at the Fuller Seminary School of World Missions, says that the Western worldview has a blind spot that makes it difficult for many Western missionaries and pastors to understand, let alone answer, problems related to spirits, ancestors, and astrology. In his article, "The Flaw of the

Excluded Middle," Dr. Hiebert speaks about the uneasiness he had as a missionary in India. He begins his article by saying:

> John's disciples ask, "Are you He that should come or do we look for another?" (see Luke 7:20). Jesus answered not with logical proofs, but by a demonstration of power in the curing of the sick and casting out of evil spirits. So much is clear. Yet when I read the passage as a missionary in India, and sought to apply it to missions in our day, I had a strange uneasiness. As a Westerner, I was used to presenting Christ on the basis of rational arguments, not by evidences of His power in the lives of people who were sick, possessed and destitute. In particular, the confrontation with spirits that appeared so natural a part of Christ's ministry belonged in my mind to a separate world of the miraculous—far from ordinary experience.
>
> Why my uneasiness with reading the Scripture? Was the problem, at least in part, due to my own worldview—to the assumptions I as a Westerner made about the nature of reality and the way I viewed the world?[9]

Dr. Hiebert answers his own question:

People in Indian villages have many diseases, curses of barrenness on women, bad tempers, bad luck, being possessed by spirits and black magic practices. The Indian villages have traditional ways of dealing with diseases:

Serious life threatening cases: With these cases they take the person to a sadhu—a "saint." This is a person of the gods who claims to heal by prayer. Because god knows everything they ask no questions. Because they are spiritual they charge no fees. But one is expected to give if a cure came about.

Supernatural cases: With these cases they go to a Mantrakar or magician. This one cures by knowledge and control of supernatural forces and spirits, believed to be here on earth. They work with chants and visual symbols to control the forces and spirits. They ask no questions, receive no fees.

Medicine: Some people would go to doctors who cure by means of scientific knowledge based on medicine. They ask no questions but diagnose by feeling wrists, stomachs, etc. They charge high fees and give a guarantee that one only pays if the patient is healed.

Quacks: These people heal with folk remedies. They ask questions, charge low fees, give no guarantees. The people being treated have to pay before receiving treatment. (At the beginning, Western doctors were often equated with quacks.)

When a person became a Christian, they substituted the missionary for the saint! Christ replaced Krishna or Siva as the healer of their spiritual diseases. For the illnesses they had, they went to Western doctors or village quacks. But what about the plagues that the magician cured? What about spirit possession, or curses, or witchcraft, or black magic? What was the Christian answer to these?

Because of the Western culture's assumptions, the only conclusion one had was "They do not exist!" But to the people who really experienced these phenomena, there had to be an answer. So even the Christians turned to the magician for cures.[10]

Let us see how this happened by looking at the following chart, which shows a three-tiered view of reality that most people apart from our Western mindset have. The Western world simply has excluded the middle tier.

TRANSCENDENT WORLD BEYOND OURS *(includes)*	RELIGION
• Hells, heavens, other times i.e., eternity • High god (African); Vishnu, Siva (Hindu) • Cosmic forces; karma • Yahweh, angels, demons, spirits of worlds	Faith Sacred Miracles Other-worldly problems
SUPERNATURAL FORCES ON THIS EARTH *(includes)*	EXCLUDED MIDDLE *(by Westerners)*
• Spirits, ghosts, ancestors, demons • Earthly gods, goddesses who live in trees, rivers, hills, villages • Supernatural forces: planetary influences, magic, sorcery, witchcraft • Holy Spirit, angels, demons, signs and wonders, gifts of the Holy Spirit	
EMPIRICAL WORLD OF OUR SENSES *(includes)*	SCIENCE
• Folk sciences to explain how things occur • Explanations based on empirical observations • Person shoots deer, attributes death to arrow • Person cooks meal, attributes cooking to fire under pot	Sight and experience Natural order Secular

• Theories about natural world	This-worldly problems
• How to build a house, plant crops, sail canoe	
• Theories about human relationships	
• How to raise children, treat spouse, have friends	

THE NEED FOR A PARADIGM SHIFT

Dealing with our worldview and going through a paradigm shift is sometimes extremely painful. Even so it may be necessary to examine our worldview and to modify or expand it in order for us to operate within a New Testament paradigm/model.

A paradigm is defined by Webster as an example or pattern. A shift indicates moving from one model or pattern to another. See the illustration of how this works:

THE YOUNG LADY OR THE OLD WOMAN

The young lady, old woman illustration[11] can help demonstrate this shifting process. The lines of the drawing do not shift. There is, however, a shift in the perception of the observer. As the observer looks at the picture, the visual pattern seems to shift. This, on a small scale, is similar to a paradigm shift or worldview change. As you go through this simple procedure, which is necessary to see these realities differently, try to imagine the complexity of a paradigm shift that leads to a radically different understanding of reality. Even though it is complex, it can be accomplished.

THE PRICE OF TEA IN CHINA THING

You may be asking yourself at this point, what does that have to do with the price of tea in China, or more pointedly, what does that have to do with loving God and the bridal paradigm? I am glad you asked that question...

When I was a new believer in Jesus, most if not all of the books my spiritual leaders recommended to me were authored by dispensational cessationists. That means that, like Pastor MacArthur, they believed and taught that the 75 percent of the works that Jesus did in the Gospels were not for today. Therefore, even though I was a radical, Bible-studying young man, my worldview caused me to see, or actually *not* to see, two-thirds of what was in the Gospels.

When I read about Jesus talking to the Samaritan woman at the well in John chapter 4, I was desirous to follow His example and to be used by God to evangelize as He did. I never even considered that in order to do that, I might have to receive words of knowledge, as He did, to prepare the woman's heart, thus making a decision possible. After all, the gifts were not for today!

After I had been initiated into the fullness of the empowering ministry of the Holy Spirit, my paradigm shifted. I found that when I read the same Bible I had been reading for over three years, all of a sudden I saw the supernatural moving and ministry of the Spirit almost on every page. It was as if I had received a new Bible.

It is the same with the bridal paradigm. I had read the Scriptures, taught them in fact, yet I had never *seen* what is everywhere from Genesis to Revelation. Maybe you are like I was—you have seen but have not seen.

ACQUIRING A NEW PARADIGM

How can we as Western Christians acquire the paradigm shift that is required to walk in New Testament reality? First, prayerfully investigate alternative worldviews by re-reading the Bible, and reading books or listening to messages by others who accept an alternative worldview; second, find a believing community whose worldview accepts the "excluded middle" tier and observe what is happening there.

As we have seen, the bridal paradigm of the Kingdom of God was God's idea and is everywhere in the Bible once you change the lens you view it through. In the next chapter, we will do a quick survey of how encompassing the bridal paradigm is throughout the Old Testament.

CHAPTER 8

The Bridal Paradigm in the Old Testament

"You just don't know what a hornet's nest you have stirred up!"

My Methodist pastor, John, said these words to me after I had filled in for him at our Wednesday mid-week service. John was bi-vocational, and because of his job as a technician, he sometimes had to travel further out on calls than what would allow him to get back in time for our mid-week service. Since I was one of his "preacher boys," he would often ask me to fill in for him.

I had come into the church from a reformed heathen background, so I knew very little of spiritual things. However, I was hungry. I had run hard after the devil, had dabbled in the occult, and had been involved in many dark areas in my life. I was determined to live for God more intensely than I had lived for the devil. Therefore, I immediately became a serious student of the Bible.

I was an avid reader; I always had a book in my hands and usually was reading two or three different books at the same time. So John was quick to feed me "good" Christian reading material, and I am so thankful for it; I learned so much from them. All of the authors I was given, though, were dispensational in their theology. Dispensationalism is a system of biblical interpretation that originated in the mid-1800s through the ministry and writings of John Nelson Darby, C.I. Scofield, and Lewis Sperry Chafer.

The dispensationalist interpretation emphasizes the distinguishable elements within the dispensations. The most characteristic hermeneutical concern for dispensationalism is the consistent distinction between National Israel and the Church.[1] Another concept developed by the dispensationalist is the doctrine of cessationalism. A cessationist believes that the spiritual gracelets,[2] or spiritual gifts, passed away with the completion of the biblical canon and the transition that occurred in the Church with the death of the original apostolic company.[3]

WHAT YOU SEE IS WHAT YOU GET

As we looked at earlier, our worldview largely determines how we read and what we believe about the Bible. It is a truism that we do not believe the Bible, we believe what we believe about the Bible. As someone trained under the dispensationalist, cessationalist worldview, I could only see what my worldview filter would let in. Even when it was in black and white and in the Book, I could not see it. However, when I was filled with the Spirit and initiated into what John Wimber termed an "advanced pneumatology," it was as if I had been given a new Bible. What I could not see before, now was everywhere on every page.

As I started to proclaim the "new" truths of the Spirit-filled life that were literally jumping out of the pages of my Bible, many who had been appreciative of my teaching ministry became less so, as I shared what they truly could not see. I had truly stirred up the hornet's nest.

John pulled me to the side and we fellowshipped as he advised me that while he was open to much of what I was sharing, many others were not, and thus it might be more profitable for me if I chose less controversial themes to teach on in the future.

My experience was much the same regarding the bridal paradigm of the Kingdom of God. Where before I had not even an inkling of such a thing, once I was exposed to it and had my eyes opened up to see, it was everywhere. In the next couple of chapters I want to present a few more of the Scriptures and the types and figures that teach the bridal paradigm so that you can see this isn't an isolated verse or two—it is literally everywhere.

IN THE BEGINNING

If we are going to look at the bridal paradigm, where should we start? I know, how about at the beginning? In the beginning before time began.

> *The Lord possessed Me at the beginning of His work, the first of His acts of old. Ages ago I was set up, at the first, before the beginning of the earth. When there were no depths I was brought forth, when there were no springs abounding with water. Before the mountains had been shaped, before the hills, I was brought forth, before He had made the earth with its fields, or the first of the dust of the world. When He established the heavens, I was there; when He drew a circle on the face of the deep, when He made firm the skies above, when He established the fountains of the deep, when He assigned to the sea its limit, so that the waters might not transgress His command, when He marked out the foundations of the earth, then I was beside him, like a master workman, and I was daily His delight, rejoicing before Him always, rejoicing in His inhabited world and delighting in the children of man.[4]*

In Proverbs, the "I" here is the personification of wisdom. Some of the attributes expressed by "wisdom" here are: eternal, being with God since before anything else was, and a master artisan at creation. Since we have the New Testament revelation, it is easy to determine that this personification of wisdom is in actuality the Lord Jesus Christ. We know Jesus is eternal and operated as the Agent of Creation:

In the beginning was the Word, and the Word was with God, and the Word was God. He was in the beginning with God. All things were made through Him, and without Him was not any thing made that was made.[5]

He is the image of the invisible God, the firstborn of all creation. For by Him all things were created, in heaven and on earth, visible and invisible, whether thrones or dominions or rulers or authorities—all things were created through Him and for Him. And He is before all things, and in Him all things hold together.[6]

But in these last days He has spoken to us by His Son, whom He appointed the heir of all things, through whom also He created the world.[7]

In Proverbs 8:22-31 quoted on the previous page, we notice the Father taking delight in the Son and the Son rejoicing before the Father; a mutual glad-hearted relationship shared by the Trinity.[8] The word translated "rejoicing" here means to laugh; to celebrate; to rejoice. It refers to a strong expression of joy: of celebration;[9] of making merry, rejoicing;[10] it means to play, to sport, to have fun.[11,12]

One thing I would like to take note of here is that the Son is taking delight in the children of men! *"Even as He chose us in Him before the foundation of the world, that we should be holy and blameless before Him. In love."*[13] Before there was a creation, He knew us, He loved us, and He chose us!

IT'S ALL ABOUT A WEDDING

The Bible opens and closes with a wedding. It has been said that Genesis is the seed plot of the Bible. If you take the first three chapters of Genesis and the last three chapters of the Book of Revelation, you would have a mini-theology of redemption. I have found that to be true. Let us look at some of the types and shadows that are seen in Genesis that help us in viewing the bridal paradigm and how it relates to Christ and redemption.

ADAM AND EVE

As we looked at previously in Genesis, after God created Adam from the dust of the ground, He revealed to Adam through the naming of the animals his inner desire for a similar, yet dissimilar, mate. Jesus desired Adam to have a mate who was like him, yet different from him.[14] That is the reason God did not create Eve at the same time as He did Adam. He wanted Adam to experience the God-like longing in his heart that Jesus has.

As C.S. Lewis has noted, hunger, regardless of whether or not it is satisfied, is an indication that food exists.[15] The fact that Adam experienced an incomplete yearning pointed to the fact that there was a fulfilling reality somewhere. We know that this did not come from Adam's experience, for he had no prior experience of ever having had this completion. This ache was a reflection of God's chosen longing to have a counterpart for His Son.

God put Adam to sleep, pierced his side, took out a rib, and fashioned his bride from that wound.[16] Why didn't God just form Eve as He had Adam? Because this was a prophetic foreshadowing of how Jesus was to be put to sleep—He died in our stead—so that from His wounded side we, His Bride, could come forth from that wounding.[17]

And after Eve was presented to him, Adam stated, *"Therefore a man shall leave his father and his mother and hold fast to his wife, and they shall become one flesh."*[18] Paul, under the inspiration of the Spirit, said that Moses was talking not only about Adam and Eve, but also about Christ and the Church.[19]

Another type we see from the Genesis account is the fact that Eve, a type of the Bride, was deceived by the serpent.[20] The devil lied to Eve and was able to deceive her into believing that God's Word could not be believed or trusted and that God was withholding something that was good from her. Evangelist D.L. Moody called this being tempted to an upward fall.[21]

The devil was inviting her into a room where she already was; she was already like God, she was one of the Image-bearers. The enemy still pulls that one out to use against us today, doesn't he? He still works to get us to *do* more for God, in order to *be* more loved by God, when the truth is we can never be more loved by God than we are now, for He already loves us to the same degree He loves Jesus.[22] We spend too much time and expend too much energy trying to get into a room we are already in!

ISAAC AND REBEKAH

Abraham, Abram's name after he had entered into covenant with God, had a son named Isaac. Their relationship is a prophetic type of the relationship between God and Jesus. Abraham gave his only son, Isaac, and he received him back from the dead in a type. Then Abraham desired for Isaac to have a bride, as God desired for Jesus to have a Bride.[23] However, Abraham did not want Isaac to have just any bride; he wanted his wife-to-be to be special, someone from their home country and relatives. He wanted her to be someone with the same background, values, and beliefs, from the people of covenant. Therefore, Abraham sent his servant back to Mesopotamia to acquire a wife for him.[24]

As the servant travels and follows Abraham's instructions to win a bride for his son, it becomes obvious that the servant's role in this drama parallels the role of the Holy Spirit in winning a Bride for Jesus. The servant went with precious gifts representing the father's heart to woo and win the heart of the bride.[25]

Once the servant arrived in Mesopotamia, he met the young woman, Rebekah, at a well at evening time. The servant had prayed asking that God would reveal to him who the chosen bride for Isaac was to be.[26] God answered that prayer and let the servant know which young woman He had chosen for Abraham's son.[27]

The servant then went with Rebekah to her family's home and told them about Abraham and his assignment.[28] As he told them his story, he constantly spoke of Abraham's virtues and how God had blessed him exceedingly. He emphasized how much Abraham loved his son, and how adamant he was that Isaac have a bride from his own family.[29]

Rebekah's family responded favorably and asked Rebekah if she was willing to wed Isaac.[30] Throughout this whole process, her heart had come alive and she said that she was willing and prepared to go with Abraham's servant.[31] The servant then acted as an escort to lead her toward her future husband, in the same way that the Holy Spirit leads us toward our Bridegroom Jesus. Aren't the parallels between Rebekah's story and ours amazing?

Before we move on to the next example, I want to point out a couple of interesting facts. Do you remember when Isaac was born we are told that his name means *"son of laughter"*? What you may not know is that the name of Eliezer, Abraham's servant, means *"God is help,"* and that the name of Rebekah, the bride, means *"snared by beauty."* Even in the names of the historical characters, we see the New Testament story of the Helper and Comforter capturing the hearts of the chosen and redeemed with the beauty of the One who was anointed with joy and laughter over all others.[32]

BOAZ AND RUTH

There was a famine in the land. Therefore, the man packed up his wife and two sons and traveled to a neighboring country. In due time, his two sons married local Moabite girls. Soon tragedy struck, killing both the father and his two sons, leaving the three women alone. In the meantime, the famine back in the mother-in-law's country has ended, so she decides to return home. One of her daughters-in-law elects to stay in her home country, but the other committed herself to her mother-in-law and travels with her.

Naomi and Ruth arrive back in Bethlehem during harvest time. In order to provide food to eat, Ruth goes out into the fields to glean what the harvesters missed. While she is doing this, she meets the field's owner, Boaz, who then offers her an invitation to stay with the servant girls in his field, and he instructs his harvesters not to harass her. By accepting Boaz's generous offer, she is able to gather more than she would have been able to otherwise.

When Ruth returns home that evening and tells her mother-in-law what transpired that day, Naomi realizes there might be a deeper relationship possible between these two. Therefore, she suggests to Ruth how she should present herself to Boaz to see what would happen. His heart is touched and the next day he proceeds to pay the required price to bring Naomi and Ruth into his household.

There are a couple of points in this story that are prophetic pictures of how God deals with us. First, there is Naomi. She is a picture of the Holy Spirit. Through her relationship with Naomi, Ruth came to love her and to be committed to both her and to her people. As the story unfolds, Naomi guides Ruth into a loving relationship with Boaz. In a similar way, Holy Spirit draws our hearts and opens our eyes to spiritual things. He brings us first to a place of repentance from our old life and to a commitment to a new one and then prepares us as a Bride for the Son.

Second, Ruth is a Moabite, a stranger to the covenant and promises. She is a great prophetic picture of those of us who are Gentile believers. We were born in a foreign country, with no inheritance and no hope.[33] Then our hearts are ignited by love and we commit ourselves to God, without really knowing what any of that means. We are welcomed into His family and become inheritors of the promises. As our relationship progresses, we move from the role of child to that of Bride. That is a clear picture of what God has always had in His heart for humanity in redemption.

Finally, there is Boaz. He starts out as a father figure, providing for and protecting Ruth and Naomi. Then, as Ruth's heart is revealed by her service to Naomi and keeping herself from other lovers, Boaz's heart is moved. He pays the price for them and the relationship moves to one of intimacy and marriage. Similarly, we tend to start our Christian walk understanding our relationship with God as a child of His; He protects us, provides for us, and meets our needs. However, as we mature and spend time with Him, we get a better understanding of the price He paid for us, and our relationship grows, deepens, and then intimacy forms. Our hearts are knitted together; we become friends.

I find it amazing to see how this mirrors the eternal heart of Jesus. He loves me enough to pay for my protection and provision. I make His heart glad. He considers it a kindness to Him when I keep my affections for Him alone, not turning to lesser loves, gazing on Him with singleness of focus and desire. In addition, as I spend time sitting in His Presence, He burns this into my heart, convinces my innermost being, and transforms me by the knowledge of His extravagant love. Wow!

A WEDDING IN THE DESERT

We have already looked at how God offered to cut the covenant with Abram so that He could bring forth a corporate people from Abram's offspring.[34] Then we saw how God approached this corporate covenant people and offered them a corporate marriage proposal. The call to exclusively worship the one true God parallels the exclusive fidelity of the covenant of marriage.

We saw how this is referred to constantly from the creation narrative into the Torah and then throughout the Prophets. It began with the command, *"You shall have no other gods before Me"*[35] (the First Commandment), and ends with the command, *"You shall not covet your neighbor's wife"*[36] (the Tenth Commandment). Our jealous God will punish infidelity not as an angry deity, but as a jealous Husband.[37] Whenever we read the prophets expressing the themes of judgment and salvation, it is with nuptial imagery; they are building on the theology and imagery of the Torah. They are judging Israel based on the covenant of Moses, anticipating the new covenant in Christ.

XERXES AND ESTHER

King Xerxes throws a six-month party for all his nobles (the original party animal?). At the end of this gala, he throws a seven-day bash for everyone in the capital city. During this festivity, he decides to display his greatest treasure in his kingdom, his queen. However, she insults him by refusing his public summons and therefore is removed from her position as queen.

Many commentators argue that the king's request was lewd and inappropriate and therefore rightly was denied. However, I am not sure that this was the nature of the king's request. Isaiah 62 talks about the people of God's glory (remember, we are His Bride) being made evident as a crown of beauty in God's hand. First Corinthians 11 says that the glory of a man is his wife as man is the glory of God. Ephesians 3 tells us that the work that God is doing in His Bride is designed to bring Her to glory so that He can use Her to reveal His wisdom to the rulers and authorities in heavenly places. This indicates that Jesus plans to do with His Bride what Xerxes was trying to do with Vashti: demonstrate his glory by the way in which his queen is dressed.

The king initiates a search for a new queen. One of the finalists from this search was a young woman named Esther, a Jewish captive whose family was taken to Babylon by Nebuchadnezzar. After 12 months of preparatory treatments, it was Esther's turn to appear before the king. Before she goes, she asks the king's adviser, Hegai, to help her dress to please the king.

In a similar way, the sanctifying work of the Holy Spirit purifies us as the Bride-to-be to help prepare us to please our heavenly Bridegroom. The things we go through, the way we respond, the decisions we make under His guidance, all work together to make us ready for that glorious day when we stand before our King face to face. We are promised that we will be ready, washed, and without spot or wrinkle when we're presented to Jesus.[38] With that in mind, we should be diligent in our pursuit of a life of righteousness[39] in order to be blameless in His sight.[40] We are to live lives of repentance (again, repentance means to change the way we think and respond) under His instruction so that we might acquire garments of white.[41]

When Esther appears before the king, her beauty, which came from her preparation, captures the king's heart and he makes her his queen. To celebrate, Xerxes throws yet another party. Traditionally this was known as a Banquet of Wine, which was the betrothal feast in Middle Eastern cultures. During the Banquet of Wine, the groom would pour a glass of wine and set it on the table, which symbolized the pouring out of himself for his chosen bride; offering all he had to her and for her. If she went to the table, took the cup, and drank it, she was symbolically saying, "Yes, I accept. I choose to live my life sustained by you. We are one."

Several years later, Haman, a man who hated the Jewish people, rose to a place of prominence in the king's court. He desired to use his position of authority to influence the king's assent to pass a law to kill all the Jews in the land. In the same way, the enemy of our soul, satan, seeks to destroy God's people, and he does it in the bounds of God's authority. Remember the examples of Job, Peter, and Jesus, all who were attacked by satan, with God's permission. There are times when God allows strategic threats from the enemy to encourage His Queen into her royal place of intercession before the King.

Esther learns of Haman's plan, and prepares herself to go before the king on the behalf of her people. When she appears before him, his heart is moved; he raises his scepter to her, granting her an audience. He watches her approach his throne, stunned by her loveliness. By the time she reaches him, he is ruined, a man in love with his bride. The king then invites her to make her request known, based on her positional authority. He promises her that she can have whatever she asks for, up to half the kingdom. Instead of immediately responding with her intercessory burden, however, Esther invites him, along with Haman, to a Banquet of Wine.

Here we see the power of bridal intercession revealed. Outside of the royal castle, the Jews are distressed. They are going around in sackcloth and ashes. They are weeping and fasting for deliverance. Inside the royal court, however, near the heart of the king, the bride is reminding him of their romance. She is reminding him of that first Banquet of Wine, reminding him of the intimacy they share, and renewing her commitment to him. That is in stark contrast to Vashti's refusal to take her place, to be seen as his bride. Esther, instead of reacting in fear, proactively responds to the situation in faith, creating an environment, in the presence of his nobles, in which she can be seen as his and his alone.

At the feast the king is pleased by his queen's actions, and again asks her what she desires. Here, Esther does a remarkable thing. Once again, rather than interceding, addressing the problem, she again invites the king and Haman to another Banquet of Wine the following night. She does not respond to the tyranny of the urgent; instead she takes full advantage of her prerogative to further stir the king's heart. Do you see what she is doing? Her request is secondary because she understands that the king's heart is ravished for her. She knows that her beloved will take care of the issues as they present themselves because of their love. Get it? So plans are made to throw another Banquet of Wine the next night, where she promises that she will let the king know what is on her heart.

Do not think for a moment that the king is not aware that there is something on her mind, something she intensely desires, but he is pleased with her approach. The next night, he again invites her to intercede from her position of intimacy and authority—and all true authority comes from the place of intimacy—again offering her up to half of his kingdom. This time Esther responds by telling him of the plot of the enemy to destroy both her and her people.

Notice that she is careful not to reveal too much or to focus in on who it is. She just lets the reality sink in and lets the king's righteous anger build. The king is outraged. Who would dare to threaten his bride?

HAMAN

Now we can see the wisdom of including Haman in the celebration. He has had two nights to firsthand observe the romance and affection between the king and his queen. Possibly, the previous night he went home and bragged to all his family, friends, and associates of his high and exalted position with the king and queen. Now, suddenly, the tables have been turned and he realizes the serious trouble that he is in. The king is so distraught that he leaves the party to think. Haman is terrified and pleads with the queen for his life. When Xerxes returns, he immediately orders Haman's execution.

This is a prophetic story that highlights our relationship with God as His Bride. First, He is not a grouch; rather, He is a joyful God who enjoys throwing parties. He is a King desiring a Bride who will prepare Herself to stand before Him, sharing the glory He so freely bestows upon Her. Our King, Jesus, gave Himself and poured Himself out for us, to bring us into an intimate relationship with Himself. Second, He strategically allows problems in our lives. In the words of Psalm 23, *"You prepare a table before me in the presence of my enemies."*[42] This gives us an opportunity, a training ground, where we can grow in our understanding of our position before Him. In addition, it provides satan an opportunity to see the mutual love between us and to be terrified.[43]

In the next chapter, we will look at a couple more of the many Old Testament examples and illustrations of frequency and pervasiveness of the bridal paradigm.

CHAPTER 9

More of the Bridal Paradigm in the Old Testament

In the last chapter, we looked at several examples and illustrations from the Old Testament that typified and demonstrated the bridal paradigm. In this chapter, I would like to examine a couple more.

The first example I want to look at is in the Book of Psalms. The Book of Psalms is a compilation of several ancient collections of Hebrew songs and poetry for use in congregational worship as well as in private devotion.[1] The Book of Psalms was Israel's "hymnal." There are many psalms that are recognized by scholars as being Messianic; that is, they refer in some sense to the Savior who will come from David's line.

One of the key ways we know a psalm is Messianic is because it is identified as such and quoted as such in the New Testament.[2] Although there are many Psalms that are Messianic,[3] I want to focus on one in particular, Psalm 45, because it is not only Messianic, it is also bridal. It is not the only bridal Psalm by any means, but it is the strongest example.

PSALM 45

Psalm 45 is identified as a royal wedding song that celebrates the wedding of a king of the house of David. The first section praises the king,[4] and the second section instructs and praises the princess-bride.[5] Christians have long seen here an image of Christ and the Church.[6,7] This Psalm is often studied alongside the Song of Solomon, which we will look at in the next chapter.

SECTION ONE

The psalmist says, *"My heart overflows with a pleasing theme; I address my verses to the king; my tongue is like the pen of a ready scribe."*[8] The Hebrew word translated "overflows" means to have strong, emotional, pleasurable feelings.[9] "Pleasing" here means something which has good, attractive, or beneficial qualities.[10] The word "theme" describes the word that a prophet bears,[11,12] which lets us in on the prophetic bearing this psalm has—it represents the heart of God. As a Messianic and bridal Psalm, it is inspired by the Spirit of God to tell us things about the King, His Bride—that's us—and the coming wedding day.

Next, the psalmist extols the King, *"You are the most handsome of the sons of men; grace is poured upon Your lips; therefore God has blessed You forever."*[13] The Hebrew word for "handsome" here means beautiful or delightful.[14] I love that, don't you? I love to tell Jesus, "Lord, You are beautiful." Men, this is not just for the women's meetings. King David was a man's man, macho to the max, yet he still loved to tell God, "You're beautiful!" Real men worship Jesus! We need to see Him as beautiful, as delightful; and we need to spend quality time beholding His beauty, for beholding His beauty results in our becoming beautiful as well.[15]

Then the psalmist goes on to extol this delightful King's many conquests. Our King wields a mighty sword, the Word of God,[16] and He uses it to defend truth, humility, and justice. *"Gird Your sword on Your thigh, O mighty one, in Your splendor and majesty! In Your majesty ride out victoriously for the cause of truth and meekness and righteousness; let Your right hand teach You awesome deeds! Your arrows are sharp in the heart of the king's enemies; the peoples fall under You."*[17]

We need to realize that our King is King of kings and Lord of lords![18] When we ask Him to move on our behalf, there is nothing that is too difficult for Him! So we can confidently cry out, *"Your Kingdom come, Your will be done"*[19] and we can rest assured He still watches over His Word to perform it![20]

The psalmist then gives us much needed information about the character of our beloved King and Husband. He tells us that the reason God gives Jesus, in His humanity, the everlasting throne is that He loves what is right and just. *"Your throne, O God, is forever and ever. The scepter of Your Kingdom is a scepter of uprightness; You have loved righteousness and hated wickedness. Therefore God, Your God, has anointed You with the oil of gladness beyond Your companions."*[21] Remember the axiom I mentioned previously that "absolute power corrupts absolutely"? The reason we can trust Jesus with our all is because He has absolute power and He has never misused it—not once!

Next, we are told that the King's robes are fragrant with myrrh, aloes, and cassia, and His palaces are adorned with ivory and filled with beautiful music—the worship of the entire heavenly host. *"Your robes are all fragrant with myrrh and aloes and cassia. From ivory palaces stringed instruments make You glad."*[22] This is referring to His wedding day. His robes are fragrant with myrrh.

Myrrh is an aromatic gum resin produced by various trees and shrubs in India, Arabia, and East Africa. It was very expensive and used in making perfume,[23] the holy anointing oil to burn incense,[24] and in preparing a body for a funeral.[25] It has a bitter taste. The three wise kings brought myrrh to Jesus' birth as a prophetic symbol of His death.[26] On the Cross, Jesus was offered myrrh.[27] Here it speaks of Jesus' death. Aloes is mentioned in the Song of Solomon, along with myrrh, when referring to Jesus' sacrifice for us.[28] Cassia is a spice like cinnamon and is one of the ingredients used to make anointing oil.[29,30]

SECTION TWO

In the second section of this Psalm, we are given a glimpse of the King's Bride: *"Daughters of kings are among Your ladies of honor; at Your right hand stands the Queen in gold of Ophir."*[31]

This signifies that the Gospel, represented here as the bridal paradigm of the Kingdom of God, will be the means of salvation to many of the kings, queens, and nobles of the earth. Whole nations shall be converted during the coming Great Harvest; and the Queen, the Bride of Christ—the Christian Church—shall be most elegantly adorned with all the Kingdom graces and works befitting an equally yoked Bride.

Ophir was a region from which the trade ships of Solomon and Hiram imported gold.[32] The gold of the region was so pure that "gold of Ophir" became a synonym for high quality gold.[33] Gold in the Scriptures often represents deity. As the Bride of Christ, we are not part of the Godhead, but we are as close as one can be without actually being there. As Paul Billheimer points out, the Church is the eternal companion for the Son, called the Bride:[34]

> This means that redeemed humanity outranks all other orders of created beings in the universe. Angels are created, not "born from above." Redeemed humanity is both created and regenerated, thus uniquely bearing His image. Through the new birth a redeemed human being becomes a bona fide member of God's family. Nothing can dim the fact that infinity separates the Creator from the created. Christ is the eternally unique and only begotten Son, "the brightness of [God's] glory," and "the express image of his person" (see Hebrews 1:3). Yet God has exalted redeemed humanity to a sublime height-such that it is impossible for Him to elevate them further without breaching the Godhead. This is the basis for the divine accolade of Psalm 8:5: "For thou hast made him a little lower than the angels, and hast crowned him with glory and honour."[35]

Next, the psalmist addresses the commitment of the Bride.[36] He instructs the Bride to accept two things: one is her separation, for she has left her parents to marry the King of Israel. *"Hear, O daughter, and consider, and incline your ear: forget your people and your father's house."*[37]

The Bride is invited to the union, which requires that she must not just resign herself to, but actually embrace her role as a chosen, separate, and peculiar people. The love of Christ as our Husband is intimately connected with the entire devotion to which we as the Bride are exhorted to love Him. We are not to love the world or the things in the world.[38]

The Bride is encouraged to fully submit herself to Jesus, honoring Him as both her Husband and Lord. *"And the King will desire your beauty. Since He is your Lord, bow to Him."*[39] The glory of the Gospel is this: the beauty that God possesses He imparts to us![40] We are dark, but we are lovely to Him,[41] not because of some inherent beauty in us, but because of the beauty that is in Him. Truly, beauty is in the eye of the beholder!

The psalmist then says, *"All glorious is the Princess in her chamber, with robes interwoven with gold. In many-colored robes, she is led to the King, with her virgin companions following behind her. With joy and gladness they are led along as they enter the palace of the King."*[42] The chamber mentioned here is the bridal chamber of intimacy. The Bride is wearing robes interwoven with gold, again, which speaks of deity—we will be the equally yoked eternal companion of the Son of God!

"In many-colored robes she is led to the King." In the ancient world, the beauty of the bride's gowns might be an expression of her family's wealth, their pride in her, and their love for her.[43] What a picture we have here of that grand day when the Lord Jesus will return to claim His Bride! He will find her arrayed in the garment of perfect righteousness that He Himself has provided, and He will escort her to His palace of glory where there will be gladness and joy that will never diminish.[44]

Now, the psalmist switches back to Jesus and speaks of His coming glory. *"In place of Your fathers shall be Your sons; You will make them princes in all the earth. I will cause Your name to be remembered in all generations; therefore nations will praise You forever and ever."*[45] The pronouns here in the Hebrew are masculine, so these statements are not about the Bride, but rather are the Bride speaking to the Bridegroom.

"In place of Your fathers shall be Your sons; You will make them princes in all the earth." Jesus' offspring and brethren, the whole Body of Christ, will be the ones who inherit the promises and the Kingdom. Jesus is King of kings, Lord of lords, and His Bride will sit with Him, ruling from His Father's throne.[46]

"I will cause Your name to be remembered in all generations; therefore nations will praise You forever and ever." We, the Bride, are the ones who preach the everlasting Gospel of the Kingdom, and as a result, there will be a ransomed people from every tribe and language and people and nation.[47]

As you can see, the bridal paradigm of the Gospel of the Kingdom is a lot bigger than just a few people serving God. It is all about love: His love for us, and our love for Him. As we have seen, this is not hidden in a few obscure passages; it is everywhere on almost every page. All of history—all of His-story—is about a love affair that God has for those whom He has created. We are loved and we are lovers.

In the remainder of this chapter, I want to look at some of what the prophets have to say about this bridal understanding of the Kingdom of God. As we will see, everything they prophesy and everything they say to Israel, to the Church, and to the world, is all wrapped up in this bridal approach to God as Husband and Christ as Bridegroom.

THE PROPHETS

If we do not view the ministry of the Old Testament prophets through the lens of the bridal paradigm, we will not be able to make sense of what they say and what they do. We end up viewing God as grumpy and angry. All of the prophets must be read within the context of the understanding of nuptial imagery when describing the relationship between God and His people. Let us look at a few of the prophets' statements.

ISAIAH

Isaiah the prophet ministered during the reigns of Uzziah, Jotham, Ahaz, and Hezekiah,[48] and is generally regarded as the greatest of the Old Testament prophets because he prophesied so much on the themes of redemption, the Kingdom, the King, and the Bride! Just look at what God says through Isaiah.

Isaiah is prophesying concerning the restoration of Israel and says:

Lift up your eyes around and see; they all gather, they come to you. As I live, declares the Lord, you shall put them all on as an ornament; you shall bind them on as ***a bride does.***[49]

He goes on to say:

*Thus says the Lord: "**Where is your mother's certificate of divorce**, with which I sent her away? Or which of My creditors is it to whom I have sold you? Behold, for your iniquities you were sold, and for your transgressions your mother was sent away."*[50]

God reminds Israel that they are married to Him and that He has not divorced them.

*"Sing, O barren one..." says the Lord... "Fear not, for you will not be ashamed; be not confounded, for you will not be disgraced; for you will forget the shame of your youth, and **the reproach of your widowhood** you will remember no more. **For your Maker is your husband**, the Lord of hosts is His name; and the Holy One of Israel is your Redeemer,*

*the God of the whole earth He is called. For the Lord has called you like a wife deserted and grieved in spirit, **like a wife of youth** when she is cast off, says your God. For a brief moment I deserted you, but with great compassion I will gather you. In overflowing anger for a moment I hid My face from you, but with everlasting love I will have compassion on you," says the Lord, your Redeemer.*[51]

God reminds Israel that their Maker is their Husband! He goes on to say He called them "like a wife"!

*I will greatly rejoice in the Lord; my soul shall exult in my God, for He has clothed me with the garments of salvation; He has covered me with the robe of righteousness, **as a bridegroom decks himself like a priest with a beautiful headdress, and as a bride adorns herself with her jewels**...*[52]

God again is speaking to Israel and says:

*You shall no more be termed Forsaken, and your land shall no more be termed Desolate, but you shall be called My Delight Is in Her, and your land Married; **for the Lord delights in you**, and your land shall be **married**. For as a young man marries a young woman, so shall your sons marry you, and **as the bridegroom rejoices over the bride, so shall your God rejoice over you**.*[53]

The Scriptures from beginning to end proclaim that God loves His people and enjoys them, but this one passage is the only instance where God emphatically declares the nature of that love and of that enjoyment—*"as the bridegroom rejoices over the bride"*!

JEREMIAH

Jeremiah is prophesying and he hears the Lord say:

Go and proclaim in the hearing of Jerusalem, Thus says the Lord, "I remember the devotion of your youth, your *love **as a bride**, how you followed Me in the wilderness, in a land not sown."*[54]

Notice, He did not remember them as servants or as adherents to a religious code or to a set of rules, He thought of them *"as a bride"*! Then, a couple of verses later, God laments Israel's unfaithfulness by saying, *"Can a virgin forget her ornaments, or **a bride her attire**? Yet My people have forgotten Me days without number."*[55] He did not count them to be just forgetful of a creed or a dogma; He says they were unfaithful to the marriage contract. Get it?

*The Lord said to me in the days of King Josiah: "Have you seen what she did, that faithless one, Israel, how she went up on every high hill and under every green tree, and **there played the whore**? I thought, 'After she has done all this she will return to me,' but she did not return, and her treacherous sister Judah saw it. She saw that for all the **adulteries of that faithless one**, Israel, I had sent her away with a decree of divorce. Yet her **treacherous** sister Judah did not fear, but she too went and **played the whore**. Because she took her **whoredom** lightly, she polluted the land, **committing adultery** with stone and tree. Yet for all this her **treacherous** sister Judah did not return to me with her whole heart, but in pretense," declares the Lord.*[56]

Again, God sees both Israel's and Judah's unfaithfulness as marital unfaithfulness.

Speaking to His unfaithful wife, God says:

*And you, O desolate one, what do you mean that you dress in scarlet, that you adorn yourself with ornaments of gold, that you enlarge your eyes with paint? In vain you beautify yourself. **Your lovers despise you**; they seek your life.*[57]

Hearing the Lord concerning the unfaithfulness of His wife, Jeremiah says:

The word of the Lord came to me: "You shall not take a wife, nor shall you have sons or daughters in this place. For thus says the Lord concerning the sons and daughters who are born in this place, and concerning the mothers who bore them and the fathers who fathered them in this land: They shall die of deadly diseases. They shall not be lamented, nor shall they be buried. They shall be as dung on the surface of the ground. They shall perish by the sword and by famine, and their dead bodies shall be food for the birds of the air and for the beasts of the earth."[58]

Notice, this is not just anger, this is a jealous anger, the anger of a husband who has been wronged by an unfaithful wife.

*Again I will build you, and you shall be built, **O virgin Israel!** Again you shall adorn yourself with tambourines and shall go forth in the dance of the merrymakers.[59]*

And a little later in the chapter:

*Behold, the days are coming, declares the Lord, when I will make a new covenant with the house of Israel and the house of Judah, not like the covenant that I made with their fathers on the day when **I took them by the hand** [in marriage] to bring them out of the land of Egypt, My [marriage] covenant that they broke, **though I was their husband,** declares the Lord.[60]*

*Thus says the Lord: In this place of which you say, "It is a waste without man or beast," in the cities of Judah and the streets of Jerusalem that are desolate, without man or inhabitant or beast, there shall be heard again the voice of mirth and the voice of gladness, **the voice of the bridegroom and the voice of the bride,** the voices of those who sing [in marital bliss], as they bring thank offerings to the house of the Lord: "Give thanks to the Lord of hosts, for the Lord is good, for His steadfast love* *endures forever!" For I will restore the fortunes of the land as at first, says the Lord.*[61]

EZEKIEL

Ezekiel is prophesying and he says:

Again the word of the Lord came to me: "Son of man, make known to Jerusalem her abominations, and say, Thus says the Lord God to Jerusalem: Your origin and your birth are of the land of the Canaanites; your father was an Amorite and your mother a Hittite. And as for your birth, on the day you were born your cord was not cut, nor were you washed with water to cleanse you, nor rubbed with salt, nor wrapped in swaddling cloths. No eye pitied you, to do any of these things to you out of compassion for you, but you were cast out on the open field, for you were abhorred, on the day that you were born. And when I passed by you and saw you wallowing in your blood, I said to you in your blood, 'Live!' I said to you in your blood, 'Live!' I made you flourish like a plant of the field. And you grew up and became tall and arrived at full adornment. Your breasts were formed, and your hair had grown; yet you were naked and bare."[62]

God says you were born and deserted. He saw you in your lost state, desolate and dying. He came to your rescue and caused you to live. Then He raised you until you were a mature woman, and here the implication is that He chose you to be His Bride. And then as we read on:

When I passed by you again and saw you, behold, you were at the age for love, and I spread the corner of My garment over you and covered your nakedness; I made **My vow** [marriage vow] *to you and entered into a* **covenant** [marriage covenant] *with you, declares the Lord God, and you became Mine* [Israel became the wife of

God]. *Then I bathed you with water and washed off your blood from you and anointed you with oil. I clothed you also with embroidered cloth and shod you with fine leather. I wrapped you in fine linen and covered you with silk. I adorned you with ornaments and put bracelets on your wrists and a chain on your neck. I put a ring on your nose and earrings in your ears and a beautiful crown on your head. Thus you were adorned with gold and silver, and your clothing was of fine linen and silk and embroidered cloth. You ate fine flour and honey and oil. You grew exceedingly beautiful and **advanced to royalty** [married to the King!]. And your renown went forth among the nations because of your beauty, for it was perfect through the splendor that I had bestowed on you, declares the Lord God.*[63]

The Lord saved her, matured her, entered into covenant with her. And what did she do?

*But you trusted in your beauty and **played the whore** because of your renown and lavished **your whorings** on any passerby; your beauty became his. You took some of your garments and made for yourself colorful shrines, and on them **played the whore**. The like has never been, nor ever shall be. You also took your beautiful jewels of My gold and of My silver, which I had given you, and made for yourself images of men, and with them **played the whore**. And you took your embroidered garments to cover them, and set My oil and My incense before them. Also My bread that I gave you—I fed you with fine flour and oil and honey—you set before them for a pleasing aroma; and so it was, declares the Lord God. And you took your sons and your daughters, whom you had borne to Me, and these you sacrificed to them to be devoured. Were your **whorings** so small a matter that you slaughtered My children and delivered them up as an offering by fire to them? And in all your **abominations** [marital/covenantal* unfaithfulness] *and your **whorings** you did not remember the days of your youth, when you were naked and bare, wallowing in your blood. And after all your **wickedness** (woe, woe to you! declares the Lord God).*[64]

Again we see the Lord is not upset because Israel was not serving Him, or because they were not keeping some religious duties. It was far more serious than that—they were being unfaithful to a marriage contract with God! When you look at it from this light, it changes everything, doesn't it?

These are not all of the examples we could look at. However, they suffice to show that all of the biblical revelation is built around two truths—God is our Father, and God is our Husband. When we keep these in view, all the pieces suddenly make sense. God loves us as a Father loves His children, but there is more. He also loves and enjoys us as a bridegroom loves his bride.

At this point, I need to stop and point out that when we are talking about God loving us as a bridegroom loves his bride, we are not talking about sexuality or sensuality. It is not about gender, femininity, or masculinity. Women are sons of God and men are the Bride of Christ. It is all about the closeness of the proximity of our hearts to God's. Angels worship Him and call Him holy. However, we call Him Abba, Father, worthy Friend, King, and Bridegroom.

No angel can cross that line. No angel, no heavenly being was made in God's image. We alone are the Image-bearers. When some of the angels sinned and fell, Jesus did not become an angel or volunteer to die in their place. We alone are His beloved ones, the ones He loves, enjoys, and desires to spend all of eternity with. We alone will rule and reign with Him forever in the ages to come. We are the Bride of Christ!

In the next chapter, we will look at the clearest and most concise picture of the Image-bearers as the Bride of Christ and God's plan for us to follow in the progression of growing in passion as lovers of God—the Song of Solomon.

CHAPTER 10

The Song of Solomon

BRIDAL PARADIGM CONCENTRATED

What a journey, eh? Have I stretched your religious sensibilities? I know when I first discovered the bridal paradigm, what all it entailed, and the implications of it, I was just blown away. It really does change everything. Serving God is no longer a chore, but a delight. I no longer have to work to get God to like me; I joyfully serve Him because He already likes me—in fact, He loves me. In this chapter, we will be examining the clearest and most concise presentation of the bridal paradigm—the Song of Solomon—and where it can take us. Because of time and space constraints, in this chapter I will be making some statements without being able to take the time to elaborate on them. I hope to write another book on the Song of Solomon in the future, but until then I'll have to speed teach, so I guess you will have to speed learn. Ready? Set? Go!

INTRODUCTION TO THE SONG OF ALL SONGS

To start off, I have to provide some introductory principles necessary to interpret the Song of Solomon (SOS). There are several ways that the Song has been interpreted throughout redemptive history. For our study, I will be interpreting the Song as an allegorical love song between Jesus and the individual believer as His Bride. This is not the only way that the Song can be studied. The key to the allegorical interpretation of any Scripture—and there are many—is that you can never use it to "read into" the text something that is not plainly taught throughout the whole of Scripture.

I have discovered, as have most believers throughout redemptive history, that the Song shows us the divine pattern for the progression of holy passion. Just to recap, God's intent from the beginning has always been to redeem all people in order to mature them into being an eternal companion, a Bride for His Son. As we have seen thus far, all of the Old Testament clearly demonstrates that fact. In future chapters, we will see that the New Testament follows that same plan and strategy. The Song brings all of that combined revelation and condenses it into one neat package, sort of like Romans does for salvation, and Daniel or Revelation does for end-time prophecy.

General Overview of the Song

The Song is divided into two sections. The first four chapters of the Song focus on the Bride's inheritance in Jesus, and the last four chapters focus on Jesus' inheritance in the Bride. It is important that we understand that while we are seeking something from God, He is also seeking something from us. He doesn't need our stuff; He wants our hearts. The focus of the book completely shifts in the middle of the Song, from chapters 4:16 through 5:1.

The first four chapters focus on the Bride's understanding and enjoyment of her inheritance in Christ. These chapters emphasize God's ravished heart of compassion to win her heart, to cause her to enjoy Him for her own pleasure and good. The last four chapters focus on the other foundational pillars of the Gospel. He desires her to live for the glory of God with wholehearted, abandoned passion for Jesus.

We will be looking at eight distinct revelations of Jesus in the Song of Solomon. Each different "face" of Jesus' beauty produces a specific response in the Bride. The eight faces are:

- Counseling Shepherd (see 1:8)

- Affectionate Father (see 1:12–2:6)
- Sovereign King (see 2:8-9)
- Safe Savior (see 3:6-8)
- Heavenly Bridegroom (see 4:1-15)
- Suffering Servant (see 5:2)
- Majestic God (see 5:10-16)
- Consuming Fire (see 8:6-7).

THE DIVINE KISS AND THE BRIDE'S LIFE VISION

This first section summarizes the Bride's theology of how to grow in holy passion. This fire of His love manifests itself by tenderizing our hearts, enabling us to feel some of what He feels as He progressively releases the sevenfold divine kiss.

"Let Him kiss me with the kisses of His mouth—for Your love is better than wine.[1] *Draw me after You; let us run..."*[2] Here the Bride states her twofold life vision: *"Draw me after You; let us run."* She wants to be drawn into intimacy, and to run with the Lord in service, ministering to others.

SPIRITUAL CRISIS YET DIVINE AFFECTIONS

The first revelation of Jesus in the Song reveals Him as a Counseling Shepherd.[3] At this point of her spiritual journey, the Bride encounters the paradox of grace. She discovers that she is dark in her heart but still lovely to God.[4] The revelation that she still can fail the Lord results in a spiritual crisis of sin and shame,[5] yet she receives a fresh revelation of her beauty in God that flows out of His divine affection. She is red-hot for God because she has experienced the love of God and wants God's kisses.[6] She starts her Christian walk with a burst of speed and zeal, but soon she runs right into a dead-end road. Over time, she finds she is losing her original spiritual focus.[7]

She experiences two pressures that are common to all of us: rejection from people[8] and the shame from her own sin.[9] But in the midst of all this, she still has a desperate cry to have more of Jesus.[10] She responds to the twofold crisis in the right way by crying out for more of Jesus. She realizes that even though she has stumbled and has lost her way, she still has hope that she can regain a passionate fire in her heart.[11]

Jesus gloriously answers her cry by revealing Himself to her as a shepherd who instructs her.[12] In essence, Jesus says, "You are the most beautiful of all the women in creation." He says, "I love you! To Me you are beautiful! You're who I want." That's powerful! She felt dirty, ugly, rejected, and shamed, but He teaches her as a Counseling Shepherd. This is the first revelation of Jesus. She cries out for help and Jesus gives her this surprising and glorious answer. He is speaking in the language of a shepherd with flocks, goats, and vineyards. He reveals Himself as a Shepherd who sees her in her rejection and shame.

UNDERSTANDING HER IDENTITY IN GOD'S BEAUTY

The second revelation of Jesus in the Song is that He is a King expressing the affectionate heart of the Father. It is reminiscent of Luke 15 where the prodigal son comes home to his father who hosted a party around a banqueting table. Jesus embraces her and puts a ring on her finger just like the prodigal son. There are many parallels between Luke 15 and this section of the Song of Solomon.

She experiences the joy of seeing the King's beauty and His desire for her. This is an especially exhilarating time in her life, when she discovers that the Lord loves and enjoys her, even in her weakness. She comes to a deep understanding of the Cross.[13] The King is pictured as sitting in His finished work—of the Cross—feeding her out of the provision of what He made available to her. As the King, He is sitting and inviting her to feast at the table with Him.[14]

Her worship is shown as a fragrance emanating out of her spirit as a picture of adoration in response to the King's provision.[15] This is her introductory revelation of the beauty and fragrance of Jesus.[16] She is beginning to see her identity in His beauty in the provision of the Cross. He says, "You are most beautiful, My love." He feeds her on the revelation of the beauty imparted to her and on His affectionate love for her. She rejoices that Jesus considers her as beautiful even when He knows her sin and weakness.[17]

Then she receives an even deeper revelation of the beauty of the King. She experiences a new, powerful revelation of her identity in Christ. She sees that she is a beautiful fragrant rose in the sight of God. The rose is the Bride confessing who she is in the knowledge of her beauty in God. It is her new identity.[18] She is beginning to realize her unique value and beauty to Him.[19]

She finds that she is developing a deep satisfaction in her new-found spiritual pleasures. She is learning to really enjoy God's Presence. His fruit is sweet to her taste. The fellowship of the Holy Spirit is so sweet. She feels an initiatory pleasure in experiencing God's affection for her. There is no greater pleasure in the human makeup than when God reveals His affection and His imparted beauty to the human spirit. She finds that she loves being loved by God. She does not yet possess mature love for Him, but He is wooing her toward a life of maturity through this process.[20]

At this point in her spiritual pilgrimage, earthly happiness is still her main goal. Though she really loves Jesus, at this point He is still only a means and not the end of her life. He is the stepping-stone to her goal of earthly happiness. She is finding that this happiness is most deeply experienced when God's Presence seems near to her. Jesus' "happiness" is not yet in her view nor is it the highest goal of her life. Rather, He is seen as the most effective way to secure her own happiness.

This is a major flaw in her spiritual life that she does not yet recognize. Experiencing the pleasure of the Presence of God is wonderful, but it is not the same thing as walking in mature bridal partnership. Mature bridal partnership will obey God regardless of what the feelings and circumstances are. She is not spiritually standing. She is sitting down, receiving His grace. She is sitting down in His shade with great delight. His shade represents the provision of the Cross, releasing to her the love and beauty of God. Jesus brought her to the banqueting table and raised a banner or a flag that describes the dealings of God in her life as filled with the love of God.[21]

However, in the midst of all this, in her heart she is crying out for a deeper intimacy. She cries out to the Lord, "Sustain me! Refresh me! I am totally lovesick! Give me more of Your Presence. Embrace me, O God!" She does not recognize that she is but at the beginning of her journey. She is not yet mature. She is only experiencing the introductory pleasures of God loving her in her weakness, which in turn is awakening the beginnings of a fierce lovesickness for God.[22]

CHALLENGING THE COMFORT ZONE

The third revelation of Jesus in the Song of Solomon is where He reveals Himself as the sovereign King.[23] She looks at Him leaping on mountains and skipping over hills. She has never seen Him like this. He is revealing Himself as Lord of the nations.[24] The mountains speak of obstacles, both human and demonic. Jesus is effortlessly skipping and leaping like a gazelle over every obstacle. He is the Uncreated God who has power over everything. In this passage, He is not coming as the Shepherd to offer counsel, or as the Father with great affection. He is revealing Himself as the sovereign King!

Jesus is calling her out of the comfort zone.[25] He is calling her out of the boat, or the comfort zone of predictability, to walk with Him on the water of risk. This represents the difficult assignments—humanly speaking—that He often gives His people that enhance their bridal partnership with Him. He desires to partner with her. She does not understand that the Father has given Jesus a mandate to disciple the nations of the earth. He does not only want her to love Him in the prayer closet, He wants her to love Him enough to go into all the world with Him.[26]

Jesus wants her to get out of the boat and meet Him on the water. Jesus has authority over the water and the storms of life. He wants her to love Him in the midst of conflict and risk with the assurance of His protection and His provision for her. She is used to being fed with grapes and raisins, at the table, under the shade tree, on the bed, and is not sure that she wants any part of walking on the water!

HER COMPROMISE DUE TO IMMATURITY

After He calls her out of the comfort zone to the mountains, she refuses Him. She turns Him away. She says in her heart, *"No I can't obey Your beckoning to ascend the mountains with You."*[27] She finds herself in the place of compromise due to her immaturity, weakness, and fear. What is important to realize, though, is that it is not due to rebellion. She is afraid. She fears that 100 percent obedience might cause her to lose something, to miss out on something. She really does love Him, but she does not have the courage and the strength to obey Him. The risks of walking by faith seem too great of an obstacle for her to overcome.

DIVINE CHASTISEMENT

In this next season of her life, she experiences the Lord's chastisement. This isn't because He is angry; it is because of His affections as a loving Father.[28] The Father lovingly promises to pry our fingers off the things that hold us in bondage.[29] The Father loves us too much to allow His immature Church to come up short of being the glorious Bride of the Lord Jesus. It is our destiny to be with Him on mountains. Again, He is not angry with her. God's correction is not the same thing as His rejection. Too many believers mistakenly confuse God's correction with rejection. In fact, His correction is the exact opposite of rejection. His correction is an expression of His deep desire to have us mature in drawing near to Him in intimacy and running with Him in anointed ministry. It is a redemptive correction, which flows out of His great affection for us. His correction is His beckoning us to come to Him.

Because of her refusal to step out of the boat, God hides His face from her.[30] As a result, she is confused because she is no longer experiencing the sweetness she loved so much earlier. God's manifest Presence is strategically withdrawn. For the first time since she has begun her journey into the knowledge of God's affection and beauty, she cannot find Him.[31]

Once we have experienced the sweetness of God's manifest Presence, then we are forever discontent to live without it. The Lord is applying the principle used in the life of the prophet Jeremiah, *"O Lord, You have deceived me, and I was deceived; You are stronger than I, and You have prevailed. I have become a laughingstock all the day; everyone mocks me."*[32] God had won Jeremiah's heart, and he told the Lord he would do anything for Him. However, preaching the truth got him into trouble, caused him discomfort and personal pain. His flesh wanted to turn and run, but his heart would not let him.

Like Jeremiah, the Bride eventually agrees to "arise" and obey the call to rise up off her bed. However, she is not yet ready to ascend the mountains until she is further equipped, though she does eventually go to the mountains.[33] Jesus' manifest Presence returns in response to her obedience. What happens? She "finds" Him again and resolves deep in her heart never to lose the freshness of the Holy Spirit in her spiritual walk. She has learned the value of her relationship with Jesus and how much He values obedience.[34]

A FRESH REVELATION OF JESUS AS A SAFE SAVIOR

The fourth revelation of Jesus in the Song of Solomon is that He is a Safe Savior. Jesus reveals Himself as the One who is safe to obey 100 percent. He shows Himself to her as the Safe Savior who extravagantly provides for her spiritual safety. The promise of safety focuses primarily on spiritual safety that protects our heart spiritually; and then secondarily, it speaks of protecting our earthly circumstances. This revelation is designed to win her heart and woo her to a deeper confidence in Jesus. This season in her life proves to be a turning place for the maiden. The depth of commitment that she manifests in chapters 4 through 8 flows out of this new insight as she learns to follow the Lord's safe leadership.

Prophetic Heart of the Heavenly Bridegroom

The fifth revelation of Jesus in the Song reveals Him as a heavenly Bridegroom, with a special focus on His prophetic heart. He speaks to her, prophetically proclaiming her "budding virtues." He really does call those things that are not, as though they were.[35] God names us according to our prophetic destiny. He looks into her heart and sees the cry in her spirit. He defines her by the cries in her spirit. Therefore, He calls her beautiful, dedicated, discerning, consecrated, etc. God names His people according to their hidden virtues that are filled with spiritual beauty. He sees the hidden cry in their spirit. He describes eight distinct virtues of her beauty that He sees emerging in her life.

The heavenly Bridegroom is preparing her, equipping her for spiritual warfare. He seeks to convince her to see how beautiful she is to Him. It is significant that He uses the words *"altogether beautiful."* This is the first time that He makes such a statement to her, adding the phrase *"no flaw in you."*[36]

A life of total commitment is foundational for all mature ministry.[37] Jesus called her to come to the mountain back in chapter 2.[38] Her first response was to refuse Him because she was afraid to leave her comfort zone. However, in this season, she commits to go with Him to the mountain. This commitment to obey is in fact the initial stages of true obedience, but it is not yet mature obedience.[39]

At this point in her walk with the Lord, it is the first time that she is called His Bride.[40] She is now called His Bride because of her new commitment in chapter 4 verse 6 to partner with Jesus on the mountain of myrrh. She is now doing what she was ordained to do from the beginning. The Bride, in essence, is one who walks in mature partnership with Jesus.[41]

THE CAPTIVATED HEART OF THE BRIDEGROOM

The fifth revelation of Jesus in the Song of Solomon reveals Him as a heavenly Bridegroom with special focus on His heart captivated with desire for her. Jesus has passionate affection for His Bride. She has been equipped, by the revelation of His captivated heart, to fully embrace the Cross.[42] Jesus describes His pleasure over her character.[43] He proclaims the sevenfold description of the Bride.[44]

The Bride then cries out for increased anointing.[45] She cries out for the north wind, which speaks of the cold bitter winds of winter. She also cries out for the south wind, which speaks of the warm refreshing winds of the summer. God, in His wisdom, knows we need both the north and south winds for maturity. This shows that she is no longer afraid of the tests of God. She says, "Blow O north wind."

We start to see her divine inheritance being established. Her garden speaks of her heart and inner life in God. *"Let my Beloved come to His garden."* Whose garden is it? Is it hers or is it His? Earlier in the book it was hers, but now it has become His. This is the transition place in her journey. In the first four chapters, she was only concerned with her inheritance—her garden. However, in the last four chapters, His inheritance is her focus. In the first four chapters, it was always *her* garden. In the last four chapters, it is *His* garden. She prays, "Blow on my garden, and make it Your garden." She prays, "Let its spices flow out." She wants His fragrances, or character, to emanate out of her life. Then she adds to her prayer, "I want You to come to Your garden to eat the pleasant fruits from my life."

Jesus answers her prayer and comes to His garden to claim His inheritance, which is His Bride.[46] Nine times He uses the ownership word "MY." He says, *I came to My garden, My sister, My bride. I gathered My myrrh, My spice, I ate My honeycomb with My honey, I drank My wine with My milk.* Everything in her is now His. She had just prayed, "I want You to send the north wind. I am willing to accept the difficult circumstances if they will enhance my ability to walk in mature partnership with You. I want to be totally Yours." The whole book is turning right now. He is going to answer the prayer for the north winds that cause the spices of His character to flow from her.

THE ULTIMATE TWOFOLD TEST OF MATURITY

The sixth revelation of Jesus in the Song of Solomon reveals Him as the suffering servant, the Jesus of Gethsemane.[47] The Jesus of Gethsemane invites her to share in His sufferings. Here she is faced with a new challenge: will she share intimately in the sufferings of Christ?[48] The Jesus who embraced the Cross in the long and lonely night in Gethsemane now says, "Open up to Me, and come with Me to Gethsemane." Remember, she just prayed, "Send the north winds so that my fragrance would increase." Jesus is now answering that prayer and sending the bitter north winds of the fellowship of suffering.

She doesn't pull back; she responds in full obedience.[49] She submits to Him. She says, *I had put off my garment.* The point is that she has worn her own garment in the past, but now she is wearing His. She had washed her feet that had been soiled because she had walked in her own way. She is committed to never defile her walk again.

She rises immediately with a heart yearning in love for Him. She opens to her Beloved. Her hands had myrrh on them, which speaks of her heart commitment to her Beloved to embrace death in any area that would hinder the working of His love in her life. It is here that she experiences her first test of suffering—His withdrawn Presence.[50] God's manifest Presence leaves her for the second time. The first time it was because of her disobedience,[51] but this time is because of her mature obedience. Some medieval teachers have called this "the dark night of the soul." Jesus wants to be the goal of her life, and not just the stepping-stone to her personal agenda of earthly happiness and self-satisfaction.

Now she experiences her second test of suffering—persecution and rejection.[52] The watchmen, who represent spiritual leaders, struck and wounded her. They take her veil, or her spiritual covering, away so that she can no longer function in the Body. Will she remain true, or will she become offended?

Recap: the Lord appeared to her with the call to join Him in Gethsemane. She responded in instant obedience. Then He gave her a twofold test related back to her life vision prayer.[53] She prayed to be drawn into intimacy—now she cannot feel His Presence. She prayed to run with Him in ministry—now the elders have renounced her, thus she has no place in ministry.

The Lord is asking her, "Will you be Mine even if the things that you so desire are withheld from you? Will you be Mine even if you cannot at this time feel My Presence? Will you still love and trust Me when you are disappointed by negative circumstances? Will you remain committed to Me when circumstances related to divine promises of blessing are not released in the timing or the way that you expected?" She responds, "Yes! Yes! Yes! I am Yours regardless." She is now saying "Yes!" at the deepest level of love.

She responds in deep humility.[54] She turns and asks for help from the daughters of Jerusalem who represent believers who are less spiritual than she is. She says, "If you find my Beloved, tell Him I *am sick with love!*" In other words, "Tell Him that I'm not offended. I love Him no matter what."

THE BRIDE'S RESPONSE TO THE TWOFOLD TEST

The seventh revelation of Jesus in the Song of Solomon is as the majestic God. The daughters of Jerusalem ask the Bride a question.[55] In essence, they ask, "Why are you so committed to Him that you would charge 'us' to go find Him? Look at what He has done to you. He has abandoned you. Why do you love Him so much?"

Her answer to them reveals her source of spiritual power—loving Jesus. She gives one of the greatest proclamations on the majestic splendor of Jesus in the Scripture. In Song 5:10-16 she gives the Church one of the most magnificent statements of worship. She speaks on ten different aspects of the beauty of God. She says:

> *My beloved is radiant and ruddy, distinguished among ten thousand. His head is the finest gold; His locks are wavy, black as a raven. His eyes are like doves, His cheeks are like beds of spices, His lips are lilies, His arms are rods of gold, His body is polished ivory, His legs are alabaster columns, His appearance is like Lebanon, His mouth is most sweet, and He is altogether desirable. This is my Beloved and this is my Friend, O daughters of Jerusalem.[56]*

She wraps up her view of His comprehensive beauty as being altogether lovely. She speaks of Him as her Beloved even when she cannot always correctly interpret what she considered harsh trials in a way that enhanced her maturity in love. She speaks of Him as her Friend, not as one who mistreated her, but as One who thoroughly understood her.

The daughters of Jerusalem then ask a second question.[57] After seeing her extravagant love and deep insight into the beauty of Jesus, they now change their question. Instead of asking, "What is He?" as in Song 5:9, they change their question to, "Where is He? We want to seek Him. We want to find what you've found." This is an example of true evangelism. Jesus isn't interested in conversion only, He is looking to make disciples!

THE LOVE LANGUAGE OF GOD

JESUS PRAISES HER AFTER HER
SEASON OF TESTING

Jesus describes the Bride's threefold hidden splendor and beauty.[58] He finally breaks the silence after the daughters of Jerusalem have been questioning her. Jesus lavishes affection and praise on her now that the season of testing is over. He describes her hidden beauty. Jesus declares, "Oh My love, you possess hidden splendor in that you are beautiful, lovely, and awesome." The army with banners speaks of a conquering army.

A returning army in the ancient world came back with banners and marched down the street. The banners in such a military processional signaled victory. He describes her as awesome as a victorious army with banners. He is saying to her that she thoroughly passed the twofold test. She defeated the greatest enemies, those found in her own soul. The strongest powers to conquer are the forces in our own heart, not the demons around us. She has come before Him as a victorious army with banners.

No force can conquer Jesus but the love of His Bride.[59] He says, *"Turn away your eyes from Me."* He does not mean it literally. He is speaking in the ultimate language of love. Her eyes of devotion have overwhelmed and conquered the very heart of God with wholehearted love. He describes His heart as overwhelmed by her.

This is one of the great passages in all of the Scriptures. Not all the armies in hell can conquer Jesus, but the eyes of devotion of the redeemed conquer Him when they are true to Him in times of testing. It is powerful when we understand how the heart of God is moved when He sees us staying faithful to Him, especially in a time of testing when we feel abandoned.

Jesus then describes the Bride's maturity[60] and her preeminence.[61] Then the Holy Spirit describes the Bride's crown of glory.[62]

VINDICATION OF THE PERSECUTED BRIDE

The Bride now has a mature commitment to serve the whole Church.[63] She shares Jesus' mature love for God's people and it overcomes her.[64] The Bride now possesses self-sacrificing love that overflows out of her heart. Then she receives a sincere response from other mature believers within the Church.[65] But she also receives a hostile response from carnal believers within the Church.[66] The Scriptures teach that self-sacrificing love for Jesus usually results in a resultant persecution. However, discerning saints vindicate the Bride[67] as does Jesus Himself.[68]

THE BRIDE'S MATURE PARTNERSHIP WITH JESUS

Bridal partnership is expressed in mature obedience to Jesus.[69] She expresses Bridal partnership in her intercession for more power.[70] She expresses Bridal partnership in her boldness in public ministry.[71] She expresses Bridal partnership in their full union.[72]

THE BRIDAL SEAL OF MATURE LOVE

The eighth revelation of Jesus in the Song of Solomon reveals Him as a consuming fire. This is the most well-known passage in the book. It is also the great climax of the book. *"Who is that coming up from the wilderness, leaning on her beloved? Set Me as a seal upon your heart, as a seal upon your arm, for love is strong as death, jealousy is fierce as the grave. Its flashes are flashes of fire, the very flame of the Lord. Many waters cannot quench love, neither can floods drown it...."*[73]

Jesus invites her to receive the bridal seal of divine love. The book starts with a cry for a kiss and ends with a seal of love. The eternal uncreated fire of God burning in the human heart empowers us to walk in supernatural love. The bridal seal empowers our hearts with supernatural love. This love is stronger than the rivers of persecution and the waters of temptation.

THE BRIDE'S FINAL INTERCESSION AND REVELATION

This is the Bride's final intercession for the Church.[74] In terms of her progression into holy passion, her journey ends in Song 8:5-7. In this passage, she intercedes for the rest of the Church to walk in what she has experienced.

Then Jesus gives a final commission to His Bride.[75] He describes His Bride as dwelling in the "gardens of the Church" taking care of the younger believers. Jesus reminds her that so many of her companions are listening for her voice. These more immature companions look to and listen for the Bride's voice, saying, "Oh, we need your help. Will you please instruct us?"

The Bride is in great spiritual demand to instruct and escort others into the deep things of God. This ministry may be private or public. There is much demand for anyone who has spiritual depth and reality. He is reminding her not to lose her focus of love as the Bride in the midst of so many on earth who want to hear her voice in ministry. He commissions her not to get too busy for prayer in the midst of her flourishing ministry by saying, "Let Me hear your voice."

He is beckoning her to be faithful in prayer and her life of communion with God. This prayer has two expressions: devotional prayer—the call to communion with Jesus. He says, "Let ME also hear your voice in worship and devotion, and intercessory prayer." He says, "Let ME also hear your voice in intercession. Cry out until I will send the fullness of My Presence." The Bride displays her faithfulness by committing to live in continual prayer to the very end.[76] She prays to Jesus crying out for the nearness of Jesus in her heart in devotional prayer and for the corporate Church in intercessory prayer.

She is praying, "Oh Jesus, quickly come near to me and to Your Church." She prays that He will be like that gazelle[77] that came leaping on mountains as He conquered all powers, both demonic and human. "Oh come quickly and manifest

Your authority over all that resists You in my heart, in the Church, and in the world." The Bride's final intercession ultimately is for Jesus' second coming.

She prays, *"Come O great stag that dwells in heaven on the mountain of spices."*[78] Throughout the Song, spices speak of the fragrant beauties of the eternal Godhead. However, the mountain of spices refers to the eternal city where the fragrant God lives. It is the city with unlimited beauty and splendor. This refers to the fullness of what she initially understood when she saw Jesus as a bundle of myrrh.[79]

She says, "You are the great stag. You are the great conqueror of the great mountain of spices. You are king of the eternal city." She is saying, "Come quickly, Lord Jesus, from Your mountain of spices. Bring Your Church to the mountain of spices, not just to the mountains of leopards. Take us to Your heavenly abode this time."

This is the same prayer as in the Book of Revelation. *"Come, Lord Jesus!"*[80]

CHAPTER 11

Overview of the Bridal Paradigm in the New Testament

We have seen throughout the Old Testament how the bridal paradigm or perspective is everywhere and how necessary it is to understand the Scriptures or to relate to God in the manner He desires us to. The bridal paradigm is not just for Old Testament saints. In this chapter, we will be looking at what the New Testament has to say about this bridal lens of viewing things.

EVERYBODY LOVES A WEDDING

In John's Gospel we read about where Jesus, His mother Mary, and His disciples were attending a wedding celebration at Cana in Galilee.[1] The hosts ran out of wine, which in that culture was an embarrassment. Mary tells Jesus that the host has run out of wine. Jesus responds that His hour has not yet come to reveal Himself. Mary tells the host's servants to do whatever Jesus says to do. Jesus instructs the servants to fill six stone jars with water.

When they have finished filling the jars, He tells them to take some of the liquid from the jars and take it to the host. As they obeyed Jesus' instructions, the water was turned into wine. Upon tasting the miracle drink, the host called the bridegroom and commended him on the fine wine, commenting that the custom was to serve the best wine at the beginning of a wedding celebration, which could go on for up to a week, and after the guests had their fill, to bring out the cheap stuff. He mentioned how unusual it was to save the best wine until the latter part of the celebration.

Although turning water into wine, especially good wine, is nothing to sneeze at, the significance of this miracle is more than Jesus ensuring that there was enough wine for the celebration. Jesus was making a prophetic statement about His wedding, the wedding supper of the Lamb at the end of the age.[2]

Have you ever asked yourself the question, "If someone had all power, what would He do with it?" Well, now we know, don't we? He would plan a wedding! Jesus was making a couple of prophetic statements that day in Cana. The first statement was that God is using His power to plan a wedding! The second statement is that God saves His best wine for last.

In the generation in which the Lord returns, the primary message the Holy Spirit will be emphasizing will be the bridal message—there is going to be a wedding. We are told that the Church worldwide, for possibly the first and only time in redemptive history, will cry out in total unity with each other and with the Spirit of God—a bridal cry—*"Come, Lord Jesus"*[3] as the Spirit of God pours out His best wine, with all of His power emphasizing the bridal reality.

MAY I INTRODUCE THE BRIDEGROOM GOD

The next instance that we need to examine concerning Jesus related to the bridal paradigm of the Kingdom of God is when John the Baptist first introduces Him to Israel. John is having a discussion with his disciples and another Jew when he makes this statement concerning Jesus: *"The One who has the Bride is the Bridegroom."*[4] Notice what John says here. He did not just say only that Jesus possesses a Bride; he says that Jesus is a Bridegroom. What John is announcing is that in the essence of Jesus' personality—how He thinks, how He feels, and how He uses His power—at the core of His being, He is a Bridegroom.

This is significant because of what we looked at back in Hosea, where we are told that God's desire was that He be thought of and related to as a Husband or a Bridegroom.[5] John the Baptist, who was the herald of the Messiah, when introducing Jesus publicly, does not announce that He is the Messiah, the Savior, Healer, or Teacher; He introduces Him as the prophetic fulfillment of the Bridegroom God.

A few months after this incident, Jesus was asked a question by several of John's disciples concerning why they fasted, but His disciples did not fast. Jesus, who often operates on several levels at once, answers their question this way, *"Can the wedding guests mourn as long as the Bridegroom is with them? The days will come when the Bridegroom is taken away from them, and then they will fast."*[6] Jesus not only answers their question, but in doing so, He also announces to everyone that He Himself is the fulfillment of the Bridegroom God prophecies that were made by Isaiah, Jeremiah, Ezekiel, and Hosea. By saying that the Bridegroom was going to be taken away, He was making His first reference in the Gospels to the fact that He would be going to the Cross. All in one sentence. Brilliant!

By identifying Himself as the prophesied Bridegroom God that was to come, He was saying that He was the God who had burning desire for His people. He was proclaiming that as the Bridegroom God He would be giving His life for His people. We see the importance of that statement because of what the apostle John wrote years later, *"Come, I will show you the Bride, the wife of the Lamb."*[7] The Lamb who dies for the people of God is also the Bridegroom who claims them as His Wife.

FAMOUS LAST WORDS

Jesus started His supernatural ministry at a wedding, and then He was introduced to Israel as the fulfillment of the Bridegroom God prophecies. Now let's look at how He ended His ministry with the message of the bridal paradigm. Let me ask you a question. If you knew you were talking to someone for the very last time, you would choose your last words very carefully, wouldn't you? Well, Jesus was no different. Let's look at His last words.

In Matthew chapters 21 and 22, Jesus is delivering His last public message to the nation of Israel. His last message has three components made up of three parables. The last of the three parables is His last public message to Israel before He goes to the Cross. In this parable, the parable of the wedding feast, Jesus summarizes all of redemptive revelation by proclaiming, *"The Kingdom of heaven may be compared to a King who gave a wedding feast for His Son."*[8]

Through this parable, Jesus is proclaiming God's eternal purpose for all that He has said and done, which is to prepare a suitable, equally yoked Bride for His Son. As this was His last public message to Israel and the world, it was critical that He drive this point home—so He proclaimed to all that a wedding is coming and we must get ready.

When Jesus started His ministry, He introduced the fact that He was the King and that He had brought His Kingdom with Him. He then spent the next several years proclaiming and demonstrating His Kingdom wherever He went. Now, as His earthly ministry is ending, He recaps the Kingdom message. He commissions His followers to go out and call those who were invited to the wedding feast.[9] Jesus' last training session for evangelism was to tell His ministers to preach the bridal paradigm, to invite unbelievers to come to the wedding.

Beloved, this is really the highest call we can give to the world, calling them to God, with the understanding that God is head-over-heels in love with them and He wants to give them the power to return that love so that they can live fascinated and exhilarated by the receiving and the returning of this love. The reason that many are living such sub-normal lives is no one has told them that the inferior pleasures of this world cannot compare with the superior pleasures of the Gospel, and that there is no greater pleasure than being loved by God, in a bridal sense, and being able to return that love as a Bride loves her Groom.

All ministry throughout the Church age, whether it be apostolic, prophetic, evangelistic, pastoral, or teaching, can be summed up in this one commission—tell them about the Bridegroom and invite them to the wedding. If we love Him like He loves us, we will have no problem going out into the entire world with this good news because loving people is an automatic thing, "a done deal," if we really love God. Religious people can love God and struggle with loving people, but true Bridal love automatically loves people.

THE SPIRIT AND THE WORD—JESUS—AGREE

Another important point we need to look at is that this is not only Jesus' final public message at the end of His earthly ministry, it is also the Holy Spirit's final emphasis at the end of the age. The Spirit releases His greatest power upon those who join with Him in giving a bridal cry for all to come.[10] As the Bride of Him who is the eternal Intercessor,[11] we join with the Spirit, crying out to God to come to the people while we are crying out to the people to come to God.

As we draw nearer to the transition of this age into the Kingdom of God, we will find that the Spirit's greatest release of power will be given to those who share His heart and are involved in proclaiming the message that He most wants to proclaim. The greatest "sign of the times" is the fact that worldwide we see the Holy Spirit releasing greater desire, revelation, and authority on those proclaiming the bridal message and inviting everyone to come.

After Jesus gave this last public message, He then meets with His disciples for the last time as recorded in Matthew chapters 24 and 25. In these chapters, He is teaching them concerning the end-time leadership principles of the Kingdom. In Matthew 25, in what is commonly known as the Parable of the Ten Virgins, Jesus refers to end-time leaders as virgins, or believers, with lamps, or ministries, whose ministry emphasis is to come out and meet the Bridegroom.

The end-time emphasis and message from the Spirit will not be to just come and receive forgiveness from the Savior, or come and be healed by the Healer, or come and meet the King who has all power, as important and necessary as each of those are. The end-time emphasis will, more and more, be to come out and encounter the Bridegroom God whose heart is filled with burning passionate desire for you.

In the middle of the parable, we read, *"But at midnight there was a cry, 'Here is the Bridegroom! Come out to meet Him.'"*[12] Midnight can represent several things throughout Scripture, but in this instance, most commentators believe that it represents the midnight of human history, or the darkest point of human history. God is going to raise up forerunners at the midnight hour, at the darkest point of human history, those whose hearts are beating as one, in unity with the Spirit; and their message will be "Here is the Bridegroom! Come out to meet Him." Glory!

THE LAST PRAYER

In John chapter 17, we see Jesus' last recorded intercessory prayer for the Church.[13] I call this Jesus' Bridegroom Prayer. Shhh, let's look in and listen to what He was praying:

Father, I desire that they also, whom You have given Me, may be with Me where I am, to see My glory that You have given Me because You loved Me before the foundation of the world.[14]

Notice He is not asking God to save them, or to keep them out of hell. What He is saying is (paraphrased),

Father, as a Bridegroom, **I desire** that the Bride that You have given Me would be with Me, that they would see My glory, gaze on Me, encounter My glory, encounter Me.

And then we skip down a little further: *"I made known to them Your name, and I will continue to make it known, that the love with which You have loved Me may be in them, and I in them."*[15] What He is saying is, "Father, I have revealed who You are to My Bride." Then He prophesies about the future, "And when I get to Heaven, I will continue to make You known." Why, Jesus? "That the love with which You have loved Me may be awakened on the inside of them."

For over 2,000 years now, Jesus has been seated on His throne, at the right hand of the Father, continuing to make the Father known—with every salvation, healing, and deliverance, every time He blessed someone financially, every time He anointed someone to do Kingdom ministry—He has been revealing how the Father feels and what He thinks. For what purpose? So that His Bride would love Him like the Father loves Him!

Remember when we looked at Mount Sinai? When the Father was showing out for His people, what was His purpose then? To win the hearts of His people. Jesus said, *"Whoever has seen Me has seen the Father."*[16] Like Father, like Son. He loves to display His power unto something—the wooing and the winning of the hearts of His people.

Again, notice with me what He did *not* pray. He did not pray that they would escape hell, or that they would be saved, forgiven, or pardoned. What He did pray was that they would be with Him, because that is what is in His heart. He likes us and He enjoys being with us. Do you see it? It is all about bridal love! All of this is to show us where His deepest desire is—us! *"Looking to Jesus, the Founder and Perfecter of our faith, who **for the joy that was set before Him** endured the cross...."*[17]

JESUS' FINAL DEED

We have looked at Jesus' final public message, His final private message, and His final intercessory prayer. Now let us look for a moment at His final deed. Let me set the scene for you. Jesus has been deserted by all of His disciples except one, John. He has been mocked, beaten, stripped, and nailed upon the Cross. He is hanging between two thieves, and one of them pours out his verbal scorn on Jesus as well.[18] Add to this the fact that Jesus is also at this time bearing the weight of all the cumulative sin of humanity—past, present, and future—and is bearing the wrath of God for our sin. What would you do, how would you act in circumstances like that?

It is imperative that we realize that Jesus does not change gears just because He is on the Cross. So many times, I have heard it preached that Jesus was born to die; He was born to go to the Cross to pay the price for our sin. It was prophesied of Him, *"Behold, I have come to do Your will, O God, as it is written of Me in the scroll of the book."*[19] Yet, when it was time to actually do it, time to actually pay the price, He started having second thoughts. He started getting cold feet, spiritually speaking.

So many preachers stand up and tell their flocks that Jesus, the God-Man, the Uncreated God of Genesis chapter 1, was a quitter! "He was just like us," they say. When the going got rough, He started looking to see if there was a back door, a plan B. He started crying out in desperation, *"My Father, if it be possible, let this cup of the cross pass from Me."*[20] Does loving God and following Him begat spineless jellyfish? No! A thousand times no! The story line is that we are supposed to be more like Jesus, not think that Jesus was just like us!

This is so very important. You must realize that Jesus never once thought about backing out, just because it got a little difficult. Well, if He was not asking God to allow Him to avoid the Cross, what was going on in the garden of Gethsemane?

It is interesting that Luke, the physician, is the only one to mention this. He says, *"And being in an agony He prayed more earnestly; and his sweat became like great drops of blood falling down to the ground."*[21]

Though very rare, the phenomenon of hematidrosis, or bloody sweat, is well documented. Under great emotional stress of the kind our Lord suffered, tiny capillaries in the sweat glands can break, thus mixing blood with sweat. This process might well have produced marked weakness and possible shock. I have heard several medical doctors state that this represented an aneurism where the main blood vessel going to the brain burst, which would have meant imminent death. In other words, Jesus was dying in the garden. I believe that Jesus was not praying for the cup of the Cross to pass, He was praying that the cup of His dying in the garden before He could get to the Cross would pass.[22]

Many modern scholars attempt to explain away this description; however, a great deal of effort could have been saved had the doubters consulted medical literature.

Back to Jesus' final deed. One of the thieves hanging beside Jesus looks at Him and says, *"Jesus, remember me when You come into Your Kingdom."*[23] How does Jesus respond? Remember, He has been mocked, ridiculed, beaten, scourged, crucified; He is bleeding and dying. He was so disfigured from the beating that He no longer looks like a man,[24] and He is bearing the eternal wrath of God. What is on His heart? The Bride![25] Jesus turns to the thief and says, *"Truly, I say to you, today you will **be with Me** in Paradise."*[26]

Notice Jesus did not say to him, "Today you will be pardoned of your sin." No! He said the same thing to the thief that He had said to His disciples in the upper room,[27] the same thing that He had prayed about so passionately in John 17.[28] He said, *"You are going to **be with Me**!"* He did not describe salvation to the thief as just getting out of the penalty of death. He did not describe it as just the pardon from sin, though it surely includes that dynamic.

Even though Jesus was just a few short minutes from His own death, that was not what was on His mind. What was on His mind, the thing that was pounding in His heart, was not His own circumstances or His own comfort. What was pounding in the heart of Jesus while He was on the Cross was that the Father would be glorified and that the Bride would be with Him. Do you see it? Oh, how glorious it is to be loved by the Bridegroom God!

Jesus' paradigm of salvation is not primarily that we are saved from something, though we are saved from many things—sin, and sickness, the curse of the law, fear, poverty, and eternal damnation—surely, we are saved from all of those. That is not Jesus' paradigm of salvation. Jesus' understanding is that we are not saved *from something,* we are saved *to Someone.*

> *This is eternal life, that they might be having an experiential knowledge of You.*[29]

> *...the only true God, and Jesus Christ Whom You have sent...Father, I desire that they may be with Me.*[30]

Do you see Jesus' perspective on this salvation thing? It is not a religious thing, or a "Dudley Do Right keep the law" system of works—He wants us with Him as His Bride forever! That is what drives and motivates Jesus! He wants the Father glorified and He wants us to be with Him because our being with Him glorifies the Father the most! Why? It was His idea, Beloved! He loves us!

Remember the scene in Mel Gibson's *The Passion* where Jesus is carrying the Cross on the way to Golgotha? He is carrying the Cross, and the guards are beating Him, and because of all that He has been through, He is weak, fatigued, and He has lost a lot of blood. He stumbles and falls to the ground. One of the Roman guards strikes Him. When you are watching that scene, it is easy to sympathize with Jesus, and the natural thought is that you want Him to get away from the soldier.

Here is the genius of what Gibson wants to bring out about Jesus as the Bridegroom who lives and dies with the Bride, as His focus comes out. Instead of doing what is natural, getting away from His torturer, instead of demonstrating His love for the Bride and the price that has to be paid if she is going to be won, Jesus crawls over and lays on top of the Cross! To me, that is the most moving scene in the whole film, for it best epitomizes everything Jesus was about and everything He did.

JESUS' LAST MESSAGE

We have seen how when Jesus was first introduced to Israel by John the Baptist, as the Bridegroom who had a Bride, He performed His first miracle at a wedding as a foreshadow of the Great Wedding to come, and to emphasize that God was saving His best wine for the end of the age. Jesus, at the beginning of His public ministry, pronounced Himself as the Bridegroom. His last public sermon to the nation of Israel was that the message of the Kingdom was about a Father who was preparing a wedding for His Son.

His last private instructions to His disciples were that they were to go out and invite people to a wedding. His last intercessory prayer was that His greatest desire was that His Bride would be with Him. His last deed, even as He was being crucified and just moments from death, was focused on sharing with the thief hanging beside Him that they were going to be together. Do you think that the bridal message is important?

Now, let us leap into the future 60 years after Jesus had returned to Heaven. Jesus appears to the apostle John on the Isle of Patmos and gives to John, and to us, His absolute, very last message to the corporate Church until He returns—a 2,000-year wait so far. This last message, recorded in Revelation chapters 2 and 3, is really one message with seven points, but it is still one message. His last public message to Israel had three points made up of three parables; His last corporate message to the Church has seven points in it. This is the final cry to the planet from the heart of the God-Man. What will He say?

In His last corporate message to the Church, He starts by saying, *"I have something that is bothering Me. You have lost the love you had for Me at first."*[31] It is like He was saying to John,

"They don't love Me like they used to love Me, John." Can you see His pain, can you hear His heartbeat?

The Book of Revelation, though it gives us much information that we desperately need as we approach the return of Jesus to the planet, the giving of that information is not Jesus' main motive. He tells John that the book is a revelation about Himself.[32] So Jesus was not so much talking about what the Church was doing, as He was expressing what was in His heart. Can you see? It is the same bridal message—it is all about love. It's all about a wedding!

WHAT ARE YOU DOING FOR DINNER?

How do you think He ends the last message He is going to speak to the Church for 2,000 years? You got it! He says, *"Behold, I stand at the door and knock. If anyone hears My voice and opens the door, I will come in to him and eat with him, and he with Me."*[33] His last words spoken directly to the Church were, "I want you to dine with Me!" It is important to realize that He is referring partially to our individual fellowship with Him, but ultimately He is talking about the Marriage Supper of the Lamb where we will *"be with Him."*[34] He is stating again His desire that drives everything that He is and does—He wants us to dine with Him. You see, it is all about bridal love from the beginning to the end.

Beloved, that was what was on His mind when He started His earthly ministry, at His final public message, His final teaching to His disciples; it was what was on His mind in the upper room and in His last intercessory prayer. It was what was on His mind with the thief on the Cross, and it was still the foremost thing on His mind when He was delivering His very last message to the corporate Church—the message that there is going to be a wedding. People, get ready. Get it?

We have seen how important the bridal paradigm of the Kingdom of God was to Jesus and how it was central in all He said and did. But that's not all, folks. There is more, much more. Let us look now at how His disciples continued this message, expounded on it, and actually expanded it as they took this good news about the bridal paradigm of the Kingdom of God to the nations of the world.

THE NORM FOR NEW TESTAMENT MINISTRY

I want to go back to John the Baptist for a moment. Earlier we looked at how John introduced Jesus to Israel as the prophesied and promised Bridegroom. But not only did John give us some vital information about Jesus, he also gave us some important information about himself at the same time.

As he is introducing Jesus as the Bridegroom, John also opens up his heart and gives us the only description, out of his own mouth, about who he was and what he was all about. Jesus gave His estimation of John by saying that there had never been a greater human being on the earth (other than Himself) than he.[35] So how does John describe himself?

John says of Jesus, *"The One who has the Bride is the Bridegroom."* Then he says of himself, *"The friend of the Bridegroom, who stands and hears Him, rejoices greatly at the Bridegroom's voice."*[36] John calls himself the friend of the Bridegroom, which is like the best man at the wedding. What a glorious privilege. What an awesome responsibility!

What John was trying to relate to us was that as the best man, he did not want to get too chummy with the Bride, know what I mean? He didn't want to draw undue attention to himself or what he was doing; instead, his desire was to get the message out that Jesus was the Bridegroom, to get the Bride to connect with the Bridegroom, and then to get out of the way. That is a big contrast to what is so prevalent in most circles, is it not?

We are not to showcase and talk about what God is doing through *us,* or to advertise *our* gifts, callings, or glory meetings. It is not about us; it is supposed to be all about Him! This is God's model for all New Testament ministry. We are to be a nameless, faceless generation. Jesus said that our left hand shouldn't even know what our right hand is doing,[37] which means that we aren't supposed to broadcast how "used of God" we are, as if we are the focus. Remember, Jesus said this, and He put it in the Word, so that when we think God is telling us to tell everybody, He has already said that we are to tell nobody.

You men, if you ask a friend to be your best man and he spends a majority of his time with your bride-to-be talking about himself, doing everything he can to draw attention to himself, and distracting the bride and the bridal party so that they aren't focused on the wedding, but instead are encouraged to keep their eyes on him, how happy would you be? Your answer of how you would feel or think about that is also how Jesus thinks and feels when He looks at the way we are doing church.

THREE REALITIES FOR THE REDEEMED

There are three distinct, yet interrelated, spiritual realities that we, as the people of God, have to juggle as we stand and live before God. The first is that we are servants of the Most High. Yes, we all have a task to perform, a job to do, a responsibility to discharge. We are called to do what we are called to do. This dynamic is specifically related to the Holy Spirit, who is the One who empowers us for our Kingdom service.

The second reality that we share is that we are all called to be mature sons and daughters of God. As we mature in the things of the Spirit, we all are offered Kingdom authority within the security of our being heirs of God and joint heirs with Christ. This dynamic is specifically related to our Father God who has invited us into Sonship.

The third reality that we share is that we are all part of the Bride of Christ; that is, we all have access to the deep things of Jesus' heart, and we can partner with Him in this age and as His eternal companion forever in the age to come.

MORE FRIENDS OF THE BRIDEGROOM

We have looked at how John the Baptist introduced Jesus to Israel, not as Savior, Healer, or Deliverer (though He was certainly all those), but instead, He announced the beginning of Jesus' ministry as fulfilling the prophetic Bridegroom God role. A few months later, John, disclosing some inside information concerning himself and his ministry focus, refers to himself as a friend of the Bridegroom.

And now, a few more months after that, and as we looked at earlier, Jesus answering the question John's disciples had asked Him concerning why His disciples didn't fast like John had taught them to, referred to Himself as the prophesied Bridegroom who was to come. He went on to expand the number of people He considered as friends of the Bridegroom to include the 12 as well as John. Jesus was saying, among other things, that being a friend of the Bridegroom isn't an exclusive club, He actually wants *everyone* to join the nameless, faceless community and to live their lives focused on proclaiming His greatness and worth instead of working so hard for their own personal recognition.

Jesus asks John's disciples:

...Can the friends of the Bridegroom mourn as long as the Bridegroom is with them? But the days will come when the Bridegroom will be taken away from them, then they will fast.[38]

Look at what He says then:

No one puts a piece of unshrunk cloth on an old garment, for the patch tears away from the garment, and a worse tear is made. Neither is new wine put into old wineskins. If it is, the skins burst, the wine is spilled, and the skins are destroyed. But new wine is put into fresh wineskins, and so both are preserved.[39]

Jesus is talking about much more than garments and canteens. He is giving a prophetic warning to all that we must not be guilty of imposing traditional or commonly held views about spiritual things on fresh revelations or fresh moves of the Holy Spirit. Dr. Jack Hayford in the *Spirit-Filled Life Study Bible* comments concerning this text that we must:

> Avoid imposing past traditional structures on present renewals. Understand that yesterday's structures and forms are often incapable of handling today's dynamic of spiritual renewal.[40]

Notice again, that Jesus is giving this warning in the context of His proclaiming Himself as the Bridegroom, and as the Savior who will be taken away (a reference to His going to the Cross to pay the price to purchase His Bride). He is saying, "It is a new day, there is a new understanding, do not miss the best and most important news you have ever heard." This is a valid warning to the Church today as well. People, get ready. As Bob Dylan sang, years ago, "The times, they are a changin'...."

PAUL DEFENDS THE BRIDE

We have seen that Jesus was all about the bridal paradigm, but it did not end there. The disciples took the baton and ran with it, and they actually released a depth of revelation on this theme greater than what Jesus did. This is only natural, as all revelation is incremental and progressive.

Paul the apostle was an amazing individual. He was a Pharisee of the Pharisees,[41] a Jews' Jew. He was zealous and pursued wholeheartedly what he believed in. Then, one day he met the Bridegroom on the Damascus road,[42] and everything changed. He ended up spearheading three evangelistic tours that resulted in the whole known world of that time having heard the Gospel.[43] In the process, he wrote over two-thirds of the New Testament, having walked in a spirit of revelation that has not been matched yet. Let's look and see if he has anything to add to our study.

Paul, writing his second letter to the Corinthians and under the inspiration of the Holy Spirit, says:

> *I am jealous over you with* **a jealousy that comes from God.** *I promised to give you to Christ, as your only* **Husband.** *I want to give you as* **His pure Bride.**[44]

Paul was a friend of the Bridegroom, wasn't he? He was looking out for what God was looking out for—the message of the Bridegroom, the Bride, and the fact that there is going to be a wedding!

Paul goes on, *"But I am afraid that as the serpent deceived Eve by his cunning, your thoughts will be led astray from a sincere and pure devotion to Christ."*[45] What is Paul saying here? Thinking back to when we looked at the Genesis account, what was the result of Eve's being deceived by the serpent? Every woe known to humanity, that's what. Paul is comparing that kind of deception and that kind of disastrous result, to the Corinthian believers being led astray from *"a sincere and pure devotion to Christ."*

One of the first rules we learn as we approach Bible study is this: context rules! A text without a context is a pretext! What that means is that no text stands alone; every text comes in a context, a series of thoughts. We have to look at the context of everything we study so that we can rightly determine what is actually being said. What is the context that causes Paul to express such concern and jealousy? Here it is: the possibility that the serpent is working to derail believers from hearing, responding, and living in the revelation that Jesus is a Bridegroom, they are the Bride, and there is going to be a wedding!

"Sincere and pure devotion to Christ" is not about making sure you do not miss too many Sundays at church, or that you do not make every Christian social event. No! Sincere and pure devotion is remembering in the day-to-day mundane routine, while under the attack of the enemy, that we relate to God, not in the context of our being sinners or in the context of our striving to get into a room that we are already in. No, no, no! How are we to

relate to God? As His beloved, as His favorite ones, as the apple of His eye. Hallelujah!

In the light of all we have studied, you tell me, how important is this? Important enough for the apostle to say that if someone comes and proclaims another Jesus than the one we proclaimed (Jesus as Bridegroom), or if you receive a different spirit from the One you received (the Spirit who is preparing the Bride for Her wedding), or if you accept a different Gospel from the one you accepted (a Gospel that is fully saturated and all about the bridal aspects of the Kingdom of God), then Paul says emphatically to let them be accursed![46] Maybe Paul thinks this is pretty important, what do you think?

Paul's paradigm of ministry was that he was taking unbelievers, or as I call them, "pre-believers," and introducing them to a God who was lovesick over them and wanted to forgive them. Then, after they responded to the good news and were now believers, he wanted to show them the excellencies of Christ—like God the Father did at Sinai, and as God the Son did in His earthly ministry and in His on-going heavenly ministry—so that passion for the Son of God would be awakened in them, resulting in their living a life-style of diligently pursuing Him, as a bride pursues her bridegroom.

PAUL'S REVELATION OF THE BRIDE

As we looked at earlier, Paul uses the natural understanding we have of earthly relationship of husbands and wives as a balancing board to express the heavenly understanding of the bridal message of the Kingdom. He says:

> *Husbands, love your wives, **as Christ loved the Church** **and gave Himself up for Her**, that He might sanctify Her, having cleansed Her by the washing of water with the Word, so that He might present the Church to Himself in splendor, without spot or wrinkle or any such thing, that She might be holy and without blemish. **In the same***

way, husbands should love their wives as their own bod-
ies. He who loves his wife loves himself. For no one ever
*hated his own flesh, but nourishes and cherishes it, **just as***
***Christ does the Church,** because we are members of His*
body. Therefore a man shall leave his father and mother
and hold fast to his wife, and the two shall become one
flesh. This mystery is profound, and I am saying that it
refers to Christ and the Church.[47]

All the other dynamics of the Kingdom, all of which are vital
and necessary, operate best and at their highest under the umbrella
of the bridal paradigm. Not that you have to necessarily use the
language, but you do have to experience the reality of it. All believers should interact with Jesus as His Bride, both in time and in eternity. Again, we are not talking about sensuality or sexuality; it has
nothing to do with gender or personality types. Women are Sons of
God and men are the Bride of Christ. It is all about us walking in
the privilege of having our hearts beating as one with His.

Another statement from the pen of Paul:

that the God of our Lord Jesus Christ, the Father of
glory, may give you a spirit of wisdom and of revela-
*tion **in the knowledge of Him,** having the eyes of your*
hearts enlightened, that you may know what is the hope
to which He has called you, what are the riches of His
glorious inheritance in the saints.[48]

Paul, praying the heart of God for the Church of God, says that
God wants us to have our hearts enlightened so that we would
understand and walk in the light of the hope[49] to which He has
called us. What hope do you think he might be referring to?

Again Paul writes, *"And He put all things under His feet and*
gave Him as head over all things to the Church, which is His body,
the fullness of Him who fills all in all."[50] Why is this important?
He is the Head, we are the Body. It is that one flesh thing. Get it?

We are members of His body. *"Therefore a man shall leave his father and mother and hold fast to his wife, and the two shall become one flesh. This mystery is **profound, and** I am saying that **it refers to Christ and the Church.**"* It is all about a Bridegroom, a Bride, and a wedding!

The Heart Impact

I want to go back to John the Baptist and his introductory statement about Jesus and himself for a third "golden nugget." Remember, John said:

> *The one who has the Bride is the Bridegroom. The friend of the Bridegroom* [John talking about himself], *who stands and hears Him, rejoices greatly at the Bridegroom's voice. Therefore this joy of mine is now complete.*[51]

John lets us in on a further detail of what makes this man that Jesus referred to as a *"burning and shining lamp"*[52] and the greatest man (other than Jesus) who had ever lived.[53] His joy was not dependent on whether his ministry was the coolest or the biggest. In fact, he stated emphatically that he knew that Jesus' ministry must get bigger and his own was to fade out.[54] His identity was not wrapped up in how many meetings he had scheduled, or how many people were attending them.

John was a friend of the Bridegroom; his joy was not about the number of people following him, or his reputation in the people's eyes, or even in his own followers' eyes. His joy came from hearing the Bridegroom's voice. Oh, that we had more pastors and preachers who cared about hearing the Bridegroom's voice, more than they care about listening to the people's voices. If we did, I tell you, we would see revival in the land!

Let me ask you a question: What is it that moves your heart? Are you caught up in the Christian rat race of bigger and better? Do you live for the day when "the power" will be so strong that multitudes flock to hear you or be prayed for by you? Or are you like the person who impresses Jesus and catches His attention?

Reader Harris, an Englishman and director of The Pentecostal League of Prayer, once challenged a congregation on this matter of power and purity. He said, "Those who want power, line up to my right. Those who want purity, line up to my left." The congregation lined up 10 to 1 for *power!*[55] What makes your joy complete? Just a character reality check.

THE HOLY SPIRIT'S LAST EMPHASIS

The last thing I want us to consider is that this Bridal reality will be the Holy Spirit's last big push at the end of the age before the Lord returns. I say the last big push, not at all meaning His only push. He is doing and will continue to do many things simultaneously, as the tsunami called the Kingdom of God breaks into this age.

The Lord who is the Spirit[56] will be increasing His activity in several arenas as we near the Day of the Lord. Bridal intimacy with Jesus[57] (manifested by a love for the Word of God and the things of the Kingdom); the spirit of prophecy being released on the people of God;[58] a spirit of prayer will be ever increasing in a global sense;[59] a return to apostolic doctrine, lifestyles, and power resulting in the greatest release of spiritual power enabling the people of God to do the works of the Kingdom that the world has ever seen;[60] and a worldwide revival[61] with the greatest ingathering of souls in the Church's history[62]—all of this will crescendo under the umbrella of the increase of the bridal message.

The Church will for the first time in history be in total unity with the Spirit[63] in the context of the bridal reality,[64] resulting in the whole Church relating to Jesus in His role as our Husband, and not just our Master.[65] This will be the result of our recognizing not only how much, the quantity, Jesus loves us, but also the way, the quality, that He loves us.[66]

THE GREATEST IMPACT

I was preaching a few years back on the subject of the bridal paradigm of the Kingdom of God. After the service was over, a sweet, elderly lady inquired if I had a moment to answer a question she had. I smiled and told her that of course I had the time.

She looked at me in dead earnestness and said, "You know, I was raised in church, in fact I wouldn't be surprised to find out that I have been saved longer than you have been alive. I have heard hundreds of preachers and thousands of sermons, but I have never heard the likes of what you preached tonight. If what you said is true, then that changes everything. But I have a question for you. If this be true, how come nobody told me this before?"

All I could do is smile, and answer, "I really can't answer that question, Ma'am. But I agree with you, that this changes everything. And at least you lived long enough to hear it now. Will you do me a favor? Go and tell everybody you can; they all need to hear this message."

The lady was right. The message of Jesus as the Bridegroom *does* change everything. It is the deathblow to the religious spirit. It is the deathblow to apathy, complacency, carnality, and lukewarmness. They all roll over, wither, and die in the glorious reality of the bridal paradigm of the Kingdom.

Like the lady said, if this be true, it means this is a new day— a whole new ballgame. God is raising the awareness of believers all around the globe in preparation for the greatest outpouring of the Holy Spirit that this world has ever seen. Bigger than the Exodus and the Book of Acts combined. The Holy Spirit Himself, He who is God, is about to bring the whole Body of Christ into the understanding that Jesus is a Bridegroom and we are a Bride. When that reality hits, there will be a gut-wrenching cry released worldwide as the Bride and the Spirit in agreement call out for the return of the Bridegroom. When that happens, watch out, because all of Heaven is going to break loose!

CHAPTER 12

Loving God—The Great and First Commandment

Let me ask a question of the men (OK, ladies, you can listen in). What does a husband want from his wife?

This is a very important and relevant question. I went to a local bookstore and was looking through the magazine section, specifically publications geared toward men or women. Almost every one of them had at least one article, and many advertisements, that had this question as its theme.

Remember, we are investigating the question, how does God our Husband, specifically, God the Son, Jesus, our Bridegroom God, want His Bride, the Church, to love Him? In light of what we have examined thus far, the fact that God desires to be thought of as our Husband, not just as our Master, and that Jesus throughout the New Testament writings is spoken of as our Bridegroom and we as His Bride, I can think of no higher or more relevant question for our consideration, can you?

OUR INHERITANCE: LOVING GOD FOREVER

As we have seen in previous chapters, everything that God has done and revealed has had one grand purpose in mind—to woo and win the hearts of His people in bridal affection. Of all the blessings God has offered to humankind throughout the ages, undoubtedly the greatest has been the gift of Himself. As John Piper so aptly entitled one of his books, *God is the Gospel*.[1]

Jesus, the God-Man, had just finished an explosive conversation with the Sadducees, a socio-political branch of Judaism that represented the aristocrats of the time. Another prominent group, the Pharisees, had heard how Jesus had silenced the Sadducees. They gathered around Jesus and one of them, a lawyer, asked Jesus a question attempting to trip Him up. He asked Jesus which was the greatest commandment in the law.[2]

During the time of Jesus' earthly ministry, there were several different religious movements, similar to the various denominations we have today, each emphasizing different aspects of religious life. The lawyer hoped, by asking this question in a public forum, to cause a religious uproar with Jesus' answer.

God had given Ten Commandments to Israel.[3] The various religious leaders of Israel had constructed a detailed religious structure based on the Ten Commandments, along with the rest of the 613 *Mitzvot* (commandments or instructions), 248 "positive" commandments, and 365 "negative" commandments, that the Lord had given to Moses in the Torah—the five books of Moses, the first five books of the Old Testament.

Over the years, Israel had added to them many clarifications, additions to the law (oral traditions), which culminated in hundreds of rules and regulations that various individuals and groups believed were absolutely necessary to please God. The lawyer hoped that asking this question would get Jesus in "hot water" with the other groups. The Pharisees' thought process was that no matter what Jesus answered, it would upset someone.

For example, if someone had recently had a run-in with someone who worshiped a false god, he would feel like the command to have no other God would be the most important.[4] If a parent was in the group who was having problems with a rebellious teenager, the command to honor your father and mother would be the most important.[5] A recent theft victim would possibly believe that the commandment to not steal would be the most important.[6] See what I mean?

Jesus answers the lawyer's question by quoting Israel's greatest Old Testament prophet, Moses, with what is commonly referred to as the Shema Israel.[7] The Shema Israel was the common denominator of all the religious belief systems in Israel: it was the basic confession of faith in Judaism.

The Hebrew word *Shema* means to hear. The Shema Israel is a command from Moses, God's spokesman, to Israel, as the people of God, to hear God's heart and to respond accordingly. The lawyer had hoped to trip Jesus up by getting Him to answer his question with something that would upset somebody. Instead, Jesus started by answering with possibly the one statement in the law that was absolutely guaranteed to please everybody! Brilliant!

Jesus answered the lawyer like this, "The most important commandment is, 'Hear, O Israel: The Lord our God, the Lord is one. And you shall love the Lord your God with all your heart and with all your soul and with all your mind and with all your strength.' This is the great and first commandment. And a second is like it: 'You shall love your neighbor as yourself.' There is no other commandment greater than these. On these two commandments depend all the Law and the Prophets."[8]

Notice that when Jesus quoted the Shema Israel, He made a few subtle changes to the wording. By the way, He could do that because He was the Author, and He knew exactly what He meant when He gave the message to Moses!

Jesus interpreted for His hearers what God meant when He spoke the Shema Israel through Moses. Jesus was saying, "Hear, O Israel (people of God): hear God's heart and respond correctly to the Lord." How, exactly, do we respond correctly, Jesus? That really is the core issue in our lives, isn't it? What does God desire of us? Those questions are the reason there are so many religions, so many movements, and so many denominations—everyone is trying to nail down exactly what we "have to do" to live a life pleasing to God.

Jesus was saying, "Here is how you respond correctly to the Lord. Not by hearing words with your physical ears, but by hearing with your heart what is on the Lord's heart. And don't stop with hearing and understanding, but follow through by aligning your heart with God's heart—love God."

Then He elaborates on what is on the Lord's heart: "You respond correctly to the Lord by aligning your heart with His heart, and that is done by loving Him with all of your heart, mind, soul, and strength." When Jesus quoted Moses, He changed might to strength and added the aspect of loving God with all your mind. In the next couple of chapters, we will be examining each of these four complementary dynamics and how they relate to our quest to "love God, God's way."

In this chapter, I want to take a few moments to look at Jesus' summarization of how He viewed these dynamics when He said, *"This is the great and first commandment."*[9]

The million-dollar questions boil down to these: How, Jesus? How do I love You with all of my heart, mind, soul, and strength? That is the cry of your heart, isn't it? Mine too. We all really want to love God; we are just not sure how to go about it rightly.

Jesus lays out for them and for us that we are to hear what is on God's heart, and then He tells us what is on God's heart—our loving Him. He defines for us what God's first priority for our life is, and then He encourages us that aligning our priorities with God's heart is the greatest way that we could live.

Notice it is the "great and first" commandment—this follows the Greek word order. Several translations rearrange the word order, placing the word first before the word great. The New King James translates the verse that way: *"This is the first and great commandment."*[10] I believe a better translation is the Holman

Christian Standard Bible's: *"This is the greatest and most important commandment."*[11]

Jesus said, *"This is the first, the most important, commandment."* It is the commandment that is first priority to God, first priority in the Kingdom, and the first and foremost emphasis of the Holy Spirit. And He said it is the great, or greatest commandment.[12] Why is it the greatest? Because it has the greatest emphasis of God's heart, the greatest impact on our hearts, and potentially the greatest impact on the hearts of the people to whom we minister.

A HERITAGE FOR HIS SON—A WHOLEHEARTED BRIDE

The Shema Israel, as defined by Jesus, reveals God's ultimate and eternal purpose for all of creation. From before the foundation of the world, God had a plan in His heart. He had a why behind the what. The what: He created the heavens and the earth. This commandment tells us why God did what He did. We know what He did on the Cross: He accomplished our eternal redemption. This statement by Jesus lets us into the why He accomplished redemption. Here, we are given the why behind the what of both creation and redemption.

God wanted a family for Himself, sons and daughters who would be loyal to Him in love. But that is not all He wanted! He also wanted to raise up an equally yoked Bride for His Son, who would be His eternal Companion. You see, the Father promised His Son a heritage. That heritage is a wholehearted people whom He would totally possess. Jesus' heritage involves much more than just the real estate of the planet, much more than just owning the 200 or so nations, much more than the rulership of the governments. Much more!

Jesus does own the right to all the real estate of the earth; the Father has deeded it to Him. We are given insight into this in Revelation 5 when we see the scroll, which is the title deed to the earth, given to the Son. Therefore, we know who has the right to the inheritance of the nations: He owns all the land. We know He controls all the governments, but to inherit the nations and to totally possess them means much more than that. It means that He would possess the heart of *the people* in all the nations of the earth.

The Father said to the Son, "Jesus, I will give You the nations—total control over the government. I will give You the ends of the earth, all the real estate, and I will give You the hearts of the people."[13] "You will possess them in their entirety" is the idea here.

When I first read that passage, I remember the thought occurring to me, "The nations are not going to like this." Have you ever thought about the fact that many simply do not want to serve God or to love Jesus? What about them?

THE FATHER'S GIFT: MANDATORY OBEDIENCE AND VOLUNTARY LOVE

In the Midwestern part of the United States during the times of the great Moody revivals (D.L. Moody was a famous evangelist who lived during the mid-1800s), many atheists toured the surrounding towns to refute the evangelists who were preaching repentance and faith. In one town, an atheist used his oratory to confound and confuse the hearers. A few Christians called out Bible verses only to have them twisted and thrown back at them. He chided the crowd, "Where is your God? If He is alive, let Him show Himself! If He is present, let Him speak!" No one dared challenge him until an old black man near the back of the crowd yelled, "Here He come! He'll be here in a minute. Then He'll shut yo' mouth, yes He will!" He pointed to the horizon and all eyes followed his finger. In the midst of the hubbub, a storm had been gathering, catching them by surprise. In a few minutes, the sky let loose a torrent of rain and wind, and, sure enough, the crowd dispersed and the atheist took cover with everyone else. God had shown Himself in the storm.[14]

In God's mind, obedience is mandatory. Do you know why? Because He thinks He is God. You know what? He is! The Scriptures are clear that God will cause all creation to obey Jesus.[15] Every knee will bow and every tongue will confess—like it or not—that Jesus is Lord. No dissenters, no no-shows; obedience is mandatory.

Jesus' heritage includes the mandatory obedience of all creation. Paul, through the inspiration of the Holy Spirit, gives us some insight into this when he says, *"that every knee will bow, every tongue will confess"*—every knee, every tongue, every human being, every demon in hell will bow down their knee in obedience.[16]

Although the obedience of all creation is mandatory, that isn't all there is to it; there is more, much more! You see, God desires more than mandatory obedience. He wants voluntary love. Jesus' heritage as King is the obedience of the nations, but His heritage as Bridegroom is the voluntary love of all of the people in all of the nations. As the King, He receives a heritage: "Every knee will bow." As the Bridegroom, He receives a heritage: "Every heart in Your Kingdom will passionately, wholeheartedly love You." Not automated, not forced, not programmed; God does not want robots that all He has to do is push the button and everyone says, "I love You, Jesus—beep, beep!"

No, God doesn't want robotic love nor automatic obedience, He longs for voluntary love. I imagine that the Father might say to the Son, *"They will choose to love You because they will see Your might, Your beauty, and Your worth and they will desire You."*[17] The Bridegroom's heritage is different from the heritage of the King. The Bridegroom's heritage is the fact that the people will be equally yoked to Him in love.

By equally yoked I mean that we should share His heart values. That is so important in our earthly relationships, isn't it? It is just as important, if not more so, in our relationship with Christ. God desires that Jesus would have an equally yoked Bride as well, one who shares His heart and His value system. We will be equally yoked in at least four ways: with all our heart, all our mind, all our soul, and all our strength.

LOVING GOD AS GOD LOVES US

The title of this book says it all: *The Love Language of God—Loving God, God's Way.* God wants us, as the redeemed Image-bearers, to love Jesus in the same manner that He, God the Father, loves Jesus. Get it?

One of the things I hated when I was growing up was when my dad would tell me to do something and when I asked him why, his answer was always, "Because I said so!" Oh, that made me so angry!

Well, God is God, and He could rightfully tell us that we have to love Him just because He said so. However, that is not how He operates. He desires us to love Him with all of our heart, soul, mind, and strength; not because "He said so," but because that is how *He* loves *us,* with all of His heart, soul, mind, and strength. This is an unfathomable concept. After walking with the Lord for over 38 years, my mind still goes tilt when I attempt to grasp it. It is beyond the comprehension of the human mind without the aid of the Holy Spirit, and without the time frame of eternity to unpack it.[18]

You may be thinking, "If that is what God is after, He is out of luck, because I cannot love Him that way...I've tried!" You are right, I'm right with you. We cannot love Him as He desires for us to love Him. Not a chance. What then are we to do? Saint Bernard of Clairvaux, a French monk who lived in the 1100s, gives us the answer to our dilemma: "It takes God to love God."

Even with the divine assistance of God the Spirit, we can only grasp a little bit of it in this age; but for the ages to come, we will continue to understand this more and more—God loves us. He loves us with all of His heart, with all of His mind, with all of His soul, and with all of His strength. It takes the supernatural power of God to understand this. It takes God to love God—it really does. One of the foundational principles of Kingdom life is it takes the power of God on our hearts if we are to love God. God knows that, so He has promised us, through the ministry of the Holy Spirit, to anoint us, to supernaturally energize and empower us to love Him—He has committed to pour His love into our hearts.[19] This involves several different dimensions of love.

FOUR DIMENSIONS OF GOD'S LOVE

The love of God has at least four dimensions. The first dimension is the revelation that God loves us. It takes the Holy Spirit to release the reality of that knowledge into our heart. The second dimension is the ability to love God back. The third dimension is the ability to love ourselves (in the love of God and by the love of God). Jesus prophesied it this way, *"You will love your neighbor in the same manner that you love yourself."*[20] The fourth dimension is that in the overflow of the other three dimensions, we then love our neighbor.

Over the years, I have had people confess to me they are incapable of loving their neighbor as they love themselves. I tell them the problem is not that they cannot love their neighbor as they love themselves; the problem is they *are* loving their neighbor exactly in the same manner as they love themselves! The reason we do not love our neighbor well is because we do not love ourselves well.

In the grace of God, we will never love our neighbor in a greater quality than the way we love ourselves. Usually, when people hear this, because in most of the teaching that is available in the Western church the principles of the Kingdom of God are not taught, they are shocked and sometimes angered. They think I am promoting carnality or narcissism. That is not what I am saying at all. Scripture is clear; we are to see ourselves as God sees us, and agree with His view instead of disagreeing with it.[21] As we love ourselves, in the grace of God, we will, in the overflow of that righteous self-love, be empowered to love others rightly, which is the fourth dimension.

To recap: first, the Holy Spirit pours out the revelation in our hearts of how God loves us, then He awakens our heart to respond by loving God back.[22] Then, in the overflow of that exchange with God's heart, we rightly love ourselves, which frees us up to love our neighbor. This is *supernatural* Christianity, which is the only Christianity that there is—a natural Christianity is not Christianity at all. It takes the operation of the Person of the Holy Spirit. This is the greatest gift and work of the Holy Spirit in a believer's life: to pour His love into our hearts in these four ways.

JESUS' PRAYER REQUEST

Jesus, the Beloved Son of God,[23] prayed for the people God promised to give Him to be supernaturally empowered to love Him with God's love.[24] Many believe that this will never happen. However, is it conceivable that God the Father would not answer the heartfelt request of His beloved Son?

God's blueprint is to equip an equally yoked Bride who would be prepared by voluntary love to eternally rule and reign with His Son, Jesus. Though to the uninitiated it may appear that Jesus' request of the Father seems impossible, I assure you the First Commandment will be in first place throughout the whole Body of Christ worldwide in the generation in which Jesus returns.[25]

Before Jesus went to the Cross, while He was in the upper room with His disciples, He prayed what has been called "the High Priestly Prayer," the great intercessory prayer of Jesus. Here it is, Jesus praying for the saints for 26 verses. It does not get any better than this—Jesus praying for His Bride. In the final verse, the volcanic explosion in which this prayer ends, He exclaims, *"Father, I made known to them Your Name for this reason, so that the very love with which You loved Me would be in them."*[26] In other words, "That they would see and love Me the way You see and love Me." This is inconceivable, except for the grace of God. Before God is finished, we will all love Jesus the way the Father loves Jesus.

A BRIDE EQUALLY YOKED IN LOVE

Beloved, that is what it means to be "equally yoked" with the Son of God. All throughout redemptive history, God has been selecting and training a Bride. His purpose is going to come to a glorious crescendo in the generation just before the Lord returns. Get this: I am talking about flesh-and-blood people, in their natural bodies, before the resurrection. This is not in the sweet by and by, in the sky, when we die stuff. It says in Revelation 19, *"The marriage of the Lamb has come, and His Bride has made Herself ready..."*[27]—we are talking about the Bride on the earth, not the Bride in Heaven with resurrected bodies. I prophesy to you there is a generation that will respond in such a way that they are prepared—a prepared Bride for a worthy Son.

The Father has a worthy Son, and He is raising up a prepared Bride, a wholehearted Bride. We will see this in the generation when the Lord returns—which will be the generation in which the Bride makes Herself ready by living lives of voluntary love, not in Her own strength, but under the supernatural empowerment of the Holy Spirit—the first commandment will be restored to first place.

Today, all around the planet, God is raising up forerunners, heralds of the greatest move of the Spirit that has ever been, who are preparing the way of the Lord's return. These forerunners, these "Friends of the Bridegroom," will be those who say in their heart, "Lord, I want to know the things that are in Your heart, the things Your Spirit will be emphasizing worldwide—in a minute from now." Of course, with the Lord a minute might be a decade or two or three. Who knows? Maybe a little bit longer, maybe a little bit shorter.

"I want to lay hold of the things on Your heart now." That is what a forerunner does. Forerunners hear the heartbeat of God and grab hold of it one short step ahead of the Holy Spirit's universal emphasis of it to the Body of Christ worldwide. The Church will be a prepared Bride before the second coming. God is preparing forerunner messengers to call others to define love as God's highest purpose. These "friends of the Bridegroom" will make the First Commandment their primary focus for both their life and ministry.

WE LOVE TO LOVE AND WE LOVE TO BE LOVED

I stated in the first chapter how much we all love to love and we all love to be loved. Have you ever stopped to think about why it is that we love being loved so much? I know, speaking for myself, I *love* to be loved. I mean I *really love* to be loved. Come on, you know you do too! It is in our DNA. Not only that, you love to love as well. The reason we all love *love* so much is because we were created in the image of God—we are the Image-bearers! God is love; therefore, we are lovers!

I have said for years that the core of my spiritual identity is that I am loved by God, and I am a lover of God; therefore, I am successful regardless of my external circumstances. Beloved, this is what I, we, you look like to God. For real! In Heaven you are not defined by your accomplishments; in Heaven you are defined and known by your love.

The church in Ephesus was a great revival center in the early Church.[28] Yet even though for a season they were the epicenter of God's activity on the earth, they did not sustain the freshness, the sweetness, of their love for Jesus. They became workers for God more than they were lovers of God. Beloved, lovers will always out-work workers.

When we attempt to work for God without living a life of intimacy with Jesus, we end up working as slaves, and eventually we develop a slave mentality. A heart of a bride is refreshed as she labors. Service without the solid foundation of extravagant devotion to Jesus will ever lead to disappointment, wounding, and eventual burnout. Thus, our service for the Lord cannot be sustained over decades. I have seen so many start in the fire of revival, but because they are more enamored with the glory than with the God of glory, after a short season, even if it is a season of decades, they fall to the wayside.[29]

The enemy of our soul's strategy is to lead you astray; to keep you from cultivating wholehearted love and devotion to the Glorious Man, Christ Jesus—at all costs.[30] To keep him from achieving his intended goal, we must make a quality decision—a quality decision is a decision from which there is no retreat—to love God with all our heart, soul, mind, and strength. We must set our hearts to make love our first priority and to have and maintain a vision to go deep in God. It takes focus and effort to go deep in God. It is not automatic. Too many wrongly believe that the blessings of God will just fall in their laps like ripe apples off of a tree. To walk in this reality requires that we must be focused on pursuing it more than we are focused on gaining things and winning influence.[31]

WHICH IS THE MOST IMPORTANT COMMANDMENT?

Over the years I have often heard the debate about which is more important, the first commandment or the second commandment? I hear it all the time: people say, "Well, you guys are into the first commandment; we are into the second commandment." You know my answer to that? That is inconceivable; you cannot separate these commandments—it cannot be done. Everyone who loves God with all their heart will always love people—always! I am not saying that they won't fail every once in a while; I am just saying that anyone who loves God the way He desires us to love Him will demonstrate that love as authentic by loving people.

It is impossible to be into the first commandment and not naturally overflow into the second commandment. Even though you might have heard that theoretical argument, it is only that—a theoretical argument—used by people who are usually not pursuing either. Seriously. If you are pursuing the second commandment without pursuing being first and foremost a lover of God, I can guarantee you will come up bankrupt in your ability to sustain it. You cannot sustain meaningful love and service for people unless you have an ongoing, fresh supply of encounter, love from God, and love back to God.

I have even seen preachers—preachers, mind you, the people who are supposed to know better—sit around tables and argue about this. Let me ask you a question. Which is more important: your brain, your heart, or your kidneys? Which one are you willing to do without? None of them, right? Why? Because you need them all. Whom do you love the most: the Father, the Son, or the Holy Spirit? Not a valid question, is it?

Therefore, which is more important, the first commandment or the second commandment? The first comes in sequence because the first is what empowers us to do the second. You cannot love God without loving what God loves, and I have news for you: God loves people. You will always love believers and unbelievers if you love God—always, always, always. To love God the way He says we are to love Him is to run straight into His passionate burning heart. The result? You love what He loves.

WE NEED TO CHANGE THE WAY WE THINK

Jesus said, *"Repent, for the Kingdom of heaven is at hand."*[32] The word *repent* means to change the way you think, and accordingly the way you live. We must constantly change the way we think. It is not a one-time thing. We must continually realign our hearts, ministry focus, and life to the first commandment. Ask me how I know? I have to realign my heart regularly—I do not mean every year or two; I mean every couple of weeks. For real. Every few weeks I have to stop and examine myself to see if I am still walking in the faith,[33] or whether I have lost my focus.

We all have to consciously and regularly realign our heart with the revelation that this is the supreme commandment. We do not have to apologize for it. We do not have to apologize for our intensity in going after it because we have the confidence from God's Word this is what God wants.

I have run into ministries for years that advise me to back away from this. People, even preacher people, get so nervous if people are locked into the first commandment. "What about…what about… what about?" I have heard so many "what abouts" over the years. The bottom line, according to Jesus, is this: it is the greatest and the first commandment. When we stand before God, this is what we will answer for. Did we volunteer for the first commandment or did we make excuses about why we did not want to do it?

Love by definition is voluntary, which means you have to step up and choose to realign your heart. God will not force you to do it, but if you love Him, you *will* do it because you will want to. As King, the Father will force everyone to obey Jesus, but as a Bridegroom, the Father woos us to love Him by showing us the loveliness of Jesus.

LOVING GOD, GOD'S WAY—THE SPIRIT OF OBEDIENCE

Loving God, God's way: massive. Jesus' definition of loving God is our being deeply rooted in the spirit of obedience to the Word of God. This is critical. C-R-I-T-I-C-A-L. *"If you love Me, you will keep My commandments."*[34] *"Whoever has My commandments and keeps them, he it is who loves Me."*[35] *"If anyone loves Me, he will keep My Word."*[36] I always wonder what part of that is so hard to understand. Could it be any clearer? He said the same thing three times in a couple of verses. From Genesis to Revelation, He has made it clear. Isn't it odd then, how many, even within the Body of Christ, waffle on this definition.

Beloved, let me reiterate, there is no such thing as loving God without seeking to obey His Word. It does not exist; it is a religious figment of someone's darkened imagination. It is religious sentiment; it is not reality. The Holy Spirit does not agree with it today, and He will not bear witness to it on the last day, at the Bema seat.

God requires more than singing to Him about love or writing poetry about love. He requires more than "warm fuzzies" about a God we have made into our own image. When we were recreated we were made in His image, but the religious culture is making a god in fallen man's image and then worshiping that golden calf. There is an unholy momentum in many believers who name the name of Jesus, making a god after their own image—the image of a fallen culture—and are calling that Christianity, then defining love according to how they worship the god of their own imagination.

We must love God in a spirit of obedience. That does not mean our obedience has to be fully mature, like the apostle Paul's. It does not mean that in our quest to be obedient we will never fail. My obedience fails all the time. I am not talking about perfect obedience. I am talking about setting our hearts to obey the Word, not just obeying the Spirit according to our own darkened imaginations. I am talking about obeying the *Holy* Spirit, according to the written Word of God, most specifically the Sermon on the Mount lifestyle.[37]

We must love God *His* way, not ours. The reason I keep stressing this is that the Holy Spirit desires to restore the first commandment to first place because the first commandment was in first place in the early Church. I recall hearing Dr. Bill Hamon say that God made the Church the way He wanted it, and He wants the Church the way He made it! In the next couple of decades, the core issue of conflict, even by people who name the name of Jesus, will be the correct definition of love. Do we love God, God's way, or do we love according to the humanistic culture around us that has no reference to obedience to the Word of God except for the verses they like?

GOD IS RESTORING HIS LOVE

Jesus is Lord, and He wants to be Lord over your life—all of it—because He loves you. He is not interested in just forgiving your sins, though He certainly wants to do that; He wants to absolutely control every aspect of your life. Many balk when I say that, but in actuality that is where our safety is, that is where our glory is, when He is in total control. He wants to control you for the purposes of love—His purposes.

Have you heard the question asked, "What is the world coming to?" A more appropriate question might be, "What is the Church coming to?" The answer? The Church is coming to God. Totally, for real. Love, by God's definition of love, is where the Church is headed. Too many define love according to the fallen, perverse culture in our nation. The Western, secular, humanistic culture has so seeped into the Church that the Church now defines love according to how the culture defines love, and uses Bible verses to back it up. That is *not* the kind of love He is restoring. He is restoring His love, the God kind of love.

Obedience to the Word of God is our glory, and it is our freedom. The yoke of Jesus is our freedom. Being love-slaves, bond-servants, to this Man who is fully God and fully man—that is our liberty, our freedom, and our easy yoke.[38] Anything less, and anything else, is deception, bondage, and leads to spiritual death.

I grew up during the hippie era of the 1960s and '70s. You know, long hair, freethinking, and free love, no rules, no restrictions, and, guess what, no freedom! That lifestyle resulted only in spiritual bondage. Beloved, I have news for you—God is not a hippie. Why do I say that? Because it is amazing the similarities of the definitions of love and liberty so rampant in the Church today with the old hippie culture.

People who were not even born during the hippie era have the same laid-back, chilled-out approach to love, to obedience, and to God. Beloved, love in the New Testament is hot pursuit, radical abandonment, total sacrifice, and self-denial. It is not, "What do I have to do to get by?" but it's "How far will You let me go, how abandoned will You let me be?" That is God's definition of love. You will not find any hippie culture in the language of the apostles, or in the lives of the saints who lived victorious Christian lives throughout the Church age.

God loves us with a fierce determination. He gave everything. Jesus gave His all—He held nothing back. He laid down His eternal riches to become a man in order to win our hearts. So I want to expose this false, cool hippie-culture paradigm of grace and liberty because the Holy Spirit wants to restore the first commandment—the true first commandment—to first place in the Church.

Beloved, we do not have to apologize for going hard after God. Our life is a stage, and what we do on that stage is for an audience of One. And He is smiling. We might not do it all that well, but we are going hard after it. I've heard John Wimber, the founder of the Vineyard Movement, say that we may not be the only thing going, we may not be the best thing going, but we *are* going. We will stumble, but we will also get back up and call sin, sin; we will repent of it, push delete, and go back to pressing hard into the heart of God.

REORDERING OUR PRIORITIES AFTER GOD'S OWN HEART

Loving God is the greatest and the first commandment. It is what God wants first. He wants it first in your life and He wants it first in your ministry. So often I am asked, "What does God want for my life?"

I can tell you for sure from the very lips of Jesus that He is saying to you, *"Hear, O Israel of God, let Me tell you what you are meant to hear—the first commandment is first and it is the greatest.*"[39] It is not the first option. We do not get a vote! It is the first commandment. Jesus wants to make it clear that cultivating love for Him is the first priority on His mind.

That reminds me of a story. Everything reminds me of a story...

There was a little girl who, every night, a couple of hours after her parents put her to bed, would roll out of bed and—thump—hit the floor. This happened night after night. One night, after she had fallen out of bed, her daddy picked her up off the floor and held her while she was crying, as he did almost every night. This particular evening he was feeling a little frustrated and he asked her, "Why do you keep falling out of bed?" His little girl answered, "I don't know, Daddy. I guess because I stay too close to where I got in."

Her problem is often our problem too, isn't it? We, like the little girl in the story, are guilty of staying too close to where we got in! We must choose the good part as Mary of Bethany did.[40] No one can make the choice for us. We have to decide to go deeper. Everyone is as close to God as he or she wants to be. Right now you are as close to God as you want to be, as you have decided to be. Do you want to go closer? Then draw closer to God and He will draw closer to you.[41] It's your turn!

Beloved, never, never apologize for developing your love for God. You do not owe an excuse to the multitudes of hyperactive people who have no focus on the love of God, even if they do name the name of Jesus. You never have to apologize for your intensity just because they are disobedient and do not want to do it. Be clear about it; go hard after it.

God has everything, yet He is searching for something. Don't you find that strange? The God who has everything is searching for something. Not because He needs it, but because He desires it. As God, He is totally complete, self-sufficient, and happy within the fellowship of the Godhead. He does not want it out of need. He wants it because He is the God of burning desire.

What Does He Want?

Have you ever noticed how many people spend all of their time and money pursuing what they want and then after they get it, they lose interest in it? That does not apply to just things either, it applies to relationships as well. Not so with God. With God, what He wants He has always wanted and He will always want forever. He never loses His desire for what He pursues. What is He pursuing?

"God is always on the alert, constantly on the lookout for people who are totally committed to Him."[42] His eyes that are burning with passion are searching. He wants something, yet He has everything. He searches for something He desires more than anything else. What is it? He is after your heart. Not your money or your talent, but your heart.

So many say, "Lord, I tell You what. I'm going to live in sin, You know, a little compromise, but if You let me do a little pornography, watch a few immoral television shows, listen to a little sensuous music, a little bit of drunkenness; I'll try to balance things out by giving a little extra in the offering. What do You say?"

He says, "I don't want your money. I want your heart. Do not give your heart away to the things of this world and then give Me your money. I am after your heart." That is what He is after.

What God Wants

One of the most important questions to ask God is always this question: "What are You looking for, what are You after?" Beloved, I have a golden nugget for you: when you find what *He* is looking for, you will have found what *you* are looking for as well—love.

The Bride asks this question. The heart of a slave and the heart of a hireling will never ask this question. The heart of obedience that is motivated by love is ever asking, "What is it You want?"

Since loving God with all your heart is the first priority to God, it has to be the first priority in your heart as well. The first thing on God's mind must be the first thing on your mind.

I am asking the Holy Spirit to mark you as you read these words, to mark you so that this truth gets hold of you, so you will say, "Love is why I am drawing breath on the earth right now; it's why I have a ministry. It is why I do what I do. It is first. This is it." I am asking, "Holy Spirit, mark us now. Mark us. Never let us be cured. Ruin us with this priority of God."

RUINED—ADDICTED TO LOVE

People visit this place or that place, go to this meeting or that conference, and they come back and say, "I went to so-and-so place and got ruined." What they usually mean is, "I heard some good music, heard a good sermon, maybe met some cool people, and now I don't ever want to do anything with anybody else." I have news for you: God does not want to ruin you in that way. God does want to ruin you, but He wants it to be by you becoming addicted to love, addicted to receiving it and to giving it. Not addicted to good teaching, good music, and disconnected from the people He has placed in your life. He does not want you disconnected from hard work and the mundane reality of day-to-day life.

RADICAL—LOVING AND FAITHFUL IN
THE MIDST OF THE MUNDANE

I hear so many today shout and sing about how they are going to live a radical life for Jesus. By that they mean being involved in the newest fad ministry or taking an exotic ministry trip for three months. However, we are not radical because we do something unusual or spectacular for a few weeks or even for a few months. Being radical is staying head-over-heels in love with the Glorious Man Christ Jesus, sustaining a fresh walk with God (and that includes reading the Bible, meditating on it, studying it, praying it, and then living it), and remaining faithful in the midst of difficulty and mendacity for decades. Now *that* is radical!

David sustained his passion for God for decades so that he could refer to his experience as *all* the days of his life. Daniel sustained his prayer life with passion for decades (from the time he was about 16 until he was 82 years of age, from 605–539 B.C., for 66 years).

To many today, *radical* means something extreme. That's cool if that's the culture's definition, but when I say "radical," I mean you live in love, in the spirit of obedience, from the inside out when nobody is looking and you are hardly feeling it, but you still are reaching for it. Radical is reaching for decades and decades—you never quit.

GOD'S WILL FOR OUR LIVES

Many are searching to know God's will, and they say something like, "I want to know God's will, I want to know what my ministry assignment is." That's a good place to start, and the good news is that I can tell you what the first issue of the will of God in your life is: that you grow in love on the inside.

I have watched people waste five or ten years searching for their ministry assignment, when 80 percent of the will of God was that they grow in love, feel His love, connect with His love, and go after love. Beloved, Christianity is an encounter with a Person. Christianity is an ongoing encounter with love.

Someone says, "Man, we've got a noble cause, a radical commitment, a fierce determination, we're going to change our city, our nation, and the whole world." Beloved, that won't hold you steady for five years. It will hold you steady for a year or two—maybe—if you get a bunch of folks in agreement, you might keep the steam in the engine going. But if you are not encountering the subtle, continual, small wooings of love in your heart, you will never stay steady for five years, and certainly not for decades.

GOING FOR THE GREATEST DIMENSION

I have been a believer for 38 years. In that amount of time, I have seen lots of flaming stars for five years. Lots. I've only seen a few people sustain their zeal for over ten years. There were so many radical people in the early 1970s when I met the Lord in 1972. There were so many radicals.

I look back over 30 years, and very few of them stayed steady for even ten years. Do you want to know the reason? They were fiercely dedicated, they had a cause, they had a mission, but they were not mostly committed to encountering a Person. Therefore the small, subtle, incremental, every-now-and-then stirrings of love did not touch them, did not affect them. You see, that was not the focus of their hearts. Changing something was the focus of their hearts.

You might have a vision to change things, or to build a ministry, but Beloved, if you are not committed to the subtle, occasional stirrings of love, where you feel loved by Him and you feel love for Him, where it overflows a little bit to yourself and a little bit to people—you will never stay in a radical posture of dedication. You may for five years. You may even stay for ten years. But you will not go for decades. It takes love, because the mission will wear you out unless you are being renewed in love along the journey.

This renewing is small. It's a little here, a little there. It's every day or two; there's no way to measure it: some days more, some days less; some weeks more, some weeks less—those little stirrings of inspiration on the heart about love—but they add up over time. The great commandment: it is not only the first commandment, it is the great one.

THE GREATEST IMPACT

As we have already noted, Jesus not only quotes the Shema Israel, He also interprets it for us: *"Hear, O people of God, I am telling you what I want you to hear."*[43] If you love God—great.

There are several dynamics to what makes it great. It impacts God's heart, it impacts your heart, it impacts the people in your sphere of influence, and it impacts your eternal destiny. And when you respond appropriately, it results in your experiencing the greatest spiritual pleasure and the greatest reward.

I am sure I haven't exhausted all the ways that this commandment is the greatest. I encourage you to meditate on this commandment. One definition of biblical meditation is when we take a Scripture or a biblical thought or concept and turn it into conversation with the Author—Jesus—the Eternal Word. Ask Jesus to reveal to you what He meant when He said this is the great commandment. When we call something great, typically we mean that it is the biggest externally. What Jesus calls the greatest is what is the biggest *internally*.

On judgment day, at the great evaluation, we may be surprised who Jesus calls great. Many of the greatest people in the Bible and throughout redemptive history had very little obvious impact. But they made an impact where it really counts—in God's heart. I love it when I can make a positive impact in the lives of people here on the earth, but let me tell you the greatest thing about my life and your life—we can impact God.

"Buddy, are you trying to say that I can impact the heart of the Genesis 1 God?" Yep.

From the overflow of having my heart impacted by God and from my impacting His heart, the overflow might impact you. Now don't get me wrong, I want to impact you, I really do, but I will not sell out the greatest and most glorious dimension of the grace of God in my life—that I can impact God and He can impact me—to impact you.

Many lose out in the area of impacting God so that they can spend time networking to make an earthly impact, and end up discouraged, exhausted, and backslidden. I have seen so many over the years who were addicted to the growth of their ministry, addicted to reaching more people, to getting more people to listen to them, and in the process they sell out the greatest thing about their lives.

As good as it is to impact people, the greatest thing you can set your heart on is impacting God. You can't stop people who live to impact God. You can criticize them, lock them away in a prison camp somewhere, take everything away from them, ignore them, mistreat them, but no matter what you do to them, their hearts are still exhilarated in love, they still have a brightness in their spirits.

If you will go after this, who knows, you could end up being one of the great people in God's eyes. Why not you? I mean, after all, somebody is going to do it. It might as well be you, right?

The great people of history will not be the people who have the big crowds, though they might be. The great people in history are the people who have great hearts, big hearts, and a big love for God. Go after it. He is after your heart. Go after His. The greatest calling in this age is to be a person who moves God's heart.

HAVING A BRIGHT SPIRIT

Beloved, I want to impact you. I do. I want to impact people; but I will not trade off my inheritance to be one of the few who impact God's heart just to try and impact a few more people on the earth. I am going to take my chances in the grace of God and go after Him, and let Him inspire me and let the brightness of my spirit impact far more people over time. If you touch the first commandment, I mean really touch it, you will become far more steady and far more effective in walking out the second commandment. People don't need more of you; they need the brightness of the Spirit in you.

I recently had a conversation with a friend who is homeschooling her children. She was expressing her ongoing struggle with time management and working out how to be everything her children need. She was saying how she felt inadequate because she did not know enough and could not do enough, and had a fear that, as a result, she might fail her kids; and that as a result of her not being able to "do" enough, her children might not turn out righteous.

The problem with that line of reasoning is that children really do not need better homeschooling moms who have it all together and who excel in every area. Even if we were able to always be there and always have the "right" answer, that would be no guarantee that our children would grow up to be what God wants them to be. That isn't what our children need.

What I advised her was that she back off some of her busyness and spend *less* time with the kids and the curriculum and spend *more* time with Jesus until she comes out of her prayer closet with a bright and anointed spirit. What homeschooling kids need is not an omniscient, omnipresent mom, but rather a mom who has a bright and anointed spirit from having spent quality time with Jesus!

I suggested, "Instead of working harder to give more, why don't you give a little less? Instead of scurrying to meet every need of the kids in the power of your flesh, why not try sitting at the Lord's feet more? You can't bail out your family without God breathing upon you and through you. Spend more time in His Presence and bring back brightness to your kids. Your children need you for sure, but they need brightness in your spirit even more." Less with a bright spirit is better than more with a dull spirit.

Too many approach all their relationships as if more of them must be the answer to ministering to the people's needs. Well, there is some truth there. More of you sometimes is an answer to a measure, but more of you with a bright spirit is far more effective than just plain old more of you.

THE SUPREMACY OF THE FIRST COMMANDMENT

As we draw nearer to the Lord's return, what the Body of Christ and the nations of the earth are going to need more and more of is people with authority and brightness, not just people with humanistic sentiment and good intentions. We need bright, anointed spirits that have encountered God in the secret place of the heart. Jesus called loving God the greatest lifestyle. He said it's the greatest commandment, which means it's the greatest lifestyle. It is the greatest ministry.

The greatest ministry I can have is the giving of myself to the first and greatest commandment. That's the great definition of life. That is the most radical, extreme lifestyle. The most noble thing you can give your life to is that. Out of that place, you can do whatever He whispers in your heart to do with a bright and anointed spirit.

There is a lot of escapism going on in the Body of Christ today. As director of a city-wide prayer ministry, one of the accusations I hear from some is that people who are praying just want to get out of work. But I just smile, for it is obvious that anyone who would say such a thing has never spent much time praying! People in the prayer rooms aren't interested in escaping, they are interested in encountering. Plus, prayer, real prayer, is hard work. But the fruit of it is that all of Heaven breaks out on earth! I'm kidding, but I'm not joking.

Let me ask you, what if the Bible were really true and God really meant what He said? What if a group of people really believed what Jesus said, and really did what He said, and latched onto the greatness of this commandment? What would it do to the atmosphere of that spiritual family?

We have looked at the fact that deep in the heart of every believer is the desire to live a radical life, to love God extravagantly. Our problem has been we don't know how. We have seen that God desires that we live that way. Jesus prayed that we would live that way. But Jesus has more than a desire, He has a plan. In the next chapter we will look at what His plan is.

CHAPTER 13

Wholehearted Love— Four Dimensions

In the last chapter we looked at the great and first commandment: loving the Lord with all of our heart, soul, mind, and strength. We also looked briefly at the four dimensions of the love of God. In this chapter, we take a closer look at these four dimensions. The first dimension of God's love is when we encounter God's love; in the second, we reciprocate love back to God;[1] in the third, we love ourselves in the grace of God; and in the fourth level, in the overflow of a bright and anointed heart, we love one another.

We love other people far more effectively if we do it according to the parameters set in the Word of God. Now, it is important that we establish on the front end that we do not wait until we have perfected dimensions one, two, and three before we start doing level four. Though we are separating them for teaching purposes, they are intertwined, and in reality we have to do all four of them simultaneously with the realization that we will do the fourth level far more effectively if the first three are being done healthily.

DIMENSION ONE: AN INCREASED REVELATION OF GOD'S LOVE

The first dimension of loving God the way He wants to be loved by us is through our receiving an increased revelation of the love that God has for us.[2] This foundational truth then equips us and makes it possible for us to love God, which is to know and feel His affection toward us. Amazingly, God loves us in the same way that God loves God. Jesus feels the same intensity of love for us that God the Father feels for Him. This is the ultimate revelation of our worth. This truth gives us the right to stand before a holy God with confidence as one of His favorites.[3]

A FALSE LOVE MOVEMENT

As we discussed in the last chapter, there is a growing love movement in the Church that is humanistic, focused on showing love for man, but it is not birthed out of having encountered the love of God. The problem with that type of love is it falls far short of being what is needed. A humanistic, man-related love only ends up with our becoming burned out and discouraged. The "love" being advocated today says that we don't need to tell people about Jesus, we only need to show them love, and that will result in their lives being affected for the Kingdom. The result is that because we aren't to speak of Jesus, only to "show the love of Jesus," we end up putting on a religious mask that is not genuine.

Although proclaiming to be a movement of light that shows love and goodwill for others, it is actually a movement of spiritual darkness. The reason I say it is dark is because it is promoting a love that originates from ourselves and is not birthed out of encountering the love of God. It is actually a statement of pride. The reason it is sweeping through the Church is that its language is confusing. The language is the same as the biblical language: "Love people." But as believers, we are to love people out of an overflow of encountering God.

As I look around, I see so many downplaying the need to connect with God, so, while it appears as though they love, at the end of the day, in the eyes of Heaven, they are arrogant about both their abilities and their virtue. I have no confidence in a love movement that is not birthed out of an authentic encounter with the love of God that results in an encounter with the Person of God Himself.

AFFECTION-BASED, DUTY-BASED, AND FEAR-BASED OBEDIENCE

There are several types of motivation for obeying God. The highest motivation is what I call affection-based obedience. Affection-based obedience flows out of our experiencing Jesus' affection for us and then responding by loving Him. Affection based obedience certainly is not the only appropriate motivation for obeying God, but it is by far the strongest, deepest, and most consistent form of obedience. Why? Because a lovesick person will endure anything for love. A life motivated by lovesickness will result in a life of full obedience.[4]

DUTY-BASED OBEDIENCE

Have you ever noticed that most of the teaching you hear related to obeying God or keeping His commandments is based on what I call duty-based obedience? Duty-based obedience tries to motivate us to depend on our personal commitment to obey God even during the times that we do not "feel" God's tangible Presence. Its premise is that, at the bottom line, God's Word requires that we obey God even when we do not feel inspired to do so—it's our duty.

First of all, let me say that duty-based obedience is valid and necessary! I have obeyed God many times over the years simply because I knew I was supposed to, whether I felt like it or not. I am the first to admit there are times I do not feel like obeying. Therefore, I have done it both ways, but in seasons of duty-based obedience, I do not feel like it at all. During those seasons, I resolve in my heart that even though I do not feel like obeying I am going to do it anyway.

By obeying, I do not mean only avoiding doing sinful things. Duty-based obedience also means doing the positive things, like spending time before the Lord in prayer, reading the Word, serving my brothers and sisters, etc. Beloved, it is your God-given duty to obey the Word of God, even during those times you do not feel inspired to do it. Remember, though it is not the most powerful motivation, it is still a valid motivation.

FEAR-BASED OBEDIENCE

The third motivation for obeying God is probably the most commonly taught—fear-based obedience. Fear-based obedience is based on imparting a fear of negative consequences if we choose to disobey. I refer it to shaking the people of God over the eternal flames of hell on a rotten stick. Those who teach a fear-based obedience are trying to motivate people to be holy through fear and shame.

Now, do not get me wrong, it is biblical to appeal to shame and fear to motivate people. Scripture is filled with hundreds of dos and don'ts, such as do not commit adultery, do not steal, do not slander, etc. And there are very real negative consequences for our disobedience. It is clear throughout the Bible that God will use His rod of correction on us if we disobey Him, because although He loves us as we are, He also loves us too much to leave us in a position of spiritual compromise.[5]

The Bible therefore does appeal to fear and shame. It is not the highest motivation, but it does motivate us. It certainly has motivated me many times. The fear of consequences, the shame of being caught—that is a biblical motivation. It is just not the highest motivation. The most powerful motivation is affection-based obedience, where we are motivated by God's love feeding our spirit, and then our obedience is the strongest.

Why do we sin? The reason we sin is because our hearts are unsatisfied with God.[6] The reason we look for other pleasures is that the inferior pleasure of sin seem more powerful than the superior pleasures found in the grace of God when God touches our spirit. When I feel drawn to a sin, it is a warning signal that my heart is not satisfied with God, and the cure for that is not running from Him, but instead running back to Him. We do not need to run *from* God when we sin; we need to run *to* Him.

DIMENSION TWO: A SUPERNATURAL IMPARTATION OF HUMAN LOVE FOR GOD

The second dimension of encountering the love of God is found when we receive a supernatural impartation of the Father's love for Jesus by the power of the Holy Spirit.[7] It takes God to love God. It takes the anointing of the Holy Spirit to love God the way He desires for us to love Him. Here is why it is so important that you understand this. Many mistakenly believe that one day they will just wake up in love with God and wake up in love with everyone else, even though they never pursue that in faith. That is deception of the highest order; it just does not happen that way.

We have to lock into this and say, "Father, I want to love Jesus like You love Him." He said I could and I should. I personally ask God daily for an impartation of His love. I spend quality time waiting on the Lord. I refuse to settle for less than this. Beloved, it is a point of spiritual focus because I understand that loving Jesus requires a supernatural impartation.

We cannot walk through life expecting to just wake up one morning in love with God or with each other. Won't happen. Loving God is a supernatural anointing that I have to intentionally pursue; it is not natural and it is not automatic. It is supernatural. It is beyond my natural ability, and I will only get more of it if I go after it. The anointing, or the supernatural ability, to receive God's love and then to return it back to Him is one of the greatest gifts the Holy Spirit imparts to the redeemed human heart.[8]

We were created with a longing to live a wholehearted and abandoned life and to know the joy of lovesickness. There is nothing more satisfying to the human heart than having the power to give the deepest affections of our heart to God and be loyal to Him in love. We soar in the Spirit when we experience the joy of holy lovesickness. We all long to possess the power to live abandoned lifestyles instead of being stuck in boredom, passivity, disloyalty, and compromise, which only leaves us broken and discontent.

LOVING JESUS IS NOT A PERSONALITY TYPE

Many have said to me over the years, "Buddy, you are so zealous for God. I wish I had your personality." Let's see, Creative, Intellectual, Visionary, and *Lover of God*. Not! Loving God is not a personality type. Every personality type can love God. It does not matter what your personality type is; you can be a wholehearted lover of God. I do not love Jesus nearly as much as I would like to, but whatever small measure I have increased in loving Him is not because of my personality. You do not get this by being a "contemplative"; you get it by recognizing that it is a supernatural reality that God is offering to you, and so you actively and diligently pursue it.

Therefore, I go before the Lord and say, "Lord, I want to love You. I know that it takes God to love God. I know it takes a supernatural impartation of Your Spirit for me to love You the way You want me to love You. So, would You give me more of it?" God's answer would be something like, "If you keep asking Me, I will."

One of the foundational principles of the Kingdom of God is that anything you can live without, you will do without. However, anything in the grace of God that you refuse to live without, God will give You—if you diligently seek after it!

GRACE TO LOVE

As the Image-bearers, we were created with a longing to be wholehearted. Beloved, you were created to live an abandoned, lovesick life. I am sure you have heard the old adage, "If you don't have anything you would die for, then you don't have anything to live for." So many have such a perverted view of grace—that somehow grace has come to mean being halfhearted, with a "maybe one day I will get around to it" attitude.

Beloved, that kind of thinking will only keep you barren and spiritually bored for decades. I have seen it so many times over the years. Christians who want to go hard after God. By going hard, I do not mean a personality type, I mean being spiritually focused, staying with it day and night. As I said earlier, we all love a good love story, and the greatest love story of them all is God connecting with the human heart.

It is yours, if you will just take it. The grace of God empowers us to get hold of it.[9] The grace of God does not give us a choice to either go after it or choose to ignore it. The Kingdom of God is not a buffet. The grace of God gives us divine ability to seize it. Do not fall for the perverse doctrine of grace that is being taught in so many circles today. It is the doctrine of "Que sera, sera, whatever will be, will be," and if we fall for it, we end up feeling comfortable with compromise, passivity, and neglect of the love of God.

The true grace of God makes us ravenous in our desires and in our focus. We refuse to be denied because the grace of God is moving on our hearts. As I observe the spiritual climate in the Western church, I see this false concept of grace that says we are living in the age of grace so we can just chill out and live carnal, worldly lives. That is a total deception; I do not care how many Bible verses people use.

CREATED TO LIVE A LIFE OF ABANDONMENT

Jesus is worthy of our living abandoned, radical lifestyles for decades, isn't He? He loves us with all of His heart; is it unreasonable that He desires that we love Him with all of ours? There is a dynamic exchange that goes on between our heart and God's when we live wholeheartedly. If you have nothing to die for, you really have nothing to live for. I want to have a heart that is on fire for God. So do you. If you are not living abandoned—if you are not red-hot for Jesus—you end up, over time, spiritually bored and thus vulnerable to darkness, and your heart is continually prone to emotional brokenness. Our hearts are far more vulnerable to the devil's devices if we are not going hard after the One who created us.

POWER IN LIVING ABANDONED

We were not created to be halfhearted. There is nothing more satisfying than the power of living abandoned. I love to be loved by God; and I love to be loved by people, too. I love to be loved, but you know what? I also love to love. I am never more alive than when I am full-scale in love with God and with others. I am never more alive than when I am in love. Neither are you. We love to love and we love to be loved because we were created that way by God. You will never be happy, never be more alive, than when you are going hard after God.

People have warned me for over 30 years, "You had better slow down, or you're going to burn out." Beloved, you do not burn out because you go hard after God. You burn out because spiritually you are bored and you are boring, and because you are motivated by the wrong things. That is what causes burnout. You get burned out because you are trying to do the work of the Kingdom with a heart that is disconnected from God, and you are wrongly motivated, so you are perpetually disappointed by not getting more money and more honor. You will not burn out if you go full-blast after God.

People in the United States are obsessed with playing and resting, playing and resting, but we are never satisfied and never rested. Forget the play and rest thing. Go abandoned for God. Live for eternity. Throw yourself into pursuing His heart the way He threw Himself into pursuing yours, and you will never be more alive. You will never be more satisfied. We were made to love God with all of our hearts.

LEVEL THREE: LOVING OURSELVES
IN THE GRACE OF GOD

The third dimension of encountering the love of God is when we come to the place where we love ourselves in the grace of God.[10] In the grace of God, you will never love and appreciate your neighbor more than you love and appreciate yourself. Now, there are two approaches to the subject of loving yourself. We can love ourselves in the flesh or we can love ourselves in the grace of God—two entirely different dynamics. What God means when He says we are to love ourselves is that we are to know what we look like to God, or another way to say that is we know who we are in Christ—His inheritance.[11]

As I stated earlier, there have been many times individuals have expressed to me their frustration that they cannot seem to love their neighbor as themselves. You ought to see the looks on their faces when I inform them the problem is not they cannot love their neighbor as themselves. The problem is that they *do* love their neighbors exactly the same way that they love themselves. They do not love themselves; therefore, they cannot love their neighbor. They despise themselves; therefore, they despise their neighbor.

Beloved, God commands us to love ourselves, not in a narcissistic or conceited manner, but righteously, valuing and, dare I say it, even rejoicing in who God made us to be physically, in our personality, and in our giftings.[12] To love who we are in the grace of God is to live in spiritual agreement with God. In fact, loving ourselves is a foundational necessity if we ever hope to live in holiness. Loving ourselves in the grace of God is very different from loving ourselves in a fleshly and selfish way. Let me explain.

Too many secretly wish they were someone else, as if God made a gigantic mistake when He made them. We have all thought that at one time or another, haven't we? Thoughts like that boil down to charging God with error. As we get our eyes off others, which is envy, and off our failures and shortcomings, foolishly despising ourselves, and set our spiritual gaze on His grace, then we will be free to love who God has made us to be.

We need to be thankful for who God has made us to be.[13] We think that if we go to a prayer meeting, witness to somebody, pray for the sick, and feed the poor, that is loving God. Loving God is much more than that. Loving yourself in the grace of God is an act of worship as you joyously exult in how brilliant, how wise, and how skillful God is. It is an act of worship.

One thing I want to add here is that when I say we are to love ourselves, I am not talking about loving our moral failures; I am talking about our gifts and passions, our mental abilities and our physical abilities. I am not talking about the moral or virtuous parts of our character right now because we should always desire to improve those. I am talking about worshiping God for who He made you to be. When you do that, it will free you up to love your neighbor as you love yourself.

DIMENSION FOUR: LOVING OUR NEIGHBOR AS WE LOVE OURSELVES

The fourth dimension of loving God is loving our neighbor as we love ourselves. How we value and treat others is the litmus test of our invisible love for God. Only when we are energized by loving Jesus and ourselves are we able to effectively and consistently overflow in love for others.[14]

When we love Jesus more, we are then able to love others much more. As I stated previously, it is impossible to love Jesus and not love people more. The greatest anointing of the Spirit is given to walk in the two great commandments of loving Jesus with all our hearts and our neighbor as ourselves. This is the greatest expression outwardly of our inner devotion to God, when we, as imperfect people, by the power of God, love imperfect people.

It is easy to love our spiritual God who is perfect and invisible. Right? To love a physical person who is imperfect, and who is sitting in the chair right next to us—now *that* is a challenge! That takes supernatural power. That takes more than just religious sentiment. Jesus said when we love the physical person next to us, then unbelievers will recognize we have had a supernatural operation of grace in our hearts.[15] They will know something supernatural is happening because they are fully aware it is very unnatural to love.

When He calls us to love, He is not talking about natural love. It is natural for a mother to love her child naturally. It is natural to have human sentiment. It is natural to hear someone's victorious or tragic story and tear up. It is natural to be moved when someone gives a testimony, and give him or her a donation. That is natural; it does not take God to do that. I am talking about interfacing with somebody on a day in and day out basis and walking out First Corinthians 13—patience and longsuffering—now, that is supernatural.

REAL LOVE IS CONSISTENT

Bible love, God's love, Christian love means substantial manifestations. It is a consistent love walked out in close relationships where there is ample opportunity to exhibit patience and humility and bridling of the tongue, and to speak only blessing. There you have it. It is an unusual work of grace if a group of people has that. When we see it, we say something like, "Wow." And that is good. However, when we do not see it, we should also be saying, "How dare you that you don't." We do not see that reaction much because our definition of love is so low.

I want to call us to something higher than someone giving you money, recognition, or friendship based on your time frame and expectations. Love is more than that. Most people evaluate love based on those criteria. If they give me a hundred dollars and they embrace me, then the group is loving. If they do not, then the group is not loving. That way of thinking is so out of sync with truth.

We need to lift the standard of reality as to what love is to a supernatural level so that we are going for something that is not just natural, human sentiment. We need to go for something that requires the power of God. If you can do it, then it is not God. When we talk about loving Jesus, being loved by Him, loving ourselves, and then loving our neighbor, we are aiming at the right definition of love because that can only happen by the power of God.

I want us to raise our sights higher, to a sustained valuing and serving of close relationships consistently. Now, I admit you do see that here and there in the Body of Christ, but it is remarkable if you see hundreds of people doing it together. It is not a given. It is not common. And when you do see it, it is awesome; it is wonderful. I want to live like that. How about you?

Loving Jesus has to end up with our loving people like that, or we are not loving Jesus. Really. Remember our foundational premise: people who love Jesus will love each other far more. You show me a people focused on receiving the love of Jesus and loving Him with all of their hearts, and those people, over time, will fall head-over-heels in love with each other. The entire emotional atmosphere of a community will change. I want to see the kind of love that is supernatural, which is the overflow of encountering the God-Man. It is impossible to love Jesus and not love people.

As I referred to earlier, over the years I have had people say, "Well, you're just a first commandment kind of guy, but we're called to the second commandment." My response? "That is absolutely the most illogical thing I've ever heard. You can no more separate your heart, liver, kidney, and brain into separate parts of the room. You cannot do the first commandment without it resulting in the second. You cannot effectively and consistently do the second unless you have done the first." I am talking about the biblical definition of the second commandment, not the sentimental, humanistic definition that abounds in so many circles. I am talking about staying steady in the First Corinthians 13 level.

The greatest anointing human beings can walk in is the anointing to walk out the two great commandments. Remember, there are four dimensions. They go together. We do not do one and then we do the other. We do all four of them simultaneously.

In the next chapter, we will be answering the question, "How do we love God?"

CHAPTER 14

How Do We Love God—Four Premises

THE FOUR SPHERES OF THE FIRST COMMANDMENT

In the last chapter we looked at the four dimensions of the love of God. In the next couple of chapters we are going to examine the four spheres in which we show our love to God: our *heart,* which speaks of our emotions and affections; our *soul,* which is our personality, the way we express ourselves; our *mind,* which is our intellect and our thoughts; and our *strength,* which is a reference to our resources. We should desire to love Him with all of our heart, soul, mind, and strength because that is the way He loves us—with all of His heart, soul, mind, and strength. It is both our holy debt and our glorious gift to love God in these four ways. This invitation into God's love brings us great benefit.[1]

In this chapter, we will be asking the question, "How do we love God?" What does the human expressions of wholehearted, bridal passion for God look like? As we discussed in the last chapter, love for God is much more than just human sentiment or extravagant expressions in a worship service. True bridal love requires heart responses with follow through. We are not content with a passion for Jesus that is merely rhetorical. We will not settle for a reputation of being radically devoted without any real expression in our lives.

LOVING GOD, GOD'S WAY

What does love look like? That really is the million-dollar question of the hour. Bridal love is more than human or religious sentiment. The love of a wholehearted Bride in love with Her heavenly Bridegroom is much more than extravagant, demonstrative expressions in a worship service, though I really do appreciate those. The reason why it is important to ask this question is that many people, when considering the bridal paradigm, think something along the lines of, "I want to be wholehearted."

If you press them, however, about what being wholehearted would look like, they are usually imagining something ethereal, maybe just sitting around in a low-lit room with quiet worship music playing in the background, smiling and thinking about love. Most people do not have concrete answers to what it really looks like to love God from Monday to Friday. We need to have a clear, practical path for what it looks like to love God.

So what is the biblical answer to the question, what does it mean to love God as a bride loves her bridegroom? Loving God means specific heart responses with follow through. As I said earlier, we are not content with only having a rhetorical passion for Jesus. If it is rhetoric, it is just words on banners, posters, or Christian T-shirts. "We are radical; we love Jesus." Our passion has to have concrete, practical expression or it is just a concept. We want more than just a slogan about being on fire, don't we?

As we have already discussed, there are many cultural definitions of love to choose from. And unfortunately, many of these natural, cultural definitions have found their way into the Church. There is a lot of confusion in many churches today about the true nature of love. One of the core issues as we near the end of the age will be how we define and walk out love because everybody will be using the term *love*—but with massive differences in what is meant by the word and how it is fleshed out.

As the Bride of Christ, we must define love on God's terms, not by the humanistic culture that seeks love without reference to an allegiance to Jesus and obedience to His Word. As followers of *"the Way,"*[2] we must recognize and renounce all the false paradigms of love that are emerging in so many sectors of the Church today.

Nothing exposes the false views of love more clearly than in how we view and preach salvation. All people, regardless of how much they "seem" to love, will go to hell without Jesus. My only hope of salvation is that Jesus paid the eternal price of my sin. Without a relationship with Jesus, Schindler and all the Jews he saved from the Nazi death camps will go to the same hell as Adolph Hitler. Yet, on the other hand, with a relationship with Jesus, anyone (even a Hitler) can go to the same Heaven that the spiritually mature apostle Paul is in today.

You may be surprised at what I am about to share with you. God's definition of love does not include extending tolerance to everyone, if by that we mean abandoning His righteous and holy standards. Love is more than romantic notions about being "happy in God." Jesus is not interested in being our boyfriend, nor is He a humanistic anything-goes hippie. Love is not about being laid back or chilling out. God's definition of love is always rooted in the written Word of God.

Our primary assignment in God's will is to grow in bridal love. God measures life differently from humankind because He already has all the money, wisdom, fame, influence, and time. When we stand before Him on that final day, the main question He will be asking each of us is, "Did you learn to love?"

It is important that we understand that God is not a power freak who loves barking out orders, all the while hoping we do not get it exactly right so He can lower the proverbial boom on us. All of God's commands are actually invitations that include with them the promise of His supernatural enabling so that we can obey them. It takes God to love God! So when He commands that we love Him, when we say yes, He empowers us so that we can love Him! Nevertheless, we do have to actually say yes!

We must actively cultivate extravagant devotion to our Bridegroom God, Jesus. This takes both time and effort. Love does not automatically grow. In fact the very opposite is true; it actually automatically diminishes unless we intentionally cultivate a responsive heart. The illustration I often use is that the Christian life is like paddling a canoe—upstream! If we are not gaining ground, guess what, we are losing ground. In light of that, the question we should be asking ourselves is, "What is the most that God will empower me to give to Him?" We are not content with the minimum requirements of salvation. We must choose the good part as Mary of Bethany did.[3]

HOW DO WE LOVE GOD? FOUR PREMISES

I want to take a moment to look at the four different premises concerning biblical bridal love. These are not the same as the four spheres of love we are going to examine later. The first premise is that loving God requires the pursuit of wholehearted obedience.[4] Jesus defined loving God as being deeply rooted in a spirit of affection-based obedience. Loving God requires more than singing love songs to Him, having ministry outreaches, or merely having spiritual "warm fuzzies."[5]

There is no such thing as loving God without obeying His Word. Love requires the wholehearted pursuit of obedience in both our attitudes, demonstrated by our living a life of purity and humility, and our actions or our service to God and to others. Many wrongly imagine that as long as they sing songs, do plays, and have outreaches, they can somehow disregard the Holy Spirit's leadership in the daily areas that He is focusing on in their lives, and somehow in the end God will equate all that with love. That is not love; that is deception.

SERMON ON THE MOUNT LIFESTYLES

Jesus defined the love of an equally yoked Bride as our living a Sermon on the Mount lifestyle.[6] A lifestyle that is pleasing to the Lord in that it denies our sinful, lustful desires—I emphasize sinful because there are righteous lustful desires—as the theatre God has chosen for us to express our love to Him. What we do, on the stage of our life, demonstrates in a concrete way how much we love God.

Each man, woman, and child has unique personal struggles according to personality and circumstances. Thus, we each have a unique assignment, a different part to play, related to how we offer our gift of bridal love to God. For instance, saying no to sin is more than our staying out of trouble; it is actually an opportunity for us to express our love to God, and Jesus takes it personally when we resist sin because of our love for Him.

Some people give God more time and money in the hope that He will dismiss an area of compromise in their life. What God wants most from us is a response of love manifested by our seeking to obey His Word. Jesus wants a love from us that allows Him to take total control of our lives to protect us and glorify us in His love.

All of Jesus' commands are related to love. For example, He commands us to pursue His heart, to seek His face, to choose love over lust, to receive eternal rewards, and to be vessels of His love to others by blessing and serving them. Everything Jesus does is about love. Remember, God does not *have* love, He *is* love. He wants us to *be* love as well.

The second premise is that love involves adoring trust, which equates to our living a life of gratitude[7] to Jesus. Adoration and gratitude to Jesus for His greatness and kindness is essential to our successfully living a life of love. It is foundational to Paul's theology of holiness and love. With awestruck gratefulness we adore Jesus and trust His wisdom, humility, and power. He is the most deserving and capable Person to rule our lives and the whole earth. We often take the wealth of God's kindness so lightly. Because of our long history of sin, we deserve God's wrath, yet His kindness brings us to repentance.[8]

Love grows in us as we grow in the revelation of the truth of Jesus' greatness and by gratitude in seeing the whole story of how He is treating us. The psalmist had an overflowing heart of adoration for the indescribable loveliness of Jesus.[9]

The third premise is that love requires our loyalty to truth, or to say it another way, we must walk in the light of the truth that we have. As we walk with the Lord, we should be progressively receiving more revelation from Him about who He is and about His Word, His Kingdom, and His ways. As we receive more light and our understanding of the truth of the Word of God grows, He requires us to be faithful to walk in the light of that truth.

But let me give you a heads up: when we choose to do that, it will often become an issue—an irritant—to many around us, even professed believers, because the Word of God is politically incorrect in the eyes of man. Natural man will not have an appreciation for the things that Jesus promises, what He requires of His people, His plans for what He is going to do in the earth (just read the Book of Revelation, for instance); all of this is massively politically incorrect.

LOVE LOVES TRUTH

True love expresses loyalty to God's Word instead of yielding to the fear of man. In the endtimes, there will be a battle for the truth as some believers give heed to doctrines of demons that promote lies about Jesus.[10] The conflict will center on defining who Jesus is and how we are to demonstrate our love for and to Him. We must love God, God's way.

Love for God demonstrates loyalty to His truth as seen in Jesus. We must express our love in allegiance with the Jesus of the Bible, not the Jesus of religious or humanist sentiments. The Holy Spirit will glorify and exalt Jesus by guiding us into all truth about Him.[11]

Three truths about Jesus offend the natural humanist's mindset, even the humanist mindset that is in parts of the Church. The first one is His deity and His resultant right to establish absolute standards for which the nations of the earth are accountable to Him. Jesus is not tolerant and accepting of everyone's view of love.

The second one is that the only way of salvation is through Jesus. And oh, they do not like that one. In the days to come, this will become one of the biggest points of contention between the Church and the other religions of the world. As Americans we are taught to be tolerant and accepting of others' religious beliefs. As citizens of the Kingdom of God, however, we are taught to stand and boldly proclaim that Jesus is the Way, the Truth, and the Life, and there is no other Way to God but through Him.[12]

The third one is that Jesus possesses the wisdom and love to judge sin in both time and eternity. As we approach the end of the age, we are going to see more and more of Jesus' temporal judgments on the earth, and more and more of man's wrath against Jesus because of them. Jesus' loving judgments are released to remove everything that hinders the working of His love in the human heart. His judgments are an expression of His passion for purity in the greatness and the glory of His people.

This issue of Jesus' judgment will be such a massive area of offense to many (even among Christians) because people will begin to debate (in fact the debate already is raging) about the various innocent groups of people on the earth. Beloved, there are no innocent people on the earth. All have sinned and fallen short of the glory of God. Before God, we are all guilty. Everyone deserves to go to hell. Everyone deserves both the temporal and eternal judgment of God.

It is only because of His great kindness and mercy that any of us have life; it is only because of His kindness our life is extended.

By kindness, we have eternal life—end of story. In the decades to come (no, Jesus isn't coming to secretly snatch us out of the world any minute), when the drama that is described in the Book of Revelation starts to transpire, when under His wise and loving leadership, His judgments begin to be poured out on the inhabitants of the earth resulting in the premature death of multitudes in the generation He returns, there is no innocent group that will have the right to challenge His leadership or question His goodness, justice, or love.

The fourth premise is that love includes a consuming desire, a lovesick abandonment to God.[13] Love is never passive but always includes burning desire. To be lovesick for God means we seek to love Jesus more than we desire anything else. Being "wounded with love" means we are sick or pained with desire for more of Jesus to the point that we are willing to remove all areas of compromise that hinder love for Him from our lives.

God is Love. He burns as an all-consuming fire of jealousy. He wants to take over our lives and consume us from the inside out by dominating our affections, thoughts, words, and actions, as He determines our destiny and establishes our eternal greatness and joy.[14] The God who has everything and lacks nothing desires us because He is love. Love is not toleration but instead is desire. The God who has everything and is in need of nothing still wants something. Why? Not because He is needy, but because He is the fountain of desire. Desire implies wanting something but not because of lack. God desires the ones He loves without lacking anything.

Jesus will reveal Himself to us as being more than our Savior (Forgiver), Healer, and Provider. He also wants to reveal Himself as the jealous Bridegroom God who will not relent in His pursuit of us until He has all of our heart. We cry, "Lord, we want more of You." He responds, "Yes, and I want more of you."

Jesus beckons us into a life of lovesick abandonment, "Take up your cross, and follow Me. Leave it all behind. Say good-bye to houses and lands for My sake." This is the voice of a Bridegroom who gave all for the sake of love.[15] Jesus defined love as laying down one's life for his friends.[16] Jesus loves us with all of His heart, soul, mind, and strength, and what He desires in return is a Corporate Bride equally yoked to Him in love. The bridal paradigm is abandonment.[17]

In the next couple of chapters, we will be looking at the four spheres of wholehearted love.

CHAPTER 15

Loving God With All Your Heart

In the next couple of chapters we will be looking at the four spheres of loving God as a Bride loves her Bridegroom. These are the four spheres in which we demonstrate our bridal love to God; the four spheres in which we show Him our love by our obedience, adoring trust, loyalty to truth, and our awakened desire in it. The four spheres while interrelated are both distinct and separate. There are a number of areas where they overlap, but each sphere has specific, practical applications for our lives.

Jesus, the great Psychologist of the ages, the one Man who truly understands what is in the heart of man,[1] is not just offering us a general definition of the make-up of a person's life before God. Some commentators say that Jesus said that we are to love God with all of our heart, soul, mind, and strength, but that really it is all the same thing. That is not correct, though. Although, as I said earlier, there is some overlap, for your life has a holistic oneness about it, there are four different spheres in which we are challenged and anointed to love God.

SPHERE 1: LOVING GOD WITH ALL OUR HEART

The first sphere—we are to love God with all of our heart. The heart speaks of our emotions, affections, longings, and the very impulse of desire that affects and directs every decision we make. The heart is the "hidden current" that moves our inner person. Our heart has powerful emotions that filter or color the way we see and respond to everything in life. Our heart defines our core reality that drives all that we say and do.[2] We all experience a wealth of emotions every day that are constantly in flux, ever changing as our circumstances change. Although what we consciously "feel," hour by hour, is very important, our spiritual "affections" go down much deeper than the obvious surface emotions that we experience. Our affections are the deep currents within us that steer our lives, much as the rudder of a boat that lies hidden beneath the surface of the water yet in actuality is what directs the course of the vessel.

If we want to be lovers of God, we first have to ask ourselves the basic question, "Where do our affections currently lie?"[3] How do we do that? To ascertain where your affections lie, all I have to do is look at what occupies your time and how you spend your money. These are the accurate indicators of what I call the interior passions. Let me see your checkbook and your day timer, and I will have a good snapshot of where your heart is. Whatever you are spending your time and money on is what has your heart.

COME ON, FOCUS

How many times have you heard someone make the statement, "I can't change how I feel"? That is true; we cannot change how we feel—directly. However, we can change what we are focusing our heart on. Really, that is all God has ever asked us to do, for He knows, because He created us, that what we set our focus on eventually becomes our treasure, and where our treasure is, our heart, or our emotions, will eventually follow. When Jesus made the statement, *"For where your treasure is, there your heart will be also,"*[4] He was revealing to us an important principle in our quest to love God, God's way. Our hearts will dwell and abide wherever it is we find our greatest treasure. In other words, for the love of God to fill our hearts, we cannot actually pursue that directly. Instead, we must seek out a great treasure and then set our heart on that treasure, and then love will happily follow along. The paradox and irony of love is that it is what we were created to experience, but it can only be obtained when it is not directly sought.

Therefore, if we desire to love Him completely, we must treasure Him supremely. When we truly recognize the glory and worth of who He is, and then set the focus of our heart on Him as our treasure, loving Him with all of our heart will be the inevitable consequence.

Beloved, as the Image-bearers, we can set our love, or our affections, on what we choose to set our focus. Our emotions eventually follow whatever we set ourselves to pursue. In doing this, we determine the course in which our emotions develop over time. God promises that if we will change our mind, He will change our heart, in time. Another way to say it is that, as we change our goals and our spiritual focus, the Holy Spirit changes our emotions.[5]

Setting our love on God not only is a positive setting, it is also a negative "unsetting" or a removing of all that works to diminish our affections; things such as bitterness, lust, being over-stimulated by worldly entertainment, and the pursuit of gaining things (even legitimate things) and influence.[6]

DAVID, THE MODEL

King David, the man after God's own heart,[7] modeled for us what is necessary if we desire to pursue living a life that is pleasing to God, when he told us that he made a choice to set his heart to love God. We, not the world, the flesh, the devil, or even God, determine the things that eventually form our emotions the most. Our decisions by themselves are not enough to change our emotions, yet they are an indispensable part of the process of emotional transformation.[8]

All things being equal, whatever you set your heart on, whatever you focused on, five or ten years ago, acted as the seed(s) that caused the emotional harvest that you are living in today.[9] The human spirit, under Jesus' great leadership, has the God-given ability to determine the course of our emotions. You change your goals, and your emotions will change in time. We set our love on Him, we set our affections to love Him with all of our heart, with all of our affections, and love Him we will!

We must choose to delight in the Lord or to set our affection on Him. We must not underestimate the power of the setting of our heart on God. In doing this, we place ourselves directly in the path of the Holy Spirit.[10] One way that we set our heart to love Him is by delighting and committing to walk in obedience even when it is costly.[11] The Holy Spirit honors the power of our decisions and often He waits on them before imparting God's love to us.[12] The power to choose where we set our hearts is part of the great dignity of being an Image-bearer—a human spirit created in God's image.

Beloved, you are changing every day of every week. Either you are growing closer to the Lord, or you are growing further away from Him in every seven-day period. There is no place in God, no quitting place, where once you "arrive," you get it, and you get to keep it, when it comes to having a relationship with God. You are gaining ground or losing ground every seven days, and the only way you will keep the ground you gain in the Spirit is by taking new ground. The only way I can maintain the love I have for Jesus is by increasing it today. If I hope to just coast along and keep what I have, I will find it decreasing.

I have to increase the areas of my life that are coming under obedience to the truth that has been revealed to me for my love to break even and/or increase. It is true: my love has to increase to keep it from decreasing. There is no such thing as neutral ground; therefore, all of our decisions are critical. They are indispensable. There are other factors involved in loving God besides our decisions, but the decisions we make are still powerful.

DELIGHT YOURSELF IN THE LORD

King David said, *"Delight yourself in the Lord, and He will give you the desires of your heart."*[13] David had such a powerful understanding of how the human heart works under God's leadership. Many people mistakenly believe that what David was saying is that if we delight in the Lord, then He will give us whatever our heart currently desires. That is not *exactly* what David meant. Delight does not mean manufactured desire. God is not saying, "If you butter Me up enough, you can get your way." He is actually saying something far better than that! You see, God is not interested in "only" giving you what you can think up; He desires to give you things far beyond what you can even conceive of.[14]

What David was telling us is that the giving of desire was God's action *after* David delighted in Him. The delight was David's part. The new desires imparted and injected into David's spirit was God's part. You and I cannot, by the force of our will, create new and righteous desires within our own heart. God's work in us is incomparable. What I mean by that is, we cannot do God's part, and God will not do our part. However, *if* we do our part, God will *always* do His part, in time.

David said, "I delight," meaning, "I am setting my heart to give myself fully to You. God, I choose that my heart will delight in You, not in the fact that I am king, or the fact that You have blessed me with favor in the sight of man or with material blessings." Now it is good, and even right, to rejoice over the areas in our lives in which God has blessed us, or that we are desiring and asking that He would bless. However, those things cannot be the supreme delight of our heart.

MAKE GOD YOUR GOLD

Job said it this way: *"If you lay gold in the dust, and gold of Ophir among the stones of the torrent-bed, then the Almighty will be your gold and your precious silver."*[15] That is a decision that we have to choose to make; and that is what it means to delight in the Lord. Make a quality decision, a decision from which there is no retreat, to make God your gold, whether you feel like it or not. Spiritually stand up and say, "I am going to choose righteousness.[16]

I am going to turn off a bunch of stuff, I am going to downsize the activities in my life, and I am going to go after Jesus. I am going to live a lifestyle of fasting and prayer and go after Him. When I don't feel anything, when I am not enjoying it, when the Word of God 'feels' boring, when prayer is even more boring, I still am going to go for it." Beloved, that is called delighting yourself in the Lord and making God your gold.

If you make a quality decision[17] to follow David's example and teachings, when he says, "You do your part. You choose that God will be your chief delight, whether you feel it or not," what will happen in time is that God will impart new desires, *His* desires, the very desires that are in His heart, into your heart. When the Word of God says God will give you the desires of your heart, it does not mean He will give you whatever you want; it means the desires of your heart will change if you delight in the Lord. He will replace your desires with Holy Spirit-inspired desires. Glory!

Do not underestimate the power of the setting of your heart on God, whether you feel anything or not. It is not about feeling. "That is good preaching, Buddy, would you say that again?" OK, I will. It is not about *feeling*. Now, do not get me wrong, I like feelings. I mean, I *really* like feelings. However, I refuse to live by my feelings. Feelings come and feelings go because they are dependent on circumstances. The Word of God never changes.[18]

Base your life on the Word, not on how you feel or don't feel. Beloved, if you choose to set your heart, if you choose to set your affections, the Holy Spirit will honor that decision. There is God-given power in your quality decision to love God with all your heart. There is Holy Spirit power released when you set your heart to love God, God's way.[19] However, it does not just fall into our laps like ripe apples off an apple tree. We have to do our part. The Holy Spirit waits for us to do it.

Moreover, we do not do it just once; we have to renew it every so often. I tell the Lord I love Him every day, but there are several times in the course of a year, maybe 5, 10, or 20 times, maybe more, that I have to stop and say to myself, "Self, slow down. It's time to renew the setting of your heart, it's time to realign," and then I get alone with the Lord and spend whatever time it takes (I don't mean it takes all day to do it), and I realign my heart to make Him my gold and my delight.

IT TAKES GOD TO LOVE GOD

We have to set our hearts on God, and one way we do that is by regularly asking the Holy Spirit for supernatural help for us to love Jesus. It takes God to love God. Another way to say it is, "It takes God's supernatural empowerment to love God the way that He desires to be loved." I want to encourage you to often ask God to pour His love for Jesus into your heart and to empower you to direct the reins of your heart into His love.[20]

Have you ever thought about the fact that no one else can give God all *your* love except for you? I cannot love God for you. You have to give Him your love yourself. The Father has entrusted a unique part of Jesus' heritage to you specifically. Only you can give your love.

I am a worship leader. I have been leading worship for over 30 years. I know the power of music to move human emotions. But I learned a long time ago that I can pick good songs, songs that provide worship language for the hearts of the people of God, but I can't make people worship. You can lead a horse to water, but you can't make him drink. I can provide the opportunity and the on-ramp, but only you can choose to worship.

The Scriptures tell us that the angels, the living creatures, the 24 elders, the heavenly hosts, and all of the redeemed from all of redemptive history are in Heaven loving and worshiping Jesus continually. And you know what I say to that? I say, "Duh!" Of course they are! They are in His literal, physical manifest Presence, standing before Him *in eternity* with no sinful flesh tugging at them, no worldly allurements distracting them, and no demons tempting them. They are healed, whole, and beholding the glory of God with their own two eyes, unfiltered and unfettered. You had better believe they are worshiping Him! Who wouldn't worship in that setting?

But, Beloved, did you ever stop to think that you and I have the opportunity to give to Jesus something that none of that innumerable host around His throne can ever hope to give to Him? Do you know what that is? A sacrifice of praise,[21] voluntary love from a heart that still has to struggle with wandering desires, spiritual distractions, lack of vision, and a dim beholding.[22] You see, it does not cost those who stand before the throne anything to offer up worship to God. However, it costs *us* something that even God cannot reimburse to us when we choose to worship Him: time. There is an old saying, "Money is power." That might be true, money might be power, but my friend, time is life! We have the opportunity to demonstrate our love to Jesus in a fallen world where it is both costly and rare. We can give Him our time!

LOVING GOD WITH OUR "ALL"

We are equally yoked to Jesus not by the size of our love but by the "all" of our love. Though our all is small, the point is that it is our all. He desires to be loved in the way He loves us—wholeheartedly. So we don't want to quit, we want to have a sustained reach for 100 percent obedience to love Him, which is different from attaining to it in our life.

When I teach on loving God with all of our heart, many times people will respond that they are afraid they might not make it; they might fall short of the goal. I always encourage them with the fact that I can guarantee that they *will* fall short! And when we do? We read and absorb First John 1:9 and renew our resolve to reach to fully obey with confidence that God enjoys us, even while we are still in process. The Lord values our journey to grow in love. The journey is the destination.[23] The reach of our heart to love Him deeply moves Him.

I HAD A DREAM

Jennifer Roberts, an intercessory missionary at the International House of Prayer in Kansas City, Missouri, tells of a vision that she had:

I was at a Saturday evening service at the International House of Prayer (IHOP) in Kansas City. I was in a season where I was feeling sorry for myself. It seemed that everyone else was receiving an abundance of revelation from God, but I wasn't receiving anything.

I am sitting on the front row and I have a vision. In the vision, I am getting ready to run a race. There beside me are several leaders from the House of Prayer getting ready to run the race with me. There beside me is Allen Hood, Dwayne (Jennifer's husband), Mike Bickle, and Deborah Hiebert all beside me on the running track. I look down at the end of the racetrack, there is the Lord Jesus, and He says, "Run." And I say to myself, "I can't compete against these people. I am not going to win this race."

And just then, a tunnel forms over my lane and I can't see anything but my lane and Jesus at the end encouraging me to run. I realize it's not a competition. I am not competing against anyone else; I am running "my" race for Jesus. I didn't have to run as fast as Dwayne. I didn't have to run as fast as Allen or Mike Bickle or Deborah Hiebert. I just had to run "my" race. It was "my" race marked before me, for Jesus. And He was at the end of the tunnel and He was cheering me on. He was saying, "Go, Jennifer, you can do it, go Jennifer, go Jennifer!" And I mean, I was slow and it didn't matter. But I ran the race for God. And when I got to the end, Jesus said to me, "Jennifer, if you run, you win!"

So then I come back to myself in the service at IHOP and I go, "Wow, that was cool!" But after a little while I start feeling sorry for myself again.

Then I have the same vision again. There's the same racetrack, and all the same people are there again. It's time for the race to start, and I'm thinking again, "I can't compete against these people; they're the leaders in the House of Prayer. I can't compete against them, I can't win this race." But this time there is something different from the first vision, I look and I notice that this time I've got a diaper bag on my shoulder, I have a stroller hooked around my ankle with a baby in it, I am holding a child on my hip and I have a toddler at my side who I am holding by the hand. Now I am really thinking, "Now I know that I definitely can't compete in a spiritual race against this caliber of people...I'm a mother with children. I can't win this race."

Then like before, the tunnel forms and I can't see anything but my lane and Jesus is at the end of the lane encouraging me to run. And the Lord says to me, "Run, Jennifer, run." But I'm thinking, "I can't run, I'm going to be so slow. I can't win this race." And Jesus says to me, "Yes, you will be slow, but it will make you strong. Run!"

So I start down the lane toward Jesus, and you know what? I am slow. I am crawling along carrying the diaper bag, pushing the stroller, carrying the baby, pulling the toddler along with me. I am so slow, but I keep my eyes on Jesus at the end, and I don't stop, I keep running the race and I finally make it to the end. And when I get to the end, Jesus is excited and jumping up and down and He says to me, "Jennifer, if you run, you win! If you run, you win!"

To Jesus, running is winning! If you are running the race, you are winning the race!

There is a real lesson for us in our pursuit of being a whole-hearted lover of God—if we do not quit, then we win. We do not find our identity in our failure but rather in the fact that He loves us, in the gift of righteousness,[24] and in the cry of our spirit to love God. Weak, immature love is not false love!

Power in our life is found in pursuing hundredfold obedience. There are powerful dynamics that occur in our heart when we soberly seek to walk in total obedience. The 98 percent pursuit of obedience has a limited blessing. The last 2 percent positions us to live with a vibrant heart. Reaching for full obedience for decades is the definition of living radically before God. We can live radical, wholehearted lives with hearts that are set on making God our gold and our delight.

In the next chapter, we will examine what we can do to love God with all of our soul.

CHAPTER 16

Loving God With All Your Soul

In the last chapter we looked at what it means to love God with all of our heart, or how to set our affections on loving Him. God created us to love Him in the four spheres of our life, which includes our heart (affections), soul (personality), mind (thoughts), and strength (resources) because He loves us this way.[1] He loves us with all of His affections, personality, thoughts, and resources.

In this chapter, we will be looking at some of what it means for us to love God with our soul or our personality. Loving God with our personality means that we are living a lifestyle of humility in our attitudes and with our speech. What we say enhances or quenches our ability to love God by the power of God.[2]

SPHERE 2: LOVING GOD WITH ALL OUR SOUL

The second sphere that we demonstrate our love for God in is in the area of our soul, or our personality. The soul is different from our affections or desires. Loving God with all our soul is loving Him with our unique personality or the animation of who we are, expressing the uniqueness of our abilities and desires including the way we walk and the way we talk. It is loving Him by laying down our personal desires, preferences, and our right to say what we think!

Our personality is expressed most dynamically by our speech. How we talk matters![3] The surest indicator that we are walking as an equally yoked Bride with Jesus is how we talk—what we say and what we do not say. How we use our tongue drastically enhances or quenches our ability to grow in love. Therefore, when we are serious about pleasing Jesus, we set our heart to express ourselves and to communicate in a way that enhances, not diminishes, love. When we allow corrupting talk to come out of our mouth, we grieve the Holy Spirit, and when He is grieved, we limit the measure, or our spiritual capacity to receive from Him.[4]

Our love can be diminished by the negative fire released in us by wrong speech that affects our inner peson.[5] Therefore, to demonstrate our love for Him, we gladly renounce all grumbling and speaking against one another, knowing that it hinders our ability to love God and to experience, or feel, God's love.

I am not talking about obvious wrong speech like blaspheming, cursing, or cussing, or what Kenneth Hagin Sr. used to call "shoot cussing"—it is still cussing, we just change the vowels. I am not limiting it to some of the base speech that is so common among so many believers like slander or gossip, which is often entered into in the name of "sharing so we can pray." As bad as all of those are, the number one issue of our speech, for all of us, is pride that is demonstrated by our complaining. Complaining is really the big one. What complaining does is quench the Spirit, and the Spirit is the key to your love being inflamed. I cannot demonstrate my love to Jesus if the Spirit and I are not in agreement. The Holy Spirit will not agree with complaint. Why? Because complaining is nothing but pride speech.

I am not talking about the complaints in prayer that are recorded in the imprecatory songs, where they are crying out, "Oh, God." There are biblical complaints. I am not talking about crying out to God for His Kingdom to come. I am talking about the normal daily complaints of life. I am talking about complaints birthed out of pride that says I think I deserve a better deal in life.

LOVERS IN WAL-MART

For instance, when I am at Wal-Mart and I complain, "Why don't they open up another lane, don't they know that I'm in a hurry, I don't have time for this." You ever used that one? Or maybe you have complained, "Who does that guy on the highway think he is, cutting me off?" (But don't mention all the times you have cut someone else off.) Or maybe this one: "Why doesn't everyone keep their hands off my stuff. Why don't they leave my stuff alone? I deserve better than this." See? At the end of the day, it is all about the "I" in the middle of pride—it is all about me, what I want, what I feel, what I think.

Can you picture the Lord Jesus standing in the checkout line at Wal-Mart just fussing and fuming about how sorry the manager on duty must be because he is holding up the Son of God? No, I cannot picture that happening either.

We are the people of God, called to be an equally yoked Bride of Christ for the Son of God. If we are ever going to live lives that are pleasing to our Bridegroom God, we will have to start choosing to bridle our tongues, and thank the Lord instead—not that we thank the Lord that somebody is annoying us, but we thank the Lord that He is watching our humility and in our circumstances we are actually having an encounter, an opportunity to encounter Jesus in that moment. God offends our mind to reveal our heart. Therefore, unpleasant circumstances in our lives are often our best friends, revealing to us how selfish we really are, and assisting us by pointing out to us the areas that we need to be taking before the throne of grace, asking the Lord for His help.

Instead of complaining that the heavy traffic is keeping me out longer than I had planned, I could choose to say something like, "Lord, You know, I hadn't planned on sitting here on this highway this afternoon, but You know what? I am not going to vocalize it. Instead, I choose to thank You for an opportunity to spend a few more minutes (or hours) giving myself to loving and worshiping You."

You know what happens when you start doing that? Something happens inside, something changes. Multiply that thousands of times over several years and your spirit will really be different. One vitamin will not make a sick person healthy, but if he or she takes vitamins for years... Get it? You choose to do the right thing thousands of times, and your spirit will really be different.

Loving God Requires a Subdued, Controlled Tongue

Our words release life or death inside our heart.[6] The most common way to grieve the Spirit is by our words. When the Holy Spirit is grieved, He still loves us; however, we cannot receive from Him and participate with Him in the same measure.[7] The Holy Spirit, through the apostle Paul, admonishes us to walk in love by purifying our speech.[8] Purified speech is speech that is not always about us, what we think, what we like, or what we want.

The Lord's half-brother, James, tells us, *"Not many of you should become teachers, my brothers, for you know that we who teach will be judged with greater strictness."*[9] I have heard that verse quoted many times over the years, and in fact, I have quoted it many times myself. It was only recently that I saw what it was that teachers would be judged for. I had always thought teachers would be judged with greater strictness because they were not living what they preached, and while that is true, that is not what James is warning us about here. Let's look at it a little more closely.

> *...we who teach will be judged with greater strictness. For we all stumble in many ways. And if anyone does not stumble in what he says, he is a perfect man, able also to bridle his whole body.*[10]

James is telling us that if we focus on and master our speech, we can actually bring all our physical appetites under submission to the Spirit! He calls this being a perfect or "mature" person. The Greek word for perfect here is the same word James uses when we are told that when we cooperate with the Spirit, allowing Him to do His work in us, the result is that we *"may be perfect and complete, lacking in nothing."*[11]

When preparing for their ministry, many teachers, or those who desire to be teachers, often focus on getting the facts right, but James points out that their greatest challenge is not what they do in the classroom, but rather how they monitor their speech *outside* the classroom. James uses three metaphors—a bit, a rudder, and a small fire—to emphasize the truth that even though the tongue is a small member of our body, it is the key to controlling the much larger issues related to our body, life, and relationships. James contrasts the vast power of our tongue that is out of proportion to its size. The tongue, if not submitted to the Holy Spirit, releases destructive wildfire in our inner being as well as in the outer circumstances of our lives.[12]

Carnal Speech Brings Judgment

And one of the most harmful ways that the tongue is used in the life of believers is when we speak in ways that dishonor others in the Body of Christ, resulting in division in the temple of God.[13] Believers who are bound up in the spirit of pride, living with loose lips, grumbling and complaining are put, by God, into the same category as those who commit sexual immorality.[14] If we are to live lives that please our heavenly Husband, the Lover of our souls, then we must hear God's call to walk in humility and renounce all grumbling and evil speaking against one another.[15]

It is imperative that we come to grips with the fact that humility is more than just a virtue; it is a plain old necessity. Walking in humility can be costly, humanly speaking, but as we have seen, not as costly as the alternative—walking in a spirit of pride that positions us in the place of having God Himself oppose us.[16] Though it may cost us something, humanly speaking, when we choose to walk in humility as an expression of our bridal love for Him, in the end there is no cost, for we get Him whom our soul loves.

Embracing humility is the theatre God chose for us as the Image-bearers and as His equally yoked bride to express our whole-hearted, voluntary love to Him. Each one of us has a different path to walk, a different part to play according to our unique personality and circumstances. We each have our own race to run, our own individualized love assignment in giving our love to God. If each of us has an individualized, unique race to run, how then are we to know how to work out our salvation with fear and trembling?[17]

A HUMBLE KING

The answer is that we have to follow Him who is our Leader and our example, the Lord Jesus, who while He was fully God, was also fully man. As we study and gain a better understanding of Jesus' humility, it will both inspire and instruct us better in how we should ask for the Holy Spirit's help to love God in the way He loves us.[18]

The world says that meekness is a sign of weakness or an absence of strength, when in actuality the exact opposite is true. Meekness is power and privilege under control. It is restraint in the use of power for the sake of promoting love. A good example is the taming of a wild horse. Wild horses are beautiful, powerful... and wild. Wild means dangerous. Once a wild horse is captured and trained, it is taught to restrain and control its power. Then its power can be used for positive ends and not for destruction.

Something that most people never consider is that the life of the Godhead is a river that flows forever out of the place of meekness. Jesus, in His humanity, put on display for all to see the riches of God's humility, endless, limitless power restrained because of love. So many times I have sat amazed by the fact that One who was so strong could stoop so low and be so gentle, just because of His great love for us.[19]

A HUMBLE THREESOME

Holy Spirit, the Third Person of the eternal Godhead, functions as the support ministry within the Godhead. He is fully God yet chooses to work behind the scenes without any selfish desire to be recognized. He is happy in His humility.[20] What an example for the rest of us! You know what? It is OK if not everyone sees what we do! Our Bridegroom, Judge, and King's humility is seen in His ultimate goal waiting for complete fulfillment until the end of the Millennium.[21] It is OK to wait awhile to see the fruit of our labor. God our Heavenly Father's humility is expressed in all that He does. Love and humility are the same.[22]

GOD'S DEFINITION OF LOVE: THE HUMILITY OF JESUS

We are told that Jesus was the exact imprint of God's nature.[23] Jesus said to Philip, *"Have I been with you so long, and you still do not know Me, Philip? Whoever has seen Me has seen the Father."*[24] *"I and the Father are one."*[25] God is love,[26] so Jesus is love. Jesus, who was the God-Man, lived a life of perfect humility,[27] being the exact representation of God's nature,[28] showing us the eternal humility of the Father.

The humility Jesus demonstrated in His incarnation openly displayed His abandonment in loving us. When we recognize that, it empowers us so that we can live a life of abandonment in loving Him, rooted deeply in humility. From eternity, Jesus has been in the form of God, which means He has always shared eternal glory with the Father. The pre-existent Christ, in the form of God, was equal with, but distinguished from, the Father. As the God-Man, being in the very form of God, Jesus eternally possessed all glory and all the privileges of being God.[29]

Humbling Himself in the incarnation, Jesus now has two natures: He is fully God and fully man, with no contradiction between the two. Jesus while on earth was never less than God, but lived as if He was never more than a man. He always retained His deity,[30] but in His humanity, refused to enjoy His unique privileges in being God because He was seeking our interests.

Jesus did not consider the privileges of being equal to God as something to be selfishly grasped.[31] In other words, He did not view the humility required in His incarnation as something that took anything essential from His core identity as a servant filled with love. He had nothing to prove to anyone because He knew who He was. In His humility as a man, He denied Himself privileges that were rightfully His. He did not deny His core identity but rather expressed His true heart of servanthood for our benefit and for our instruction.

JESUS—THE SON OF MAN

Jesus did not see the incarnation as a scandalous injustice when He laid aside His glory to eternally become a man to make a way to exalt us forever.[32] Did you catch that? Jesus laid aside His glory and became a man. He lived as a man. He died as a man. He rose from the dead and ascended to Heaven as a man. He is seated at the right hand of God—forever as a man. He did not quit being a man after salvation was accomplished. Part of salvation was the requirement that Jesus, the eternal Son of God, had to humble Himself and to live forever as a man in the incarnation.

Jesus did not empty Himself of His deity; however, He chose not to use His divine power for His own ends while on earth so that He would qualify to be our High Priest. Jesus was God hidden in the obscurity of humanity. While on earth, He never once drew upon His own omnipresence, omnipotence, or omniscience as God. As a man, a flesh-and-blood man, He lived dependent on the anointing of the Holy Spirit every time He performed a miracle.[33]

Jesus is God and man with two distinct natures existing in one person. Jesus remained as the head of the universe during His earthly life. He forever is the Creative Word who sustains and holds all things together.[34] Yet He emptied Himself[35] and made

Himself poor.[36] He possessed all the majesty of deity, performed all its functions, and enjoyed all its prerogatives. Yet, He was vulnerable to hunger, fatigue, pain, frustration, and embarrassment.

As God, Jesus displayed to us the fact that God's core identity is love expressed in humility, "If you have seen Me, you have seen the Father." Jesus' main identity was gained from His power and uniqueness as the Son of God. Satan sought to tempt Jesus with this because that is what motivates satan. If Jesus' core identity was in His power, then the incarnation would have been robbery or a denial of what was in His heart. Our culture, because it is earthly, unspiritual, and demonic,[37] places a high value on gaining our identity from emphasizing our uniqueness—because that is what satan does.

Jesus, as the sinless Son of God, never deserved to experience any of the "benefits" of the fall of man. In fact, He deserved the opposite. Yet He did not insist on His rights to live free from rejection, pain, and humiliation. He came incognito instead of in the glory He possessed, as was seen in the Mount of Transfiguration.[38]

GOD AS SERVANT

It was precisely because Jesus was in the form of God that He sought to give and serve.[39] What most expressed both His glory and His love was His humility. In His humiliation, He saw nothing un-Godlike in washing the feet of the people He created. In His mind, His servitude was expressing His true God-like self. He saw the lowliest tasks as opportunities to show who He was as the humble God. To serve is at the core of who God is.[40] If we desire to be godly, we must take on that same mindset.[41]

Jesus demonstrated for us that love is not self-absorbed, but rather absorbed in the good and ultimate welfare of others. He was not preoccupied with His own preeminence, but rather was consumed with the eventual exaltation of others. Jesus did not live for "now," He lived for eternity. If we allow that attitude to capture our hearts, we can live the humble lives of service He did. He was already rich from all eternity.[42]

Jesus made Himself nothing,[43] He made Himself of no reputation.[44] He willingly embraced shame and bore disgrace in coming as a *doulos,* a servant. This was a new dimension for Jesus who came as a servant without rights to honor. Jesus concealed His divine glory. This is the most profound incognito imaginable while maintaining the full power of God. Jesus hid His glory under the veil of humanity.

Jesus embraced a life of weakness, rejection, homelessness, poverty, weariness, shame, and pain. For love. If Jesus had faltered for even one moment, it would have affected our eternal destiny drastically. Jesus did not come down openly as the God of "jasper glory,"[45] but instead He came as the man who expressed this glory. He wanted to identify with us, not just dazzle us. He could not do this without becoming one of us.

We are by nature preoccupied with our image and being recognized for our good traits and our good deeds. Jesus willingly embraced a position where everyone totally underestimated Him and His abilities. When they saw Him, they saw nothing to distinguish Him. He was totally ordinary in every sense.[46] He embraced death on the Cross.[47] In His eternal form, He was immune to death. Now He would willingly become its victim. He embraced a type of death that involved indescribable physical pain and emotional shame. Dying on a cross was viewed as being under God's curse.[48]

God is love. The core definition of love: love gives. Love by definition is what is given, not what is gained. We are the reward of His suffering. His passion for God and people are first to Him above His own immediate well-being.[49] Jesus existed eternally as a servant. He did not become something that He was not already.[50]

Jesus was a servant when He came the first time to die, and He will be coming as a servant when He returns to be crowned as King. The eternal government of God is servanthood. When

Jesus takes the scroll in Revelation, He pledges the leadership of the earth forever to servant rulers who will perpetually wash the feet of others. When Jesus returns at the Second Coming, it will be all about love. He will gird Himself to serve His creation forever. As the reigning King, He loves to use His power to enrich the ones He loves.[51]

JESUS—THE FATHER'S STORY OF LOVE

Jesus loves to tell the Father's story so that He can make the character of the Father known.[52] Jesus is God's self-exposure. Jesus is God telling the Father's story. This is one of the grand reasons for the incarnation. Jesus is the expression of the Father. He said to see Him was to see the Father.[53] We would never have known about God's kindness without Jesus going to the Cross to demonstrate it to us. God is love and He desires a people He can express His love to forever.[54]

Jesus is God expressing Himself. Each Person in the Godhead expresses Himself through the other. Holy Spirit is behind the scenes manifesting power at the Word of the Son under the Father's authority. Jesus did not minister out of the resources of His deity but depended on the anointing of the Spirit.

The Father hides until the Son reveals Him and the Son hides until the Father reveals Him. No one within the Godhead tells His own story. They do not talk about Themselves. Each gives His part of this grand mystery of love. Jesus gives us the Spirit who is the great Friend of the Bridegroom preparing us for the wedding. The Father gives us to the Son. Then the Son gives everything back to the Father. Jesus trusts and depends on the Father and the Father the Son.

LOVE FOR JESUS: HUMILITY IS EXPRESSED THROUGH OUR SPEECH

Now, in the light of Jesus and His example of humility, let us revisit the things we opened the chapter with. In Philippians chapter 2, the Holy Spirit through the apostle Paul gives the believers at Philippi, and us as well, an exhortation to walk in humility as Jesus did.[55] What is interesting is how he models how that is to be fleshed out in real life. When Paul tells the Philippians they should walk in humility, he focuses on their need to "speak" with humility. Beloved, this is one of the most practical applications of loving Jesus. We must not hide our complaining under the guise of just being honest.[56] Love grows in us as we are moved by Jesus' humility as we see the story of how He treats us.[57]

To love God with all our soul is walked out best as we love Him with our unique personality in deep humility. This is expressed most dynamically by our speech. We set our heart to express ourselves and to communicate in a way that enhances not diminishes love. When Holy Spirit is grieved, we do not receive from Him in the same measure. What we say enhances or quenches our ability to love Jesus by the power of the Holy Spirit.[58]

Love is diminished by the fire released in wrong speech that affects our inner person. We renounce grumbling and speaking against one another knowing it hinders our ability to love Jesus.[59]

WHAT ABOUT WHEN WE ARE MISTREATED?

In the case of our being mistreated or enduring disappointments, we must interpret them according to truth as seen through Christ's eyes and example. Offense that comes from our disappointments can paralyze our spiritual life if we fall prey to blaming and accusing others—it hinders our walk with God. The past attacks our confidence: who we are—those loved by God; what we do—we love God by how we act out the play of life; and where we are going—our eternal destiny in God. Beloved, we must face disappointment God's way in order to be free to grow in love for God.[60]

We must entrust our enemies into the hands of Jesus' powerful and wise and loving leadership. To neglect this is to be diminished in our ability to respond to Jesus in love.[61] We must forget our "noble" sacrifices that tempt us to pride or to feel we deserve better treatment from God and others in our ministry and circumstances, thus undermining our gratitude for His goodness. We were once lost in the state of darkness,[62] but now we are the children of light. Jesus pointed out the danger of relating to Him based on how much we feel we deserve instead of with gratitude.[63]

Beloved, we must walk in humility and speak in humility if we are to love God with all of our soul.

In the next chapter, we will look at how we can love God with all of our mind.

CHAPTER 17

Loving God With All Your Mind

God created us to love Him in the four spheres of our life, which includes our heart (affections), soul (personality), mind (thoughts), and strength (resources), because He loves us this way.[1] We can only love God with all our heart by seeking to love Him with our soul, mind, and strength in practical ways.

When you hear the First Commandment referred to, most of the time it is quoted as loving God with all of our heart, or our affections. The problem is, as we looked at in the chapter on loving God with all of our heart, we cannot control our affections directly. We cannot just "choose" how we want to feel about something. We do play an active part, even the deciding part, on what our affections are going to be directed toward, but only indirectly. You cannot just will affection and emotion and then, within the next hour or two, there you have it.

You have to choose where you want your affections to lie, then you have to feed your mind accordingly, and later, based on your decisions, your affections are formed. Through the engaging of the mind—and that really is God's strategy—loving God with your intellect drives the transformation process.

We have to expose our emotions to the grace of God and to the power of the Holy Spirit, and when we do, our emotions come alive with wholehearted love. There is no greater delight, no greater spiritual reality than having our emotions bright with love. That is what all human beings crave; it is in our DNA.

Everyone in his or her heart of hearts desires to live in that bright place where our hearts are alive. The problem that most of us run into is that we mistakenly focus on the emotional side of it instead of directing our emotions through the setting of our mind; we just *wish* our emotions were different. We do not actually set them in a determined way according to the Word, and feed our emotions in a biblical way through our intellect.

So many wish they were red-hot in love with God, and when they are not they become discouraged and depressed; and because they have not been taught the biblical solution to the problem, they believe where they are living is normal and so they settle for living as second-class citizens in the Kingdom.

There is good news in the bridal paradigm—we do not have to live discouraged or depressed, and we do not have to live bored with a dull heart. We can follow the biblical pattern and see our emotions come alive in a bright, supernatural way under the anointing of the power of God. In this chapter, we are going to focus on what it means to love God with all of our mind.

Sphere 3: Love God With All of Our Mind

Loving God with all of our mind includes several different dynamics of our mind. First, we love God with our mind by meditating on the Word of God. Meditation on the Word is to our mind and emotions what fuel is to an automobile. You can purchase an expensive car, but if you never put any fuel in it, you are not going anywhere. You cannot drive a car without fuel and you cannot have a heart that is full of bright affections for God unless you fill your mind with regular loving meditation on God's Word. Though this is a non-negotiable, most believers never actually get around to this on a consistent basis.

Now, everyone who has been a believer for any length of time at all knows that, but knowing isn't the same as doing, and very few understand what all that entails and fewer still ever get around to actually meditating on His Word.

We as the Image-bearers were created to intimately know God as our Husband and to love Him with all of our hearts as His Bride. We will never walk in the reality of that truth unless we live a life of meditation on the Word. Get it? The devil will do anything and everything to keep us from meditating on the Word of God because he knows how our minds were designed to function. Without fuel, we are not going anywhere.

My dad was an over-the-road truck driver. As I grew up, I spent a lot of time around truck stops, truck terminals, and truck drivers. To be honest with you, most of the drivers I was around were a little "rough around the edges." Know what I mean? Many of them were social drinkers. I mean "really" social drinkers. Therefore, as I was growing up, I spent a lot of time looking up at, and sometimes looking down at, many of Dad's friends.

In that environment, I heard and learned a lot of "worldly" wisdom. I heard things like: "You can't understand the Bible," "It's always boring anyway," "I know I should read it, but I don't know where to start," "I'm too busy to read the Bible." Ever hear any of those before? You have? Did you hang out at truck stops?

You know what, those aren't just "wise" sayings from truck stops, are they? You hear those same statements repeated every day in bars, factories, or in high-rise office complexes no matter where you live. In fact, those same words are spoken in most churches all over this nation every week. Why do you think that is? Because the devil knows that if the Image-bearers open the Bible, read it, and meditate on it, over time their emotions will come alive, and they will love Jesus with all of their heart. And we can't have that now, can we? Get it? The devil does! That is why he preaches that party line so hard everywhere you go.

Another scheme of the enemy is to keep God's people running around with a Messianic complex trying to solve everybody else's problems—because after all, we are the only ones who know how to fix everyone's life, right? He has to keep us busy in a whirlwind of "good" activity so that we never actually stop and put fuel in the car, for he knows if we do....

Loving God Takes Time

In this present age, everything related to the Kingdom of God transpires in time and space. It is not about theory or concepts[2] because faith without corresponding action is ineffective.[3] If we desire to love God with all of our heart, then we have to respond to God by loving Him with all of our intellect, and we accomplish that through long and loving meditation on His Word.

What Does It Mean to Meditate

When I speak to people about the need to meditate, I get mixed responses because there is so much misunderstanding that abounds about what it means to meditate. One of the big misunderstandings is caused by the fact that there are so many different types of meditation. Buddhists meditate, Hindus meditate, and New Agers meditate. When I mention meditation, there are those who immediately think I am talking about one of those types of meditation. I am not.

It is important to remember that the devil is not a creator or an innovator: he is only an imitator, a counterfeiter, a perverter. He has never come up with anything new; he only corrupts and perverts what is already there. Just because there are false forms of meditation does not invalidate the true form of meditation. Instead, the fact there are false forms of meditation encourages me to pursue the true form of meditation.

Have you ever heard of someone being arrested and convicted for counterfeiting $3 bills? Of course not. Why? Because there are no real $3 bills. You can only counterfeit something that is authentic. Our emphasis should never be on the counterfeit; it should be on the authentic. Just because there are fake $100 bills does not mean that I will stop accepting a $100 bill someone offers me.

Yes, there are false and even dangerous forms of meditation. But, that does not deter me from pursuing the true, biblical form of meditation; in fact, it encourages me even more to go after the real thing.

I have been told that when bank tellers are being trained to recognize counterfeit money, they spend lots of time examining not the counterfeit, but the real thing. If you are familiar with the real thing, you have less chance of being fooled by the false. I do not spend excessive amounts of time examining what the devil is doing; instead, I focus all of my attention on what God is doing. When the devil tries to throw something fake in, it stands out like the proverbial sore thumb. So I do not want to spend any time examining the wrong ways to meditate; instead, I want us to take a few minutes looking at the right way to mediate.

Thus Saith the Lord—Meditate

One of the first verses that made a mark on my life after I became a believer was Joshua 1:8:

This Book of the Law shall not depart from your mouth, but you shall **meditate** *on it day and night, so that you may be careful to do according to all that is written in it. For then you will make your way prosperous, and then you will have good success.*[4]

I memorized that verse and it has done me good for well over 30 years.

God had raised up Moses to be the deliverer of Israel from their bondage in Egypt. Moses had facilitated the exodus so that the people of God could go out into the desert, where, as we saw in a previous chapter, God could "propose" to them. Now Moses had died, and Joshua was chosen by God to take over the leadership of Israel in Moses' stead to lead them over the Jordan into the Promised Land.[5]

The Lord tells Joshua:

Every place that the sole of your foot will tread upon I have given to you, just as I promised to Moses...No man shall be able to stand before you all the days of your life. Just as I was with Moses, so I will be with you. I will not leave you or forsake you. Be strong and courageous, for you shall cause this people to inherit the land that I swore to their fathers to give them. Only be strong and very courageous, being careful to do according to all the law that Moses My servant commanded you. Do not turn from it to the right hand or to the left, that you may have good success wherever you go.[6]

Amazing promises. God commits to Joshua that He would be with him in an obviously supernatural way just as He had been with Moses. Then Joshua is given a warning:

Being careful to do according to all the law that Moses My servant commanded you. Do not turn from it to the right hand or to the left, that you may have good success wherever you go.[7]

God says that the promise is contingent on Joshua keeping all the covenant stipulations that had been given through Moses. Heavy responsibility. The Lord gives specific directions to Joshua on how to fulfill God's will for his own life, his ministry, and as the leader of the nation of Israel's entrance into the Promised Land. Let's look at it:

This Book of the Law shall not depart from your mouth, but you shall meditate on it day and night, so that you may be careful to do according to all that is written in it. For then you will make your way prosperous, and then you will have good success. Have I not commanded you? Be strong and courageous. Do not be frightened, and do not be dismayed, for the Lord your God is with you wherever you go.[8]

God told Joshua that in order to have the courage to faithfully walk out God's plan for him, he had to keep the Word of God *in his mouth* day and night. If he did so, then the result would be that he would be divinely empowered to walk out all that God desired to do in and through him. The deciding factor, according to this passage, was not what God desired to do; it was what Joshua decided to do.

For Joshua to have God with him like He was with Moses—to be spiritually strong and courageous; spiritually prosperous, resulting in success; to walk free from fear and not be dismayed concerning the many obstacles that stood in his way; to experientially walk out having God in his life and ministry—then Joshua would have to faithfully respond to God's method of meditation and spiritual warfare.

Human nature is such that we all naturally think that if God wants something to happen, we can just sit back and it will fall into our laps like ripe apples off a tree. But alas, it isn't so. As mentioned previously, there is a biblical principle called the comparability of responsibility. God has His part and we have ours. We cannot do God's part and He will not do ours. We need to know and understand God's promises, but we must then respond appropriately in order to see them fulfilled in our lives.

OUR INHERITANCE: GOD'S POWER IN OUR HEART, MIND, AND MOUTH

God made a promise to the people of God. The author of Hebrews expressed it this way:

> *"This is the covenant* [or the promise] *that I will make with them after those days,"* declares the Lord: *"I will put my laws* [His Word] *on their hearts* [their emotions], *and write them on their minds* [their understanding]."[9]

God promises to write His Word on our heart and mind[10] as He wrote the Ten Commandments on tablets of stone.[11] God said that His desire was to put His desires on our emotions and to write them on our understanding. He writes them on our minds, or reveals them to our understanding by releasing a spirit of revelation to our mind until we progressively gain living understanding of His Word. We are promised enough insight to succeed in the assignment that God has given us in this life. God is not so much interested in us quoting Bible passages about what He wants us to do as He is in our understanding and personally embracing, at the heart level, why He wants us to do what He wants us doing.

Hebrews goes on to say that after God releases revelation about who He is and what He wants, God promises to empower our emotions until we are filled by the power of His Word with new holy desires. It is not enough to know what God wants. We have to want what God wants as well. We must share His desires.

In the Gospel bearing his name, Luke relates what happened when the risen Christ appeared to a couple of His disciples on the road to Emmaus. After Jesus appeared to them, they share with us the result of that encounter: *"Did not our hearts burn within us while He talked to us on the road, while He opened to us the Scriptures?"*[12] Then Dr. Luke adds, *"**Then** He opened their minds to understand the Scriptures."*[13]

God writes His Word on our heart as we walk with Him meditating on His Word. Life comes when we live it. We are to live by, or be spiritually healthy in our heart by, feeding on God's Word, which is the holy transcript of His heart. Our heart lives and becomes strong and healthy by feeding on God's Word in spirit and in truth. The opposite is also true. Our heart dies and becomes weak and sickly when we neglect regularly feeding on God's Word in the context of a living, loving, vital relationship with God Himself. Without fuel…

The most substantial way in which we feed our spirit and bolster our spiritual strength is by feeding on God's Word in spirit and truth. There is no set method in which to do this because Christianity is not a belief system, or a religious list of dos and don'ts; it's a relationship. So each person will walk it out a little differently, based on who he is and the depth of his relationship with the Lord. However, there are some foundational principles that are necessary to everyone.

Many today are in the spiritual ICU with a sick heart and a diminished spiritual appetite. The reason is that they do not relate to God as a Person and they do not meditate on His Word rightly and regularly. When we do it right, the voice of the Spirit and the Word is stronger than the voice of sinful lust, or the spiritual obstacles that would like to take us out of our race. We do not live by the things of this earth alone; we have to feed on every word that comes from the mouth of God.[14]

A lifestyle of prayer, fasting, meditation on the Word, and a life of obedience positions our heart before God to freely receive all that He desires to give us. It is important, however, that we understand that although these activities are important, they do not earn us God's favor or blessing. It is never God *has to;* it is always we *get to.*

I like to say it this way. We take our cold hearts (we all naturally have cold hearts), and we faithfully place them before the bonfire of God's Presence, His burning heart, by seeking Him in the Word in spirit and truth. The result—our cold hearts thaw and come alive in His Presence. Not because of some inherent goodness in our hearts, but because any old ice cube will melt if you place it before the fire. Get it?

God opens His Word to us progressively, in small portions, in direct proportion to the amount of *time* we feed our spirit on His Word. If you want to thaw quicker, then spend more time before the fire!

God's Word has to be in our mouth as well as in our heart.[15] Why? Because for the promises of God to be fulfilled in our lives, we have to meditate on His Word day and night. One of the main ways we meditate on God's Word is by saying it. The Hebrew word translated *meditate* in Joshua 1:8 means to muse, to speak with oneself, murmuring in a low voice, growl (like a lion over his prey), groan or moan (like a dove), sigh, utter, soliloquize, meditate, to read syllable by syllable, to contemplate, imagine, the muttering of enchanters, to sing.

If we are limited to meditation based on written material, i.e., a piece of paper, notebook, flashcard, or a book, if we leave home without it, we are up the creek without a paddle. Or if we are driving a car, peddling a bike, climbing a ladder, etc., you get the picture, we cannot access the written material even if we have it with us. However, if we have it memorized, then we can speak it, sing it, mutter it under our breath, think about it, pray it, etc. That is why this exhortation in Joshua is so important for meditation.

The second aspect about meditation that I have found helpful is the aspect of turning the verse or verses I am musing over into conversation with the Author! Remember, the basic premise of the bridal paradigm of the Kingdom of God is that everything God does is relationally based. He wants to be our Husband, not just our Master.[16]

ENCOUNTERING GOD BY PRAY-READING THE WORD

Well then, how do we acquire a thawed heart, a burning heart? Simply by daily relating in a healthy way with the Living Word through the written Word. Jesus said, *"You search the Scriptures* [Bible study] *because you think that in them you have life; and it is they that bear witness about Me, yet you refuse to come to Me* [and dialogue with Me like I am a real Person] *that you might have life."*[17]

When I first became a Christian, one of the first things that I was told to do was to study the Bible. And study it I did. In the beginning, the words on the pages jumped off at me. After awhile, however, I found that there were days, and then weeks, when the Bible became dry and dusty. I still believed it was true, but it just was not "happening" for me anymore. Have you ever been there?

I found that it is not enough to study the Word alone. We must also give our heart to God and receive from Him as we study. You see, Bible study must result in an active dialogue, or a vital relationship in our heart with God. To hear many tell it, the Christian walk is all about the Father, Son, and Holy Book. However, the Book is not the end; it is the means to the end—Jesus.

The apostle Paul who authored over half of the New Testament warns us that the letter without a proper relationship actually kills instead of bringing life.[18] Scripture is meant, among other things, to give us the conversational material for our prayer life. It creates the language that our heart uses to relate with God. Incorporating the Word into our prayer language with God makes prayer both easy and enjoyable.

We must actually speak the Word audibly back to God and against satan in response to his attacks on our lives. Many believers believe the Word but they do not follow through by actually speaking the Word back to God or against satan. If they do speak it at all, they only speak it to other believers. The power of God's love touches us deepest as we declare it not just to each other, but also back to God. We are most moved by His love as we thank Him for the love that He declares over us.

I want to look at two broad categories of truth related to meditating on the Scriptures or what I call pray-reading the Word. These are not all-inclusive, but they cover the majority of the Scriptures.

PRAY-READING

The first category I want to look at are Scriptures that focus on *promises* that we are to believe in God's Word. For example, Scriptures that declare that God loves us, forgives us, leads us, protects us, or provides for us. Let's use these two passages:

But God shows His love for us in that while we were still sinners, Christ died for us.[19]

Give and it will be given to you. Good measure, pressed down, shaken together, running over, will be put into your lap. For with the measure you use it will be measured back to you.[20]

We take the Scriptures and we actively dialogue with God by praying or speaking the promises that we are to believe from His Word. This is one of the most effective forms of spiritual warfare as we speak these truths against satan's attack on our lives.

First, we thank God for the truths we are considering. We turn these truths into simple declarations of thanksgiving or trust in the Lord. For example, we declare, "Thank You, Lord, that You love me and have forgiven me. I trust that You have promised that You would lead, provide, and protect me."

Then, we ask God to reveal, or release deeper revelation concerning these particular truths to us.[21] For example, pray, "Father, please reveal to me the certainty of Your provision, or how much You love me, forgive me, or how I have ravished Your heart." Alternatively, "Father, would You release Your promised guidance, provision, and protection, etc."

The second category of Scriptures are those that focus on *exhorting* us to obey God's Word. For example, Scriptures that command us to bridle our tongue, serve others, or give of our time and money to God. We actively dialogue with God by praying and speaking truths back to Him that exhort us to obey His Word. This is spiritual warfare. We also speak these truths against satan's attacks on our lives.

First, we commit ourselves to obey God in the specific way(s) set forth in a biblical person or passage. We make simple declarations of our resolve to obey the Word or imitate the faith of the godly.

...You shall love the Lord your God with all your heart and with all your soul and with all your mind.[22]

For we all stumble in many ways. And if anyone does not stumble in what he says, he is a perfect man, able also to bridle his whole body.[23]

For example, you might declare, "Father, I set my heart to love You and obey You with my speech, time, and money, etc." Or, "I set my heart to love You like David or to endure hardship like Paul." "I set my heart to pray like Daniel or do miracles like Paul in the Book of Acts."

Second, we ask God to empower us to obey that particular truth or to imitate the godly examples of people in Scripture. Ask God for His help to give you wisdom, motivation, and power to obey in specific areas. For example, pray, "Father, help me to love You, to bridle my speech, or use my time and money in full obedience." Or, "Father, I resolve to love You more. Give me power to love You like David." Or, "Father, would You lead me away from temptation,"[24] or "Deliver me from the works of the evil one."[25]

THE POWER OF GOD'S WORD IN SPIRITUAL WARFARE

One last aspect I want to emphasize before we move on is the principle that the Holy Spirit hovers and waits to move in power wherever the Word is spoken by those in covenant with the Father.

*The earth was without form and void, and darkness was over the face of the deep. And the Spirit of God was **hovering** over the face of the waters. God **said**, "Let there be **light**," and there was **light**.*[26]

The Scriptures tell us that Jesus creates, sustains, and governs everything under the Father's authority by speaking God's Word.[27] Jesus was the One who spoke God's Word to create in Genesis chapter 1. We find the phrase, *"And God said"* ten times[28] along with *"Let there be…"* eight times.[29] We see the Spirit's work in the phrase, *"It was so"* seven times[30] and *"God made"* seven times.[31]

Jesus, as the God-Man, gave us a model of how to do spiritual warfare as He spoke the Word in power to drive satan back. When Jesus was tempted in the wilderness, He used the Word to strike like a sword cutting into satan's domain. This was a clash of powers that sent satan reeling into retreat. Satan had never confronted a Man saturated in God's Word and moving in such authority.[32] When we speak the Word to satan, anointed by God's Spirit, then it strikes him as a sharp sword that injures his domain.[33]

Beloved, we must fill our hearts with the Word as part of our daily lifestyle as well as use the Word in an intentional way during times of temptation or oppression. When we fill our heart with His Word, we receive divine strength; and then when we use the Word, it is like bullets out of a gun. One of the main keys to successful spiritual warfare is a lifestyle of meditating and speaking God's Word, first to God in our daily conversation with Him and then to the enemy when he attacks us.

So how do we love God with our mind? We fill our minds with long and loving meditation on God's Word, we turn that Word into conversation with a real and living Person, and we resist putting anything in our minds that weakens or diminishes our love for Jesus and quenches the Spirit.

In the next chapter, we will look at how we can love God with all of our strength.

CHAPTER 18

Loving God With All Your Strength

In the last couple of chapters we have looked at how God desires us, as the Image-bearers, as His Bride, to love Him with the four spheres of our lives—with all of our heart, which means with all of our affections; with all of our soul, which means with all of who we are in the uniqueness of our personality; and with all of our mind, which means with all of our thoughts. In this chapter, we will examine how we are to love Him with all of our strength, which means with all of our resources, with all that we have.

SPHERE 4: LOVING GOD WITH ALL OUR STRENGTH

There is an old axiom that says, "God doesn't have your heart until He has your wallet." There is gold in them there hills! Jesus said, *"If you love Me, you will keep My commandments."*[1] Many erroneously teach this verse as a command: "You have to prove you love Me by keeping My commandments." In other words— here comes an English grammar lesson—they present the phrase "you will keep" as an imperative, or a command.

The Greek verb here is not an imperative, or a command; rather, it is future indicative. That means the verb phrase "you will keep" is a guaranteed event because of the fact of the love: "If you do love Me, it is a guaranteed money-in-the-bank fact that you will demonstrate that love by keeping My commandments." The Greek verb here means particularly to watch, observe attentively, keep the eyes fixed upon, keeping for the fulfillment of the prophecy. Figuratively, to obey, observe, keep, fulfill a duty, precept, law, custom, or custom meaning to perform watchfully, vigilantly.[2]

Let me restate it using the wallet example. Because you love God, it is a given that you will willingly submit your resources to Him, which is the proof, the result of your real love. If you love Jesus with all your strength, then it is a given that you will submit your resources to Him. Your resources can be defined as your time, money, talents, reputation, and influence. Because we love God, we use our resources, in relationship with the Spirit, in a way that causes our love to grow.

We love Him with all our strength as we pursue Him in prayer *with* fasting. Fasting involves investing our natural strength in our pursuit of loving Jesus more. This is one of the main spiritual rationales behind why we fast unto the Lord.

We voluntarily fast in the area of our strengths, especially related to the five activities listed in Matthew 6:1-23. These five areas express *voluntary* weakness because we desire to invest our natural strengths—our time, money, energy, reputation, etc.—into the hands of the Spirit as a demonstration of our love for Jesus. Remember, we do not legalistically work in order to earn anything from God. Instead, we lovingly volunteer to align ourselves with the things Jesus asks of us so that we are in a position to receive from Him what He desires to give us.

In the verses referenced in Matthew, Jesus describes five grace-releasing activities that position us to receive more. We serve and give through our charitable deeds: our giving of our loving service and money;[3] through our prayer life;[4] through blessing our adversaries, by forgiving them—giving them a gift that they do not deserve, like Jesus forgave us, a gift we did not deserve;[5] and by fasting.[6]

The normal way we use our strengths is in order to increase our personal comfort, wealth, and honor. But when we choose to live a fasted lifestyle, we lay down our natural strengths as an offering of voluntary weakness, trusting God to return our strength to us in a way that enriches us and transforms us with meekness.[7] Therefore, our devotional lives are the means of our appropriating free grace, not of earning it. In these five areas we position our "cold heart" before the "bonfire of God's enabling grace" so as to receive the Spirit's empowerment.

LOVING GOD REQUIRES ALL OUR STRENGTH

Loving God with all our heart requires that we love Him with all our strength. Fasting works to both express our love to Jesus and at the same time positions us to receive the Spirit's power to love Him more. Our capacity to love Jesus is enhanced by engaging with the Spirit through our living a fasted lifestyle. We do not fast to gain influence with others but so we can position ourselves to receive power to fully love God.

The anointing to love God is our greatest possession. It takes God to love God. It takes the anointing of the Spirit to enable our hearts to receive God's love and to enable us to return our love to Him. The greatest reward of being loved is found in our receiving the enablement to love. It is the supernatural ability to feel love for Jesus. The joy of lovesickness mixed with our loyal obedience frees us from the burnout of spiritual boredom.[8]

The grace of fasting is God's gift to us and is one practical way we can posture our heart to experience God's power to love Jesus more. Fasting is not an optional part of New Testament Christianity. So many treat fasting as if it is just one more item on the buffet that we can choose or ignore. God gives more to us according to our hunger for Him. Therefore, in a real way fasting makes us hungry. For real. I like to say it this way: some people eat because they are hungry, and some people eat in order to get hungry.

Just as fasting makes our natural hunger grow, it also helps our spiritual hunger grow faster as well.[9] If we do not have something to die for, we do not have anything to live for. To have something to die for means there is a cause worth investing all our strength and resources into. Jesus loves His Father with all His strength.[10] The 24 elders imitate Jesus' love for God by casting their rewards before the Father.[11] We can follow their example, and the good news is, it's legal!

RECEIVE GRACE: VOLUNTARY WEAKNESS

Fasting is a call for us to embrace voluntarily weakness unto more than just hunger. We fast because we are hungry to experience more of God's Presence. As I referenced earlier, Jesus points us toward five expressions of voluntary weakness in which we can invest our natural strengths—food, time, money, words, energy, and influence—in our relationship with Jesus.[12]

We embrace weakness, in the voluntary laying down of our natural resources, to position ourselves to receive supernatural strength from the Spirit. God made something so simple—such as praying and not eating—so very powerful. Paul was not referring to moral weakness due to failure but voluntary weakness due to godly choices.[13]

We normally use our strength and resources to increase our own comfort, wealth, and honor. By the fasted lifestyle, we bring our natural strengths to God as we express our love to Him and trust Him to return our strength to us in a way that transforms our heart and blesses our circumstances, more than we would have experienced had we done it ourselves.

Paul received a divine revelation that embracing voluntary weakness was the doorway into more of God's power. In many circles today, there is much discussion about walking in "perfected power," but little time is given to the doorway into that perfected power—the pathway of weakness.[14] A lifestyle of voluntary weakness includes prayer, fasting, and simplified living, so that we would have more money to seed into the Kingdom, as well as joyfully embracing persecution and reproach for Jesus' sake. The Kingdom paradox is that He releases spiritual power in the context of natural weakness.

FIVE EXPRESSIONS OF THE FASTED LIFESTYLE

In the Sermon on the Mount, Jesus taught His disciples (that's us) five specific ways to embrace voluntary weakness. He embraced these in His life as did all the great men and women of God in the Bible including Moses, Elijah, John the Baptist, and Paul. The five expressions of the fasted lifestyle include giving, serving, praying (with the Word), blessing our enemies, and fasting food. Each is a form of fasting in that we are to embrace weakness, declaring to God that we acknowledge that we derive our strength from Him and therefore feel perfectly safe to offer it back up to Him, trusting Him to make up the difference.

In giving, we fast our money or our financial strength and security. In serving and prayer, we fast our time and energy by investing it in seeking God and helping others. In giving up food, we fast our physical, emotional, and mental strength. In blessing our enemies, we fast our right to use our words against others and our reputation. We do all this as an expression of our wholehearted, bridal love for Jesus and in our quest to position ourselves to receive more spiritual power to love Him. The fasted lifestyle is a long-term commitment to these five expressions.

GIVING MONEY: OUR FINANCIAL STRENGTH

Jesus said:

*But when you **give to the needy**, do not let your left hand know what your right hand is doing, so that your giving may be in secret. And your Father who sees in secret will **reward you**.*[15]

Do not lay up treasures on earth, but lay up for yourselves treasures in heaven. For where your treasure is, there your heart will be also. No one can serve two masters, for either he will hate the one and love the other, or he will be devoted to the one and despise the other. You cannot serve God and money.[16]

In this text, Jesus is referring to giving to the needy and acts of servanthood as two expressions of fasting. Our money is a significant part of our financial and social strength. When we give some of our money away to build God's Kingdom, our personal resource base becomes weaker as we fast our financial strength. This is an expression of our love for Jesus and others, as we trust God to multiply the money we give away back to us. Jesus urges us all to use money now to lay up for ourselves treasures in heaven.[17] In the process, our hearts grow in love for Jesus, as we are freed from our dependence and trust in money. It is impossible to love God and money.[18]

Jesus said that the widow who gave her last two mites showed much more love for God than those who gave much more money but at less of a personal sacrifice.[19] Giving money requires emotional dynamics that force us to wrestle with our deep-seated covetousness and our fear of living in lack as we demonstrate our love for Jesus.

King David, the man after God's own heart, set his heart to live radically by loving God with the proper use of his money.[20] David gave over $100 billion (according to today's prices) to God's house out of his personal finances. One talent equals about 75 pounds (1200 ounces). At $800 an ounce, a talent of gold would be worth about $1,000,000. Thus, 100,000 talents of gold would be worth about $100 billion.

We give our money, or our financial strength, to express our devotion and love to Jesus. Love is not minimized because we believe that God promises to give us more money when we give our money to Him. God told Israel, *"Return to Me, and I will return to you....Bring the full tithe...put Me to the test, says the Lord of hosts, if I will not open the windows of heaven for you and pour down for you a blessing...*[21]

When Israel withheld their money from the Lord, they were demonstrating their lack of love for their Father.[22] The Lord told Moses to ask people to give money for the construction of a worship sanctuary so that He could dwell in their midst.[23] True bridal love does not see the giving of money as a sacrifice because lovers see love as the goal, not money.

SERVING PEOPLE: OUR STRENGTH IN TIME AND ENERGY

Serving others is another aspect involved in our giving to the needy. In serving others, we are investing our time and energy to partner with God to see His purpose fulfilled in the lives of others that could have legitimately been used to further our own interests. We show our love to Jesus by serving the saints and in the serving of others, and when we do, we find that we come face to face with the Servant of all. He wants us to encounter Him in serving others, for service is where that encounter takes place.[24] You will find a portion of Jesus in serving others that cannot be found in any other way.

PRAYING: OUR STRENGTH IN TIME AND EMOTIONS

Jesus made an astounding declaration:

But when you pray, go into your room and shut the door and pray to your Father who is in secret. And your Father who sees in secret will reward you.[25]

Prayer and reading the Word is a form of voluntary weakness because we are fasting our time and emotions.[26] When we invest time in prayer, we are passing up opportunities to network, socialize, or be entertained. In prayer, we fast our emotional energy as we pour ourselves out, interceding for God's Kingdom blessing to fall on others. In fasting our time, we are entrusting ourselves to the Lord for our promotion, instead of working to promote ourselves.

Instead of living like the world, using all of our time to seek our own comfort and success, we sit in a room praying to an invisible God, telling Him what He tells us to tell Him, knowing full well that sometimes He delays His response to us as we seek to love Him and entreat Him to release blessing on others. We position our cold heart before the bonfire of God's grace to receive the Spirit's empowerment. Beloved, the most needed and less heeded exhortation that Jesus gave to help the Church prepare for the endtimes is to "watch" or develop a heart connection with the Spirit in prayer.[27] If we have grace for prayer, we will have courage and direction.[28]

FORGIVING AND BLESSING OUR ENEMIES

One of the best indicators of where we stand in loving God with all our heart is in the area of loving and forgiving those who have hurt us. If we love God, it is a given that we will forgive and bless our enemies.[29] Forgiving and blessing our enemies is a form of fasting related to our words and relationships; we fast our words and reputation by refusing to come to our own defense.

Instead of using our right to choose and use our words to defend and promote ourselves, the Lord calls us to restrain our speech and trust Him to fight our battles. We actively bless our enemies by refraining from speaking words to expose our enemy as we defend our position and gain the sympathy and support of others. An enemy in the most general sense is one who blocks us from achieving our goals. Enemies are those who hinder our plans, in our estimation, and cause us to lose honor, time, money, and relationships. This loss is often real and painful.

This includes fasting our reputation as well. A good reputation is a significant part of our life, strength, and resource that can be used to influence others. When we fast our reputation, we are showing our love to Jesus by obeying Him and gaining our "higher" identity and comfort from God instead of people. When we bless our enemies, we fast some of the social strength (and satisfaction) we would normally gain from fighting back. We fast from defending our reputation, and trust the Lord to fight for us when we are silent. In what I call "bridal" silence, we are committing ourselves to God, trusting Him to answer for us. This is by far the most difficult form of fasting.[30]

FASTING FOOD: OUR STRENGTH PHYSICALLY AND MENTALLY

Now we come to one of the most controversial subjects throughout the whole Body of Christ—the fasting of food. Fasting is something that is accepted and commended if you believe it or talk about it, but is very disruptive on many levels if you actually do it. It is important to remember that Jesus never said "if" you fast—He said "when" you fast.[31]

Fasting or abstaining from food is more about our voluntarily embracing physical, emotional, and mental weakness than it is about hunger. When we offer up our physical strength to God, we often miss opportunities to build our personal success. When we are fasting, our mental processes are often blurry, our body becomes weak, our communication skills are feeble, and our memory is foggy.[32] At first, these things may seem to be liabilities, but not when they are contrasted with the alternatives. Overindulging in even legitimate physical appetites often quenches the Spirit's activity in our hearts and lives. Lawful, God-given pleasures often will dull our spirits if they are allowed to reach a point of excess. It is sin to let any pleasure become more important to us than our bridal love for God.

Many people are hindered by the fear of fasting; it paralyzes them. Actually though, the fear of fasting is worse than the fasting itself. Once the choice is made, one of the major hurdles to be overcome is removed. Fasting is a spiritual discipline that requires that we deny ourselves various legitimate pleasures that are not sinful in themselves, but neither do they enhance our life in the Spirit. Most people overindulge in the natural, permissible pleasures of recreation, abundant food, comfort, and money.

The Internal Rewards of Fasting

The Father rewards us when we fast in two different ways, internally and externally. The internal benefit includes the increase of our heart's capacity to encounter Him. The external benefits include our circumstances changing and being blessed. Fasting also greatly impacts our eternal rewards. Fasting tenderizes and sensitizes our hearts over time to receive greater grace to love Jesus more. We love Him with new focus, consistency, and intensity, with a new zeal for righteousness. John the Baptist was the greatest man ever born.[33] His greatness was not because of miracles in his ministry,[34] but rather because of his obedience and intimacy cultivated in a fasted lifestyle.

It should be pointed out that even though we engage in a fasted lifestyle, that does not guarantee that our problems will just disappear. Rather, we are transformed so we can see them in the divine perspective, which frees us up to be preoccupied with loving Jesus instead of being focused on our problems. As the Spirit reveals to us the big picture of God and eternity, we become increasingly freed from being unhealthily preoccupied with our temporal circumstances.

When we mix fasting with prayer (the power twins), it spiritually positions us to receive deliverance from our various sinful addictions (which we all have). Again, as I stated before, we do not earn freedom; rather, we position ourselves before God in a better posture to receive what He is offering. God has offered grace, through fasting, as a means for pulling down demonic strongholds in our mind.[35]

Some of the most common sins that beset people, even many Christian people, include bondage to pornography, immorality, anger, alcohol, drugs, and different eating disorders, either eating too much or too little. Isaiah exhorts us to fast to *"loose the bands of wickedness,"*[36] that we might be freed from sinful behaviors to which we are addicted. Strongholds are demonically energized; they are an established territory in our lives that we have given satan the right to hold, either through our sin or that of the generations before us.

PRACTICAL SUGGESTIONS

Fasting is basic to the Christian life—it really is Christianity 101. Some mistakenly see fasting as radical, advanced Christianity and therefore as optional. There is no such thing as biblical New Testament Christianity that does not include fasting. I urge all to fast at least one day a week. In our finances, we should give beyond a tithe and out of our surplus—we should give until we feel the cost of giving. We must serve others and bless—love—our enemies.

I encourage you to establish a personal Bible study plan. If you have one already, great. A majority of believers do not have any sort of plan when it comes to studying the Bible. If you do not have a plan, may I suggest one for you? I suggest reading ten chapters of the New Testament six days a week; if you follow this plan, you will read through the entire New Testament each month.

Develop a personal prayer list to help you to focus in prayer. Pray for breakthrough for your heart in receiving more grace to love Jesus,[37] and ask for direction for your life and for revelation of the Word.[38]

Many believers diminish their life in God in the evenings and weekends then seek to recover spiritual ground during the day. The evenings are the time when most spiritual losses take place and spiritual ground is given up. We must not continually take one step forward and one step back. The territory that we gain in spiritual war can be lost again through our own neglect or sin.

CHAPTER 19

The Relationship of the First Commandment to the Second

We have been looking at how we can love God, God's way. As I have referred to earlier, there are several arguments that I hear when I teach on the importance of the First Commandment. One is that many believe in some sort of "call" to one commandment or the other, such as, "I'm an outer court, second commandment person." As we have seen, that just is not so. Everyone is *called* to the First Commandment and to *do* the Second Commandment. The question is not whether people are inner court or outer court oriented; it is whether or not they understand God's priorities and how they function together. In this chapter, we will look at that.

THE TWO MOST IMPORTANT COMMANDMENTS

"Teacher, which is the great commandment in the Law?" He said to him, "You shall love the Lord your God with all your heart and with all your soul and with all your mind. This is the great and first commandment. A second is like it: You shall love your neighbor as yourself. On these two commandments depend all the Law and the Prophets" (Matthew 22:36-40).

One of the foundational premises of the bridal paradigm of the Kingdom of God is this: people who love Jesus will love others much more. It is impossible to love Jesus and not love people more.[1] The greatest anointing of the Spirit is offered to us as we walk out the two great commandments by loving Jesus with all our heart and our neighbor as ourselves.

As we looked at earlier, there are 316 commandments in the Torah. Jesus didn't come to do away with any of them.[2] However, He did prioritize them. Dr. Bob Jones Sr. used to say, "You can do what you ought to do. Responsibilities never conflict." What he meant was that we all have to do what we have to do. The problem is, of all the things we have to do, which one do we do first? The real issue is prioritization. Jesus recognized that, so He told us that only one of His commandments is the great and first commandment. Let's do the math on that. If one commandment is 1 and *has* to be 1, then if it is 2, 3, or 316, it isn't 1 any longer. At that point, not only is that commandment messed up, but every other commandment is messed up as well. The First Commandment has to be first, or everything is upside down.

If the First Commandment is first, then God is first. If any other commandment is first, then that commandment has become an idol. More precisely, to put what Jesus said is the Second Commandment in first place is to make our ministry an idol in our heart. We are to love Jesus, and then out of the overflow of loving Him, we love and serve others. Even serving Jesus cannot be put in front of loving Jesus. First things first. Keep the main thing, the main thing.

Jesus answered the question presented to Him concerning which was the greatest commandment by quoting Deuteronomy 6:5, *"You shall love the Lord your God with all your heart and with all your soul and with all your might."* In doing so, He added three new ideas. First, that loving God is the first and greatest thing. Second, that loving people is like loving God. Third, the purpose of God as seen in Scripture hangs or originates from these commandments—in the right order.

REVIEW: THE FOUR STAGES OF LOVE

The first stage of love is our receiving the revelation of God's love for us.[3] Knowing how God feels about us, as our Father and Bridegroom, is the foundational truth that equips us to properly respond by loving God.[4] The second stage is our receiving an impartation from the Holy Spirit of the Father's love for Jesus. This anointing is qualitative and not quantitative. It takes God's power to love God.[5]

The third stage of love is us loving ourselves in the grace of God. We can only love our neighbor as we love ourselves in the grace of God, which is only possible as we know who we are in Christ[6] along with rejoicing in who God has made us to be. This means we are thankful for our personality, giftings, callings, physical features, etc.[7] Remember, agreeing with God about our value is far different from loving ourselves in a selfish way. It is as we get our eyes off others (envy) and off our failures (condemnation) that we can value, and yes even love, who God has made us to be.

The fourth stage is that we end up loving others. When we are loving others as God loves them, it is the greatest work of the Spirit and is the ultimate proof of His Presence and work in our heart and life. As we love God and ourselves, we automatically overflow in love for others. It is the visible measurement of our invisible love for God.[8]

LOVING OUR NEIGHBOR IS "LIKE" LOVING GOD

"And a second is like it: You shall love your neighbor as yourself."[9] First, loving God flows from regularly encountering God's love for us. So does loving others. Without an ongoing encounter with the love of God, the well of love for others will dry up.[10] Second, to walk in genuine love, as defined by God, is much more than sentimentalism. We must consciously seek to love Jesus with *all* our heart, mind, soul, and strength. It is the same with loving others. It is not just a nice little ideal. We have

to consciously seek to be a vessel of honor in regard to loving and serving others. Third, to walk in love requires the Spirit's power to energize us by regularly having our emotions stirred and strengthened by the subtle impressions of the Spirit. Christianity is an ongoing encounter of love with a Person.[11] Likewise, we need the Spirit's anointing and assistance if we are to love others as we are called to.

Only when we wholeheartedly love Jesus and ourselves are we able to consistently overflow in a life of love for others. We are energized in a way that sustains true compassion by the gratitude and joy of being loved by God. We must love God first and ourselves second if we ever hope to attain a proper love for our neighbor. Again, let me emphasize, we must love ourselves first to have power and energy to love others. We can only love our neighbor in the overflow of loving God. For only in being loved by God and in loving God can we properly love others.

These truths really do change everything. Hearing this, and saying yes to it, demands that we pursue a comprehensive reordering of how we think and how we process life. We are, as fallen spiritual beings, by nature self-consumed, so it takes the power of the Spirit to walk this out. Loving God and loving ourselves are bound up as one; they cannot be separated. We will only properly value others in the overflow of seeing how valuable God is and how valuable we are to God. The Second Commandment never stands by itself. In the few instances where it appears to, this is because its connection to the First Commandment is assumed.

Many mistakenly think that we are called to love others instead of ourselves. This is both incorrect and impossible. We are to love others *as* we love ourselves by using the same standard in measuring love for others as we use for ourselves. We do this by seeking our neighbors' benefit *as* or "with the same focus and energy" as we seek that for ourselves. For example, we are to seek for more money and blessing so we can give more. In this way,

God's generosity is manifest both *to* us and then subsequently *through* us.

When we love others as we love ourselves, we will recognize and value their longing for significance, acceptance, and success as being as important as our own. Since everyone is an Image-bearer, created in God's image, they deserve to receive unfeigned love from us, just as we receive unfeigned love from God. We owe others an encounter with the love of God through us.

Moreover, while we are committed to and involved in demonstrating a life of love and service to others, we are not to make the mistake of dismissing our responsibility to love ourselves—we are rather to enhance it by loving others with new depth. We experience the deepest measures of God's tender compassion as we show it to others. This radical command touches the very core of our being. This command also many times exposes a deep root system of sin within us. As we seek to love people as ourselves, we often run right smack into the wall of our own sin and spiritual lack.

Love Is the Source and Goal

Love is the source and goal of the Law and Prophets. When Jesus stated that, "On these two commandments hang the Law and Prophets," He was emphasizing their importance and how connected they are to each other and to God's eternal purposes for His Kingdom. God's purposes, as declared in the Law and Prophets, depend or hang like a bucket on a rope on love. Love is the source behind all of God's eternal purposes.[12]

Our love for God and the focus for our lives out of the Scriptures are fulfilled as we walk out a life of love toward others. Love empowers the practical expression of what the teaching in the Law and the Prophets really mean.[13] The apostle Paul gives us more insight into love when he exhorts us to offer it from a pure heart, which means that we love others out of a motive to enrich others without seeking personal benefit, and from a good conscience that is free from condemnation,[14] and from sincere faith that stands steady in difficult circumstances.[15]

Let me summarize: love is both the goal[16] and the source of the Law and Prophets. In other words, all of God's Kingdom purposes in the Scripture hang on these two great commandments. To properly understand the "Golden Rule," we must see it in the context of the Sermon on the Mount, which calls everyone to an all-consuming bridal covenant relationship with God. In this passage, Jesus taught us that the Father gives good things to those who ask in prayer. Next, He said, "Therefore, whatever you want men to do to you, do also to them." In other words, this commandment is given in context to the call to prayer.[17]

Our call as the Bride of Christ to walk in love is given in context of God releasing His supernatural provision to us by prayer. The foundation of this commandment is a revelation of the Father's love resulting in a prayer life based on trusting His leadership. An important aspect in loving people is seen in embracing a lifestyle of prayer and fasting so that we are prepared to release more of the power of the Spirit to them. The life of John the Baptist, Elijah, Paul, and the apostles testifies to this.

Love is rightly focused on meeting people's physical needs with food and clothing. However, do not confuse this as being the same as secular good works. The difference is that we, as believers, are to remember that people are eternal spiritual beings; they need more than having their physical needs meet. The God-kind of love requires more than sentimental humanism that is content to meet people's physical or emotional needs apart from bringing them into a relationship with Jesus. Our allegiance to Jesus provides us the standard and source to be properly motivated and energized in our service of love. One of the main core issues at the end of the age will be in how love is defined. We must define and demonstrate love on God's terms, not by the humanistic culture that seeks love without reference to obedience to God's Word. The true definition of love and good works is found in our allegiance to Jesus.

God is not interested in giving love simply for the giving's sake. God loves the world,[18] and He gave His unique Son to demonstrate His love for them. But He still expects that the recipients of His love respond by believing, receiving, and walking out His purposes for their lives.[19] God uses love to awaken the human heart to the truth about Jesus, which meets their greater eternal need. His desire is always all about producing gratitude to God and a love for truth in them. Demonstrations of God's love should always draw people to truth and not to us, providing for them the opportunity for their greater eternal need to be met in a personal encounter with the Person of the eternal Bridegroom—Jesus. Secular humanism is content to help people without meeting their deeper spiritual need. We, as the Bride of Christ, demonstrate our love for God as we seek to enrich others on Jesus' terms.

THE SUPREME VALUE OF LOVE: IT IS THE ONLY THING THAT LASTS

The supreme value of love can only be understood when it is seen in context of the eternal realm of the judgment seat of Christ.[20] The Holy Spirit had Paul emphasize that all believers will give an account of their life and ministry to God.[21] What good is it if we give people food, shelter, and clothing, and meet all their earthly needs and wants, if at the end of their life, they die and enter into an eternal separation from God? Duh! We have to keep the big picture in mind—there is a purpose in what we do and how we do it.

The character of love[22] is the eternal nature of God, which is holiness. Paul gives us the essence of love as patient—by not judging harshly—and in being kind.[23] Paul defines how love does *not* act by using eight negative statements[24] and how it *does* act in using five positive statements.[25]

The superiority and preeminence of love is seen in its permanence in eternity.[26] Love never ends because every movement of our heart in love is remembered and rewarded by God forever at the judgment seat of Christ, whether it is recognized or appreciated by people on earth or not. No investment of love is forgotten, wasted, or lost in God's sight.[27]

Love is the greatest because God is love.[28] Faith, or agreement with God's Word, is the God-appointed way to release the gracelets, or gifts, of the Spirit. Love is the purpose for them. Faith is how the gracelets function; love is why they function. Hope, or a trustful expectation,[29] stabilizes us. We must be strong in faith and anchored in hope to walk in love.[30]

CHAPTER 20

Practical Ways to Pursue the First Commandment

INTRODUCTION

All of God's commands are actually invitations that include with them the promise of His supernatural enabling to obey them. It takes God to love God. The Father delights to give us a supernatural impartation to love Jesus, if we will but just seek it. Love for God does not just fall into our laps. Even for believers, loving God does not automatically happen without our choosing intentionally to cultivate a responsive heart. However, when we choose to respond by setting our affections on Him, we find that the power to love God that He imparts to us includes the supernatural ability to feel love from Him and to give back to Him. There is a supernatural element in being energized by stirrings of love in our emotions by Him.[1]

An old adage says the road to hell is paved with good intentions. There is a lot of truth in that. Over the years, I have watched hundreds of believers who were truly born again, Spirit-filled, and on fire for Jesus who ended up sitting on the sidelines with nothing but memories of what used to be. I have also seen individuals who stayed on the road for decades and are still burning brightly for the Lord. I have asked the Lord as to the why of both of those.

One of the common reasons for sincere believers who started off correctly but end up drifting off course while in pursuit of the

First Commandment is the mismanagement of their time, resulting in their not being energized in love by the Spirit. Another common issue is that there are those who despise the process required in being a wholehearted lover of God because they neglect to regularly renew their vision to intentionally pursue loving Jesus.

One of the most common mistakes is that many see the time they invest in prayer as being "First Commandment time" that competes with being with people, which is their "Second Commandment time." Terrible and deadly fallacy. Beloved, the time we spend sitting at the feet of Jesus is the place where we are energized to walk out both commandments. We walk out the First Commandment by obeying God with affectionate, grateful trust even when we are outside the Prayer Room.

It is an absolute must that we regularly position ourselves to receive the power to walk in love. Sitting before God to "get oil" is a statement of humility. It is saying and demonstrating that we believe God's testimony that we need to be empowered to love with clarity, consistency, and with right motives. Getting the oil of intimacy is about getting spiritual fuel so we can walk out both commandments more effectively. Jesus, the One who created us and so knows exactly how we function as well as how we should function, testifies that He knows that we cannot love well if we are not living connected to the Spirit's Presence.[2] We can be active with people but we cannot love well. There *is* a difference. If we are not empowered by the Spirit, though we are doers of the work, we will be far more angry, offended, and/or proud in our service.

PRACTICAL WAYS TO PURSUE LOVING JESUS

One of the things that is necessary if we are going to pursue a life of loving Jesus is the determination of a quality decision. A quality decision is a decision from which there is no retreat. Beloved, we must make a determined quality decision to love God. It does not just happen. Our response to His love starts as a choice we make to have a heart of affectionate obedience. Life in the Spirit is all about choices. And after we make that choice and start moving in that direction, we must regularly realign our heart by intentionally renewing our vision to make loving Him our first priority and to continually go deeper in God.[3]

We have to be like Mary of Bethany; we must choose the good part.[4] No one can choose it for us. I remember as a young believer watching many of my friends just floating along, ever busy but never going anywhere. Then I got hold of some books by A.W. Tozer, Leonard Ravenhill, Charles G. Finney, and John G. Lake. I started listening to the teachings of David Wilkerson and listening to the music and teachings of Keith Green. One day I was sitting on the edge of my bed, and from somewhere in the depths of my being[5] arose a cry, "Why everybody else? Why do they get to know You? Why not me?" Ask yourself that question, "Why not me?"[6] David and John leaned on Jesus' heart or set their heart to love and be near Him.[7] Why can't you?

I learned a valuable lesson from the Spirit of God. Every person is as close to God as he or she wants to be. You are as close to God, right now, as you want to be. You see, God is not withholding from us. The Spirit is saying right now, *"Draw near to God, and He will draw near to you."*[8] Every command is an invitation that includes the promised assistance to empower us to obey it—if we respond.

Another thing we need if we are going to pursue loving God, God's way, is a spirit of revelation concerning His love for us. Revelation of God's love is what equips our heart to love Jesus. It takes God to love God. We love God with all our heart *only* as we see that He loves us with all His heart. He empowers us to love by revealing His love to us. We love *because* we understand He first loved us.[9]

We gain revelation of God's love for us by meditating on it from God's Word. We position ourselves to receive from His heart by feeding on His Word.[10] We can behold how the Father feels about us by meditation on the Word.[11]

The next thing that we can do to help us on the path to passionately loving God with all our heart is by asking. *"You do not have, because you do not ask."*[12] We must ask the Spirit to pour love and revelation into our heart.[13] One day I was reading an article by Dr. Jack Deere[14] in the *Last Days Ministries* newsletter.[15] In that particular issue Dr. Deere had contributed an article entitled, appropriately, "Passion for Jesus." In this article Dr. Deere says:

> More than anything else, passion for the Son of God has to be guarded and cultivated or we will lose it. I find that almost every good thing in my life is all too ready to compete for my time and intimacy with the Son of God.
>
> I have begun praying a prayer that has done more to generate passion in my heart for the Lord Jesus than anything I have ever done before. This prayer is found within what is perhaps the greatest prayer in the entire Bible. I am referring to the high priestly prayer of the Lord Jesus in John chapter 17. I have turned the last verse of that prayer into my own personalized prayer. *"And I have declared to them Your Name, and will declare it, that the love with which You loved Me may be in them, and I in them"* (John 17:26 NKJV).
>
> Jesus said that He had declared the name of the Father to His disciples, that is, He showed them what the Father was like. He did this for one overriding purpose. Jesus wanted His disciples to love Him as His heavenly Father loved Him. He wants the love that His Father has for Him to be in His disciples. I read this verse many times before I really saw it. The first time I actually understood what Jesus was saying I found it difficult to believe. How could I love Jesus as God the Father loves His very own Son? Of course, no one can love anyone to the same degree or quality that God loves them. On the other hand, neither can we be as holy as God, yet God says to us, "You shall be holy for I am holy." It is through the power

of His Spirit in us that we can walk in holiness. By that same power, we can live our lives with a consuming passion for our Lord. The Father loves the Son more than anyone or anything else. He is devoted to the Son. His eyes never leave the Son. All that the Father does He does for the Son. Jesus prayed that we would be driven by that same single-eyed passion....

...As I said earlier, I have paraphrased John 17:26 and turned it into my own personal prayer. I pray it like this: "Father, grant me an impartation of the Holy Spirit to love the Son of God like You love Him." I pray this in the morning when I get up; I pray it during the day when my mind slips into neutral; and I pray it when I fall asleep at night. My heart has been captured by this prayer. When I pray it, I am confessing to God that if He does not grant to me a work of the Holy Spirit in my life, I will never acquire passion for the Son of God. I am confessing to Him that my godliness, my discipline, my knowledge of the Word, though all good, are alone insufficient to produce passion for the Son of God. I can change my mind but only the Holy Spirit can change my heart. It is the task of the Holy Spirit to "shed abroad the love of God in our hearts" (see Rom. 5:5). Divine love can only be divinely imparted....

If you begin to pray this prayer on a regular basis, passion for the Son of God will begin to permeate your heart. It may take you months, even years, before you notice a significant difference. In fact, you will probably never be able to point to the day or the hour when you began to be consumed with passion for the Son of God, but others will notice. They'll say you've changed; you seem different. They'll say there's a kindness, a gentleness in you they hadn't noticed before. There's an infectious quality in your love for the Son of God that didn't seem to be there before, and they'll want to know what you've been doing.

Don't be passive about acquiring passion for the Son of God. Make it the focus of your life. Put your eyes on the Son of God and leave them there (see Heb. 12:1 ff.), and you will find yourself becoming like Him. You'll find yourself falling in love with Him as you ask God day after day to consume you with passion for His glorious Son. And that passion, as it begins to occupy your heart, will conquer a thousand sins in your life. You will begin to love what He loves and hate what He hates....[16]

When I read that article, something went off inside of me. John 17:26 has been my life verse for years, the verse that was my mission statement for my life and my ministry. I started praying that prayer every day, several times a day. I have been praying that prayer for over 13 years now. And guess what? It works. Oh, how it works. Over time, a passion for the Glorious Man, Christ Jesus, has been released inside of me and has grown and intensified until truly He is the love of my life.

The good news is that it is not just for me, or for Dr. Deere. Start praying that prayer, and meditating on that verse, throw in a little fasting here or there, and just watch what happens over time. I dare you!

Just Say It

Another practical thing you can do that will rush you along in your pursuit of being wholeheartedly in love with Jesus is confessing that you love Him. Years ago, I was at a Charles and Frances Hunter conference in Faith Memorial Church in Atlanta, Georgia. Frances Hunter was speaking at one of the afternoon sessions. She was speaking on how to have a Christian marriage. She said that if you want to love your spouse more, you have to say you love him or her more—sometimes in faith. If you tell your spouse every day, many times a day that you love him or her, and then follow up by acting as if you love your spouse while refusing to allow yourself to say or do anything that remotely resembles anything to the contrary, God will supernaturally energize your heart and you will fall madly in love with your spouse. Then, with a twinkle in her eye, she said, that since Christians are the Bride of Christ, if we would do the same thing to Jesus, He would energize our hearts and we would fall madly in love with Him as well, as the Lover of our souls.

Well, I took Frances up on that. I started confessing, speaking to Jesus, what I did not have, but wanted to have, "Jesus, I am Your beloved, Your favorite one. I am a disciple whom You love. Your delight is in me. You feel about me as the Father feels about You. I belong to You and You are mine." I started confessing in my daily prayer times and many times throughout the day, "I'm loved by God and I am a lover of God; therefore, I am successful!"[17] Over time, mixed in with the other things we have been discussing, a dynamic change started occurring in my heart. A love started growing and growing. I have shared this principle with others over the years and have seen unbelievable results in those who have actually committed to do them.

BIRDS OF A FEATHER

Another necessary dynamic to fuel your passion for Jesus is Christian fellowship. We receive a massive positive backlash of God's love when we are involved in a lifestyle of serving our neighbor by sharing the love of God and in receiving it from others. The fullness of God's love can only be experienced as the whole Body functions together. A significant portion of our appointed inheritance in God is linked to our receiving it from the hands of others as they reveal and release God's love to us.[18]

The Greek word translated fellowship is *koinonia*. This word is used in the context of a marriage contract (surprise, surprise) where the husband and wife agree to a joint participation in the necessaries of life.[19] The New Testament usage is clear that Christian fellowship is not sanctified human fellowship, but is a dynamic that is unique to believers in Jesus. Kingdom fellowship is about God, not the things of the flesh.

One afternoon Jesus asks His disciples concerning what the multitudes thought about Him. Their response was that they thought He was a prophet, maybe even one of Israel's great prophets come back from the dead. Jesus then probes deeper, asking them who they thought He was. Peter spoke up and said, *"You are the Christ, the Son of the Living God."* Jesus responded, *"Blessed are you, Simon Bar-Jonah! Flesh and blood has not revealed this to you, but My Father who is in heaven."*[20]

Moments later, Jesus starts sharing with them the Father's plan, how He would go to Jerusalem and suffer many things, would be killed and on the third day following would be raised from the dead.[21] Immediately, Peter, who had just received the greatest revelation from the Spirit of God that a human being can receive and who had just been commended by the Son of God, pulls Jesus to the side and begins to rebuke the Uncreated God of Genesis chapter 1, the Creator of Heaven and earth, saying, *"This shall never happen to You."*

Jesus' response is one that is very informative to us if we desire to be equally yoked to Him. Jesus turned and said to Peter, *"Get behind Me, Satan! You are a hindrance to Me. For you are not setting your mind on the things of God, but on the things of man."*[22] Another translation says, *"You are an offense, a hindrance and a snare to Me."*[23]

Why did Jesus react so strongly to Peter's words? Because Jesus saw, as we need to see, that the natural, fleshly way of seeing things is not normal—it is abnormal, or a better way to say it is that it is subnormal. People often say of Christians, "They are not normal." Actually, it is the exact opposite: the Christians are heading back toward normalcy, and the rest of the world is subnormal.

James, the Lord Jesus' half-brother, talking about "normal" wisdom or ways of thinking, described it this way:

This is not the wisdom that comes down from above, but is earthly, unspiritual, demonic.[24]

Another translation says:

This [superficial] wisdom is not such as comes down from above, but is earthly, unspiritual (animal), even devilish (demoniacal).[25]

Yet another translation says it this way:

Wisdom like that doesn't come down from heaven. It belongs to the earth. It does not come from the Holy Spirit. It comes from the devil.[26]

Jesus says, if anything is of this earth, if it doesn't originate from Holy Spirit—the things of the Spirit, the things of God, things of the Word, of Christ—then in God's view it originates from and is pushing us toward the devil, the enemy of God.[27] If this is true, then Houston, we have a problem!

Not Legalism—Liberty

God is not saying that you cannot eat pizza or go bowling. However, He is saying those things cannot be called Christian fellowship and will not, in and of themselves, help you be a lover of God. In fact, if they are the mainstay of your life and enjoyment, they will over time actually push you away from God. Good, not evil, is the worst enemy of best.

It is no secret that if we choose sinful activities we will not naturally draw closer to God. But the big secret is this: if we choose the natural things, even the things God blesses us with, legitimate blessings, without large and regular doses of the things of the Spirit, those legitimate things will eventually often pull us away from intimacy with God. If you do not believe me, ask Old Testament Israel.

We are fallen beings, living in a fallen world, surrounded by natural people who naturally think the devil's thoughts. Unless we take seriously the call to holy living (Oh no, Ethel, he used the H word!), we are going to find it difficult, if not impossible, to live a life pleasing to our heavenly Bridegroom.

OUR EXAMPLE

Our model in the New Testament is the apostolic company. How, and with who, did they fellowship?

And they devoted themselves to the apostles' teaching and the fellowship, to the breaking of bread and the prayers.[28]

The cup of blessing that we bless, is it not a participation [koinonia] in the blood of Christ? The bread that we break, is it not a participation [koinonia] in the body of Christ?[29]

Do not be unequally yoked with unbelievers. For what partnership has righteousness with lawlessness? Or what fellowship [koinonia] has light with darkness?[30]

That which we have seen and heard we proclaim also to you, so that you too may have fellowship [koinonia] with us; and indeed our fellowship [koinonia] is with the Father and with his Son Jesus Christ.[31]

SETTING OUR HEARTS TO LOVE JESUS

As we have already discussed, the only way that we will receive the fullness of a life consumed with loving God is in the context of our having a sustained vision to go deep in God. In this age, everything in the Kingdom of God happens in time and space. It takes focus and effort to go deep in God, not so we can earn it, but so we can position ourselves to receive it. Our soul prospers as we grow in the anointing to love God and each other. To walk in this requires that we must focus on pursuing it more than we focus on gaining material possessions and influence.[32]

"Where there is no prophetic vision the people cast off restraint...."[33] Those without a vision of obeying the First and Second Commandments are usually only concerned in knowing what is required of them: "What do I *have* to do?"

Remember the story in Chapter Twelve about the little girl who kept falling out of bed? People seeking to love Jesus extravagantly should not be content to say where they got in. They should not be asking, "How far do I have to go?" Instead, they should be asking, "God, what is the most that You will empower me to give to You? How far will You let me go, how abandoned will You let me be?" Lovers are not content with the minimum requirements of salvation. Satan's strategy and priority is to lead us astray from cultivating wholehearted love and devotion to Jesus.[34]

Sustaining a fresh walk with God through decades is the definition of living radically before God. We are not radical because we do something unusual for a few weeks or months. David sustained his passion for God for decades so that he referred to it as "all" the days of his life.[35]

Daniel sustained his prayer life with passion for decades, from about age 16 to 82 years old.[36]

> *Now when Daniel knew that the writing was signed, he went home. And in his upper room, with his windows open toward Jerusalem, he knelt down on his knees three times that day, and prayed and gave thanks before his God, as was his custom since his early days.*[37]

In all of this let me encourage you that we are on a lifelong journey. As John Wimber used to say, "The journey is the destination." Moreover, while we are on this journey of intimacy with the Lord, we must not despise the day of small beginnings.[38] We must learn to value the small stirs of God's Word and Spirit on our heart. The Kingdom starts as a seed in our heart and grows slowly but surely. We cannot accurately measure it during the process.[39]

CHAPTER 21

Running for the Prize—Being Complete in Our Love

LOVING JESUS ON HIS TERMS

We can only love Jesus on His terms. He defined it as being rooted in a spirit of obedience. There is no such thing as loving God without sincerely seeking to obey His Word. Obeying God is not just the cosmetic Christianity that is so prevalent in the Western church. Jesus said that our day-to-day righteousness had to exceed the outer garment religiosity of the scribes and Pharisees if we desired to live a Kingdom lifestyle.[1] Loving God requires more than having sentimental feelings about God;[2] it requires deep-seated, heart-level agreement with Him. We must love what He loves and hate what He hates.

Expressing our love to Jesus always includes denying our sinful, lustful desires. Each of us has a different struggle according to our individual personality and circumstances. Thus, we each have a different assignment on how we offer our gift of love to God. One of the commonly shared dynamics is that we all must say no to sin as an expression of our love to Jesus.[3]

Jesus called us as His Bride to live "perfect," meaning we should seek to walk in all the light the Spirit gives us. We can only do this by reaching from our heart to live in hundredfold obedience in our thoughts, words, and deeds. Yes, it does take diligence.

One thing I have learned over the years is that lazy people never inherit the Kingdom.

By inheriting the Kingdom, I am not talking about going to Heaven when you die. God does not just want you to die in order to see the Kingdom. He wants you to "die" while you are still walking around so that you can see the Kingdom while you are still here on the earth. Get it? You will not need the Kingdom in the sweet by and by when you die; you need the Kingdom now, here in the dirty now and now.

There are no lost people who need to hear the good news of the Kingdom in Heaven. There are no sick people who need you to lay hands on them so that they will be healed in Heaven. You will not see demonized people on the streets of gold who need you to cast out their tormenting Klingons (you know, aliens onboard—thank you, Bill, very much). We need the Kingdom now. The people all around you need the Kingdom now. We owe everyone we meet an encounter with the Kingdom and with the King. That will only happen as we walk in the light as He is in the light.

Walking perfectly in obedience to the light we receive is relative now and absolute in the age to come. Jesus said it this way, *"You therefore must be perfect, as your heavenly Father is perfect."*[4]

Jesus is not saying here that He expects that we walk in sinless perfection—if He did, we would all be in trouble, wouldn't we? What He is saying is that we must be faithful to walk in all the light that we have.[5] The reason for this is that we are to be an equally yoked Bride with the Son of God, and He walks in all the Light that He has. We must live a lifestyle that is reaching for 100 percent obedience.

Reaching for 100 percent obedience is not the same as attaining to it in this life. It is a given that we will miss the mark. We will miss the mark; but when we do, we repent, change our mind and our direction, and renew our resolve to fully obey with the full confidence that God enjoys us while we are still in the process of maturing.[6] When we obey the Spirit's light, then He gives us more light and we experience more of God.[7]

Enoch received the testimony that he pleased God by a lifestyle of comprehensive obedience.[8] I heard someone tell the story of Enoch once.[9] He said that one day Enoch was walking with God because they were friends, and as they walked and fellowshipped together, God said to His friend Enoch, "Enoch, you know, we are closer to My house than we are to yours, so why don't you come and spend the day with Me?" Enoch said, "OK, Lord, I will!" And you know what? Enoch is still there spending the day with Jesus, for in Heaven there is no night.

At the end of our natural lives, each of us will stand before Jesus to receive His testimony about our life.[10] He will reveal to us the truth about the quality of our obedience and love. On that day, everyone will long to hear Jesus say, "*Well done, good and faithful servant.*"[11]

We are to ask the Lord for wisdom into areas we lack complete obedience in. We ask the Lord to shock us now with insight into our lack of obedience instead of at the judgment seat. David asked the Lord for insight into areas in which he lacked complete dedication to Him.[12]

THE PRIZE: OUR TESTIMONY OF BEING COMPLETE IN LOVE AND OBEDIENCE

The prize which Paul sought was to receive God's testimony about his life that he walked in complete obedience. Paul's highest goal was to win the prize of presenting the testimony to Jesus on the last day that his obedience was complete—thus his love for Jesus was perfected.[13]

The prize involves offering to Jesus a life of complete obedience and then receiving His response, which includes eternal rewards that express how He feels about us loving Him in this way. Paul wrote toward the end of his life that he had not yet obtained the prize of the testimony of perfect obedience.[14] God's testimony about our life is not given until after we complete our race. Paul had several years before his race—life—was over. The prize of the upward call of God is to receive the testimony that we finished the race in full obedience; thus, we receive a full reward.[15]

Paul was assured of the prize of the crown of righteousness as his race was nearing completion.[16] We only have the few short years we are on this earth to bring every area under the Spirit's leadership as our way of demonstrating our love to God. All who are wise will make this their greatest single goal, for which they will gladly sacrifice pleasure, money, and even honor in ministry.

The pursuit of complete or comprehensive obedience includes bridling our speech,[17] making a covenant with our eyes that refuses to look on anything that stirs up lust,[18] disciplining our physical appetites, managing our time for service and prayer, and using our money to increase the Kingdom beyond personal comfort.[19]

THE LAST 2 PERCENT

God granting us spiritual power in our life is found as we pursue hundredfold obedience. There are powerful dynamics that occur in our heart when we soberly seek to walk in total obedience. The 98 percent pursuit of obedience has only a limited blessing. The last 2 percent is what positions us to live with a vibrant heart.

Maintaining a sustained reach for full obedience for decades is the definition of living radically before God. We are not radical because we do something unusual for a few weeks or months. When we neglect to confront sin in our life we are not loved less by God, but we do suffer loss in minimizing the full gift of our love from this life to Jesus on the last day.

God daily gives us many opportunities to make quality decisions that demonstrate our love to Him. Yes, we will make wrong decisions that we regret, but we also have opportunities to change them. If we make right decisions in our pursuit of obedience, He gives us many opportunities to confirm them or prove them in our character.[21]

Scripture presents two aspects of being complete before God. First, at the new birth, we are instantly made complete in Christ in our legal position (justification) because of Jesus' work on the Cross. Second, we progressively become complete in our obedience in our living condition before God (sanctification). Both are foundational truths.[22]

There are different terms in Scripture for this truth of those pursuing 100 percent obedience: complete,[23] perfect,[24] mature,[25] blameless,[26] without spot,[27] worthy,[28] stand,[29] steadfast,[30] do His will,[31] guiltless,[32] and above, without, free from reproach.[33]

Paul prayed and preached so that people would receive a testimony of "complete obedience."[34] Paul believed and prayed that people would become complete in their responsiveness to the Spirit of the Lord. To perfect what is lacking in their faith included being perfected in their heart responses and knowledge of truth.[35]

LOVE—LIVING WITHOUT COMPROMISE

To live perfect and blameless simply means to live without compromise. This is not the same as receiving the free gift of righteousness.[36] Jesus spoke to the rich young ruler of perfect or complete obedience that included his money.[37] To live in complete or perfect obedience is also referred to as God's love being perfected in us.[38]

Complete obedience comes as a fruit of lovesickness. What does it mean to be lovesick? First, it means to love God first and most. We want to love Jesus in a deep and steady way, not just blow kisses to Him on the run as we pursue His blessings. Second, to be sick or pained when compromised in our life hinders our love for Jesus.[39] Lovers of God are not just afraid of the consequences of their sins; they are mainly grieved because they have grieved the Lover of their soul.

Our greatest calling is to love Him in a complete way with love that is perfected. Every movement of our heart seeks to demonstrate our love to Him knowing that our obedience moves Him and thus is never in vain. Do you know the way that even the small movements of your heart touch Him? Each time we repent of compromise, it moves Him. The Lord values our journey as we seek to grow in love. If we do not quit in our pursuit, then we win!

What is your greatest dream in life? Is it to be empowered to walk in complete obedience? True freedom is found in the yoke of Christ by refusing to be trapped in bitterness by those who mistreat us or to be caught up in seeking wealth and fame as our primary goal in the Kingdom.

Jesus, as the jealous God, reveals Himself to us as much more than our Savior—Forgiver of our sins—and Healer, but also as the jealous Bridegroom God who will not relent in His pursuit of us until He has all our heart.[40]

The Scriptures tell us that there will be some believers who are saved, but only as through fire. They are like one who is pulled out of the fire just in the nick of time. They escape through the flames yet they lose all that they had worked for in their life.[41] We can suffer the loss of some of our potential if we live halfheartedly.[42]

A SAVED BUT WASTED LIFE

Years ago I heard Mike Bickle, director of the International House of Prayer in Kansas City, relate a supernatural encounter he had with the Lord as a young man. In this encounter, Mike was standing before the Lord in Heaven, and he "knew" he was at the end of his life before the judgment seat of Christ. He also knew that he had lived a Christian life, had a good marriage, raised his kids to serve the Lord, and had a successful ministry serving God and man—although at the time he had this encounter, Mike was still single, so he didn't have a wife, children, or a ministry.

Jesus looked at him with burning eyes and said, "Saved, but what a wasted life." Mike protested and told the Lord, "You must have me confused with somebody else." Jesus did not respond. He just stood looking into Mike's eyes with sadness in His eyes. Mike continued protesting, when a thought came to him that it is impossible to manipulate the Man Christ Jesus. Mike cried out to the Lord, "Please, give me another chance?" Then another thought came strongly that it is appointed for man to die once and after that comes the judgment.[43]

Mike said he fell before the Lord weeping with a profound sense of loss and regret for having avoided living a sinful life, but not having lived a wholehearted life that pleased the Lord. Several years later, he had another encounter with the Lord where the exact same thing happened. Again, at the end of the encounter he found himself weeping before the Lord because he had lived a "Christian" life but not a wholehearted life that was pleasing to the Lord Jesus. He said those two encounters made an indelible mark upon his heart concerning the importance of living a life that is more than life as usual.

The fear of the Lord is the beginning of wisdom. When the Scriptures talk about the fear of the Lord, it does not just mean living in terror of going to hell or reaping the consequences of our sinful decisions on earth. It also means realizing that there will be some who live like their neighbors next door and their neighbors on the pew next to them, and don't go for the gusto, living whole-hearted lives of abandonment, radical lives of seeking the Lord, living lives of doing the works of the Kingdom. As a result, they will suffer the loss of all they have—with a foundation of wood, hay, and stubble, when they could have had a foundation of gold, silver, and precious stones.[44]

Beloved, what matters most about our life is not what we think or what our neighbors think; it is not what the television evangelist or our favorite Bible teacher teaches. All that will matter on that day, and therefore all that should matter on this day, is what will

Jesus think and what will Jesus say about how we lived our lives when we stand before Him and look into those burning eyes.

Why have I been gripped by the need to live a radical, wholehearted life before the Lord? Because of all the things I fear in life, fear of making mistakes, fear of failure, fear of the displeasure from my fellow man, the thing I fear most is regret. You see, if I wait until that day to find out that I did it all wrong, there will be nothing to do but fall down before the Lord and weep. I will not be able to change anything. However, if I seek His face today, I can hear His words, I can know His heart, and I can repent—I can change my mind, my heart, and my direction before it is too late.

> *Therefore, we must pay much closer attention to what we have heard, lest we drift away from it. For since the message declared by angels proved to be reliable, and every transgression or disobedience received a just retribution, how shall we escape if we neglect such a great salvation?*[45]

I encourage you to take a few moments and to think about what your encounter with Jesus and His evaluation of your life so far would be like if it were to happen tonight. If you do not think you would be satisfied with the outcome of that meeting, spend some time, just you and Jesus, and ask Him to let you know what areas need to be addressed while you still have a chance to do something about them. My cry for years has been, "Lord, shout at me now, so You won't have to shout at me then."

Here is my prayer for you: "Jesus, I pray for my friend, and I ask that You draw him or her to Your loving side and help prepare this person for the glorious day when the two of you sit down at that great evaluation. May it be a day of rejoicing and not a day of sorrow. Amen."

CHAPTER 22

A Bride Without Offense

In this chapter, we will be looking at one of the key dynamics of loving God, God's way, and that is living with an unoffended heart. It should go without saying, but attempting to walk in love while living with the dynamics of walking outside of love is counterproductive. When we try to live that way, it is not like matter-antimatter where they just cancel each other out and we are back at square one. When you have love and add offense, the opposite of love, there is no canceling each other out; instead, the offense wins. It is imperative that we win this battle, or we will not win.

LOVING GOD WITH ALL OUR HEART REQUIRES WE OVERCOME OFFENSE

As we looked at earlier, we are empowered to walk out the First Commandment to love Jesus with all of our heart to the measure we are thankful to Him and to the degree we trust His leadership. On the other end of the spectrum, we are hindered to the measure that we are offended at His leadership.

You might be thinking, "Well, I'm not offended at Jesus' leadership in my life." Over the years, I have found that many sincere believers have levels of unperceived offense at Jesus and His leadership in their lives. It is truly one of the main factors that has to be settled if we desire to live as lovers of God. In the days, months, and years ahead, it will be more and more the major battleground as we approach the end of the age. To be victorious in the Christian walk, we must have a deep foundation of bridal love based on the foundation of the premise that Jesus' leadership is good because He possesses perfect love and wisdom in all that He is and all that He does.

Because we are living in a fallen world, we all have opportunities to enter into offense. If we do not learn to recognize it and it is allowed to remain in our hearts, it will develop an entire root system that will grow and function unperceived beneath the surface. It will cause negative, sinful actions to spring up. These outward manifestations of offense will defile us, trouble us, hurt us, cut us off from the grace of God, and hinder our experience of God's Presence. When undealt with, offense will eventually turn into bitterness that will not only affect us, but will spread to others, causing them to be defiled and troubled as well.

AN EXAMPLE OF OFFENSE

John the Baptist was a relative of Jesus—some believe he might have been His cousin, but we are not sure. It is believed by some scholars that John as a young man possibly joined the Essenes, one of the Jewish sects in Judea at that time. We know for sure that he grew up in the wilderness of Judea.[1] While living in the wilderness, John received a supernatural prophetic call around A.D. 27.[2]

After the Spirit of prophecy came on him he started preaching a message of repentance.[3] He was the partial fulfillment of the return of a prophet in the style of Elijah.[4] He was the forerunner of the ministry of Jesus in Israel. John had received a prophetic word that, as he baptized people in water, one of the people he baptized would receive a supernatural baptism in the Holy Spirit, and when that occurred, he was to proclaim that this person was the Messiah.[5] When John baptized Jesus, there was a voice from Heaven,[6] and the Spirit descended upon Him[7] just as John had been told.

John proclaimed that Jesus was greater than he,[8] and was the prophesied Christ.[9] He announced that Jesus was the Lamb of God who would take away the sins of the world.[10] John recognized Him to be "God's Chosen One,"[11] which was one of the terms for the promised Messiah. After John baptized Jesus, a transition took place where John's ministry started coming to a close and Jesus' started gaining momentum.[12]

Shortly after Jesus started preaching, John was arrested by Herod and put into prison because John had confronted him about the unlawfulness of Herod living with Herodias, his brother Phillip's wife.[13] While in prison, John sent some of his disciples to Jesus, asking Him, *"Are you the one who is to come, or shall we look for another?"*[14]

Instead of answering John's question, Jesus turned and ministered to the people around Him, healing many people and ministering deliverance to the demonized. Then He turned to John's disciples and said:

> *...Go and tell John what you have seen and heard: the blind receive their sight, the lame walk, lepers are cleansed, and the deaf hear, the dead are raised up, the poor have good news preached to them. And blessed is the one who is not **offended by Me**.*[15]

Jesus warned John and his disciples to not be offended at His leadership in John's life. Many are offended at Jesus both for what He does and for what He does not do—or what He allows to happen.[16] Jesus vindicated John's unwavering commitment and set him forth as the model of spiritual violence. Overcoming all offense concerning Jesus' leadership requires spiritual violence.[17]

One of the fundamental truths of the Kingdom of God is that Jesus offends our mind to reveal our heart. He does this so that our offenses will be brought to the surface so they can be healed. Jesus in His wisdom does this in His leadership over our lives individually as well as over all history.[18] There is a special blessing in store for those who trust Jesus' leadership in this age before the breakthrough. While we are here on the earth, in this age, is the only time in history we can express this aspect of love to Jesus.

The saints in Heaven cannot give this gift to the Son of God—only we can. It requires extravagant love to trust Jesus' leadership as perfect in love and wisdom before seeing the outcome.[19]

Satan is always lying to us, telling us how we are being mistreated by God. Love lets us know that we are getting better treatment than we deserve. We must not fall for the strategy of the evil one; we must face our disappointment with expressions of love that trusts Jesus' leadership. Our true view of His leadership comes to the surface in context to His redemptive disciplines as seen in our personal lives and in the nations of the earth. We choose to trust even in the face of disappointment.

THE LORD IS GOOD

The anchor of our faith is our confession that *"The Lord is good, His steadfast love endures forever."*[20] When we stand, even in the face of apparently contradictory circumstances and proclaim the good leadership of Jesus, when we speak only of His perfect love and infallible wisdom—it is the supreme form of spiritual warfare. When we declare that His steadfast love endures forever, we are saying that no one is disqualified from the benefits of His leadership if they will trust in Him.

The following song was sung during some of the strategic times in redemptive history. For example, at the dedication of the Tabernacle of David; the dedication of the Temple of Solomon; and in the war led by Jehoshaphat:[21]

> *And they rose early in the morning and went out into the wilderness of Tekoa. When they went out, Jehoshaphat stood and said, "Hear me, Judah and inhabitants of Jerusalem! **Believe in the Lord your God, and you will be established; believe His prophets, and you will succeed.**" When he had taken counsel with the people, he appointed those who were to sing to the Lord and praise Him in holy attire, as they went before the army, and say, "Give thanks*

*to the **Lord**, for His steadfast love endures forever." And
when they began to sing and praise, the **Lord set an ambush**
against the men of Ammon, Moab, and Mount Seir, who
had come against Judah, so that they were routed.*[22]

The Lord is good, His steadfast love endures forever.[23]

Forever in Heaven our song will be *"worthy is the Lamb."* Our
eternal banner is that Jesus is worthy.[24] We declare, in time and in
space, that Jesus is worthy of our unqualified trust in His good
leadership. We declare that Jesus is worthy of our sacrificial obedience in our diligent pursuit of Him and His Kingdom rule.[25]

We declare that Jesus is worthy of being the supreme leader
over all created order. Our banner confession is that Jesus' loving
leadership works all things for good in our life.[26] This banner confession is the place where we find spiritual protection, revelation,
and spiritual pleasure now and forever.[27] This confession is our war
cry against the enemy's false accusation against Jesus' leadership.[28]

THE DEVIL'S GREAT LIE

The devil's great lie is that you are not getting what you deserve. This was the lie he used on Eve.[29] He is not coming up with
new lies; he does not have to, for so many are still falling for the
same old ones. Beloved, our ability to receive God's love and to
love Him back is directly related to how we view the difficulties
in our life. When things go south, many heed the lie and end up
in a place of bitterness with incorrect paradigms of God with no
sense of gratitude, which is the very foundation of loving God.
The devil seeks to hinder the working of love in us by accusing
Jesus' leadership over our life. He wants to convince us that we
are not receiving the good that we so rightly deserve. A mindset
of complaint and self-pity always destroys love.[30]

Jesus taught on the danger of relating to Him based on supposedly getting what we think we deserve, instead of relating to
Him from the place of gratitude being thankful that we do not get

what we deserve! Satan tells us we deserve better treatment from God in our life, our family, and our ministry, undermining our gratitude for the goodness of God. How quickly we forget that we were once lost in darkness.[31]

We have to resist the spiritual attacks of the enemy—lies are spiritual attacks just as much as if we were being swung at with a baseball bat—and counterattack by proclaiming our love to Jesus by actively trusting His leadership in difficulties in our spiritual life, our personal circumstances (physical, financial, relational), or crises in the nations of the earth (temporal judgments).

We should not be reactive, waiting for the enemy to attack before we do something; instead, we should be proactive and daily pray that our love will abound so that we respond correctly when offense presents itself. People who are loved by God, who love God, who love themselves and live a life loving others, are untouchable. However, we have to set our heart to love God without getting trapped into the bitterness of feeling mistreated.[32] We have to ask the Holy Spirit to reveal even the smallest pockets of unperceived offense that might be working in our heart.[33]

THE BATTLE FOR LOVE

We must contend for the correct insight that fuels gratitude in our hearts for the love of God and the blessings of God. His judgments are perfect. They are not too severe nor are they too lenient. They are never too late, but they are not often early either. They are perfectly chosen to expose and remove all that hinders the working of God's love in our lives.[34]

As we get closer to the endtimes, many will be offended with Jesus and with one another, which will result in our love growing cold. Jesus warned us that many will fall away because of offense[35] and will betray one another and hate one another, and that the love of many will grow cold.[36] This will cause many to rage against the Lord, which will only result in their placing themselves under the wrath of God.[37]

The Power to Love

One of the common misconceptions that many have about the age to come is that after we receive our resurrected body and we no longer have to struggle with sin any longer, we will be on autopilot and will just love God naturally and continually. It is true that we will not struggle with sin, but that will not make love automatic. This kind of thinking comes from not having a healthy understanding of the bridal paradigm of the Kingdom.

God is all about relationship. Wholehearted love and full obedience will not be because we are programmed to love God in a robotic sense. Rather, we will forever love Jesus voluntarily by being empowered by gratitude,[38] just as we are here in this age. Since it is true that we are going to love Him forever that way, doesn't it make sense that we will have to start sometime? My question to you is, if we are to do it in Heaven and we have to start sometime, why don't we start now?

True love requires that the lovers have the full freedom to voluntarily choose. No one can make you love; you have to choose to love. God's integrity will never allow Him to force some sort of robotic, automated behavior void of choice or devoid of true heartfelt intimacy

The good news, the glorious news, is that satan and all his demons will be locked away in prison and therefore there will be no lack or harm, thus no "fear"[39] tempting us. Thank God, our resurrected, glorified body will no longer be burdened with a sin nature, and everyone around us will share this same glorious condition. We will behold Jesus face to face. Remember, Adam and the angels who sinned also saw God face to face. However, they did not behold Him as a Redeemer; they only beheld Him as the powerful King.

The absence of a sin nature did not keep Adam or one-third of the angels from sinning, and it will not keep you from sinning either. The two-thirds of the angels who refused to follow lucifer's plan to overthrow God and His righteous Kingdom were not on autopilot then, nor are they on autopilot now. They chose to be loyal then, just as they are choosing to be loyal now. Get it?

Jesus' Bride has always had to choose whether they would love Him or serve Him. Not having a sin nature doesn't guarantee whether you will love God or not—choosing will. Remember, everyone is as close to God as he or she wants to be, whether he or she has a sin nature or not. We choose to love Him or to serve Him by our choices—it is voluntary love. Our grateful love will grow throughout all of eternity. Eternal love, like sin, is a mystery.[40] Whether it is in time or in eternity, voluntary love takes cultivation.

God in His wisdom has led history specifically to create the context that would allow us to live forever with gratitude as being the foundational dynamic to eternal loving obedience.[41] Our human soul was created with the capacity for eternal increase in either love or hate—we choose which it will be. Love will continually grow in the redeemed even as anger continually will grow in the heart of the eternally damned. So if it is not automatic, what will keep our love for God, for ourselves, and for others fresh and growing for billions and billions of years? Choices. It is all about choices.

The human spirit was designed to never lose its capacity to increase in its feelings and its need to be fascinated.[42] The saints in Heaven will be forever having their love for Jesus fueled by growing in their gratitude for His leadership, His grace, and His goodness. Forever we will cry, "Worthy is the Lamb."[43] It is important to realize and to take advantage of the fact there is dynamic continuity in the gratitude and love formed in our heart now—in this age, on the earth—and with what we will have in our heart in the age to come. The same gratitude that will energize us in the age to come is being worked in us now.

What Now?

She had everything a girl could want in life: she was beautiful, talented, and popular. At the prime of her life a freak accident caused her to lose her sight. However, being a survivor, she knew she would just have to make the most of it. God would surely make a way for her. It wasn't long before she was enrolled in a school for the blind and began to make lots of new friends.

One very special friend who worked at the school taught her not only how to survive in a sightless world but also how to laugh and play. She called him her knight in shining armor and he called her his beautiful princess. She didn't know how she would have made it without his friendship. Finally, after an especially wonderful evening, her friend asked her to become his wife. Instead of the joyful response the anxious young man expected, his princess broke into uncontrolled sobs.

She screamed at him and told him to get out, saying that didn't he know that she could never be a good wife unless she could see. He desperately tried to calm her fears and explained that he loved her just like she was, but she was adamant that unless she could see she would never become his wife because he deserved someone who could see. She was unfit.

Every day for weeks her prince would try again to persuade her to conquer her fear and marry him, but every day he was greeted with the same reply. Unless she could see, she could not say yes. Finally the young man came to her room with exciting news. He had talked to a surgeon and arranged transplant surgery that would allow her to see. A donor had been found and she could have the surgery the next day. Now would she marry him? Joy of joys, her dreams were coming true.

The surgery took place, and on the day she was ready to take the bandages off and see for the first time, she and her prince stood together holding hands as they unwrapped her eyes. Was she as beautiful as he said she was? She was about to find out. He lovingly kissed the top of her head and she opened her eyes.

The light was bright as she looked in the mirror. She was beautiful! She focused on her prince. Oh, no, it couldn't be. Instead of a handsome prince, there stood a man with empty eye sockets. How could he have deceived her like this! She couldn't marry a blind man! She turned on him and unleashed her pent-up anger. Why had he never told her he was blind? She ordered him to leave her presence. The young man sorrowfully left. He made several attempts to come back and check on her progress, but she refused to see him.

On the day that she was to be released from the hospital, the nurse asked her what to do with all of the precious gifts the young man had continued to send daily. She replied that they should just be thrown away because she would only be able to love someone who could see how truly beautiful she was. The nurse shook her head sadly and said, "Don't you know that the very eyes that you are seeing with were once his?"

Sad story, isn't it.

The young woman had been blind, and even though the young man in the story helped her to see, she refused to see, and so even though her physical eyes had sight, she remained blind.

Well, I hope that like the young man in the story, I have helped you to see in areas where maybe you were blind before. And I pray that now you can see, you will rejoice in your newfound sight and go forth rejoicing in the new knowledge that you are loved and you are a lover, therefore you are successful.

I trust you will go forth and tell everyone everywhere that there is going to be a wedding, and that they are invited.

May I pray with you as we close our time together?

Abba, I pray for my friend—may You give him or her a spirit of wisdom and of revelation in the knowledge of our glorious Bridegroom, Judge, and King. I ask that You give my friend an impartation of the love You have for Your Son, by Your Holy Spirit. May the all-consuming passion of his or her life ever be the pursuit of knowing You and Your Son in an ever-increasing manner. I ask that You empower my friend to live an abandoned, radical lifestyle in pursuit of living out the Great and First Commandment. May this special person love You with all of his or her heart, soul, mind, and strength, and in the overflow of that love, learn to love himself or herself and pour out a life in service to others. May this child of Yours be one of the nameless, faceless generation, a friend of the Bridegroom, a lover of God. And on that grand and glorious day when this friend of mine and Yours at last stand before You, may he or she hear the words, "Well done, My good and faithful servant, enter into the joy of Your King." In the Name of Jesus, I ask all of this. Amen!

Not My Will, But Yours Be Done

DID OUR BRIDEGROOM PRAY TO AVOID THE CROSS?

"Father, I know You want Me to go to the Cross, and I know that unless I do humankind will be eternally lost. But I am afraid, and I have been thinking, maybe there is another way to get the job accomplished. I know that I always said I wanted a corporate Bride, but, You know, being single isn't that bad..."

STOP!

That conversation never transpired.

But many theologians and Christian leaders believe that it did happen much like that. They believe that Jesus had second thoughts, cold feet, and began looking for the back door. Though martyrs throughout human history have bravely and boldly died for their faith in Christ, some think that Jesus Himself—the One whom the martyrs died for—just didn't have what it took.

In Chapter Eleven, we looked at how the New Testament builds and expands on the foundation laid throughout the Old Testament in presenting the whole of biblical redemptive revelation in the light of the bridal paradigm of the Kingdom of God. Starting with Jesus' first miracle at the wedding at Cana to the consummation of this age at the Marriage Supper of the Lamb, we have seen that truly the love language of God is all about a wedding, and all about an eternal bridal companion who loves God, God's way.

We looked at the initiation of Jesus' earthly ministry at the wedding in Cana of Galilee, His first public introduction by John the Baptist as the fulfillment of the Old Testament prophecies that in the last days God would be known not just as Master but as Husband, with his proclamation that the One who has the Bride is the Bridegroom.

We examined how all of Jesus' teaching and ministry was in the context of the bridal paradigm of the Kingdom. He is the Bridegroom, and the Church is the Bride called to love Him with all of our heart, soul, mind, and strength because that is how He loved us, with all of His heart, soul, mind, and strength. Everything in the Kingdom is working toward the day when the Bridegroom and the Bride will consummate their relationship at a wedding establishing the Kingdom of God.

Everything Jesus modeled and taught is to be interpreted in the light of that bridal revelation—it is the glue that holds it all together. Jesus, as the Bridegroom, like Hosea, "went again" after His wayward Bride even to the point of being willing to go to the Cross, pouring out His life's blood as an atonement for Her sin, and bearing the wrath of God on Her behalf so that She could be cleansed and brought back into full relationship with God the Father and into bridal fellowship with Himself.

We looked at Jesus in the garden of Gethsemane. There we find the only possible glitch in the story. Jesus, the Uncreated God of Genesis chapter 1, took upon Himself the form of a man, and was born as a baby in a stable. He lived 33 sinless years as a human being. At the young age of 12, He already was showing signs of knowing who He was and what He was all about—His Father's business.

At the age of 30, He submitted Himself to being baptized by John the Baptist to fulfill righteousness. As He was coming up out of the water, He was powerfully baptized with the Holy Spirit and fire, empowering Him to proclaim and demonstrate the Kingdom of God on earth with signs, wonders, healings, and miracles. Immediately, He was led by the Spirit into the wilderness where He underwent intense spiritual warfare at the hands of the devil himself.

He then spent the next three and a half years preaching and teaching the Gospel of the Kingdom. He preached the good news to the poor, healed the sick, cast out demons, raised the dead, and confronted and exposed the corrupt spiritual leaders of the religious systems of that day. He called the multitudes to press into the things of God by seeking the Kingdom of God and His righteousness. He was a stalwart of righteousness, a model of what a man could be who knew His God.

When the religious and political leaders wanted to silence Him, they had to make up lies because they could find no chinks in His lifestyle—He was a man of God. He was a man with a purpose and a focus, a man who could not be bought or sidetracked. That is, until we see Him in the garden of Gethsemane where He was found asking God to relieve Him of His call and commission because now He was starting to feel a little uncomfortable. *What?*

Things aren't as they seem. Let's look at what was *really* going on.

Jesus had announced that in order to fulfill the prophetic Scriptures, God was going to raise up a Messiah who Himself was the Bridegroom God, who would give His life to ransom God's people to pay for their sin to woo and win their hearts so that they would recognize who they were and take their place as the Bride of Christ.

He told His disciples that it was time, the hour had come, and He was going to Jerusalem where He was going to be betrayed, beaten, and killed; but on the third day, He would rise from the dead. They travel to Jerusalem where He and His disciples share a last Passover meal together. Afterward He prays the great intercessory prayer recorded in John 17 when He intercedes for His disciples and those who would believe their testimony concerning Himself and His message. He then prays for all believers through-out the rest of redemptive history until He returns.

Then, knowing that He is about to be arrested, tried, and cru-cified, that night He goes to the garden of Gethsemane. He asks three of His disciples to wait nearby, praying for Him. Luke tells us He went off from His disciples to pray alone. He knelt down and prayed, *"Father, if You are willing, remove this cup from Me. Nevertheless, not My will, but Yours, be done."*[1]

Matthew records that Jesus made that request of His Father in prayer twice: *"And going a little farther He fell on His face and prayed, saying, 'My Father, if it be possible, let this cup pass from Me; nevertheless, not as I will, but as You will.'"*[2] and *"Again, for the second time, He went away and prayed, 'My Father, if this cannot pass unless I drink it, Your will be done.'"*[3] Mark's record of this prayer adds a little more positive aspect: *"And He said, 'Abba, Father, all things are possible for You. Remove this cup from Me. Yet not what I will, but what You will.'"*[4]

DID JESUS RECOIL FROM HIS COMMITMENT TO DIE FOR OUR SINS?

Some interpret this to imply that Jesus, without sinning, was personally reluctant to endure the Cross but was prepared to set aside His personal desires to comply to God's will in this mat-ter. This interpretation assumes "cup" to signify "dying on the Cross," and *"not My will, but Yours"* to imply that Jesus hoped, if at all possible, to avoid going to the Cross.

Some commentators use this text as an illustration of how Jesus was tempted in His suffering: *"For because He Himself has suffered when tempted, He is able to help those who are being tempted,"*[5] and, *"For we do not have a high priest who is unable to sympathize with our weaknesses, but One who in every respect has been tempted as we are, yet without sin."*[6]

It is typically stated that our comprehension of Jesus' "weakness" in the garden enables us to be assured that He identifies with us in our personal weakness, and therefore He is sympathetic and forgiving. While I fully agree with both the texts in Hebrews and I also agree that Jesus is sympathetic, compassionate, forgiving, and sinless, I do not agree that this position is the true meaning of Jesus' statements in His prayer to the Father in the garden.

GOD THE FATHER ANSWERED JESUS' PRAYER

I believe that, in the light of Jesus' role as the Bridegroom God, it was not dying on the Cross that Jesus desired to avoid, but rather His dying in the garden before He ever got to the Cross. It is inconceivable that Jesus as the Bridegroom God had personal desires contrary to the Father's. In everything, Jesus' will was in harmony with the Father's. I believe Jesus was in danger of dying in the garden, and therefore He called out to His Father for the grace and supernatural power either to remain alive through His garden experience, or, if He did die in the garden, to be revived by the Father so that He would be alive for His coming crucifixion. Incarnationally,[7] He had the intrinsic power to sustain Himself or revive Himself; but, as in all things, Jesus lived by the Father's power and not His own.

I believe the meaning of the prayer was something like this: "Father, I am dying. If I die here in this garden, then I cannot fulfill My prophetic destiny at the Cross to woo and win the Bride. Abba, as I have My entire life, I am asking that this would be accomplished by Your power, not by My own."

And, in fact, God answered Jesus' prayer, and supernaturally strengthened Him in the garden by means of angelic ministry, enabling Jesus to remain alive to face His crucifixion to save us from our sins and win our heart and our love.

This might, to some, be a new perspective, while it is not at all a fringe understanding of these Scriptures. To those who have not been exposed to this understanding, it might sound at first unreasonable and unscriptural—remember the worldview thing? It is hard for us to see what we do not *see*. So for those who aren't familiar with this, let us examine it carefully and scripturally and you will see the strength of this interpretation contextually, theologically, and biblically.

JESUS CONSTANTLY PROCLAIMED GOD'S PLAN FOR HIS CRUCIFIXION

The concept that Jesus would, at the last moment, waver in His commitment to go to the Cross and to paying the Bride-price for the redemption of the Bride is cross-grain to everything we see concerning His steadfast commitment throughout His ministry. Jesus clearly declared His intentions when He proclaimed, *"I am the good shepherd. The good shepherd lays down His life for the sheep. ...I lay down My life for the sheep."*[8] Jesus echoes this same thought a little later, *"Greater love has no one than this, that someone lay down his life for his friends."*[9]

PETER'S DESIRE THAT JESUS NOT DIE

From that time Jesus began to show His disciples that He must go to Jerusalem and suffer many things from the elders and chief priests and scribes, and be killed, and on the third day be raised. And Peter took Him aside and began to rebuke Him, saying, "Far be it from You, Lord! This shall never happen to You." But He turned and said to Peter, "Get behind Me, Satan! You are a hindrance to Me. For you are not setting your mind on the things of God, but on the things of man."[10]

Does it seem reasonable that Jesus would rebuke Peter for the very sentiment He Himself supposedly expresses in His prayer in the garden?

JESUS WAS COMMITTED TO DYING TO PAY THE BRIDE-PRICE

As we have seen, Jesus openly and repeatedly announced that He was committed to die to fulfill the prophetic Scriptures to pay the price for sinful man.[11]

After Jesus was resurrected He rebuked two of His disciples for failing to understand the necessity of His death, burial, and resurrection, saying, *"O foolish ones, and slow of heart to believe all that the prophets have spoken! Was it not necessary that the Christ should suffer these things and enter into His glory?"*[12] These words were spoken after His resurrection, but there is no evidence to point that He came to this conclusion as a result of His struggle in the garden. In fact, He is saying the exact opposite. He is saying that even the disciples should have always known and understood the inevitability of the Cross because of the message of the prophets. If He held the disciples accountable for what the prophets said, how much more would He, the very One of whom they prophesied, be held accountable?

The death, burial, and resurrection is at the center of the Gospel.[13] The Gospel without the Cross is no Gospel at all.[14] Jesus Himself summarized His commission of the disciples by stating:

> *Thus it is written, that the Christ should suffer and on the third day rise from the dead, and that repentance and forgiveness of sins should be proclaimed in His name to all nations, beginning from Jerusalem.*[15]

A SECOND LOOK AT THE GARDEN PRAYER

Now that we have looked at the overwhelming scriptural evidence that Jesus both recognized and was committed to the necessity of His crucifixion to save us from our sins as the Bride-price, let's look at what happened in the garden. As we do, I want you to notice four important principles. First, we will see that there is a strong indication that Jesus was in danger of dying in the garden. Second, there is no scriptural evidence that

Jesus—our *"holy, innocent, unstained, separated from sinners and exalted above the heavens"* high priest[16]—ever wavered in His commitment to the Cross, as the text we have already examined amply attested to. Third, there is ample biblical evidence that Jesus' will was never at any time, even in the garden, at variance with the Father's will. He was always in agreement with, and submitted to, the Father's will. Fourth, it is apparent that His prayer was answered, and as a result, He was strengthened in order to be able to leave the garden and continue on to the Cross.

IMMINENT DEATH

Jesus went to the garden of Gethsemane to pray. While He was praying, we read, *"He began to be greatly distressed, sorrowful, and troubled. Then He said to them, "My soul is very sorrowful, even to death; remain here, and watch with Me."*[17] Then Luke adds, *"And being in an agony He prayed more earnestly; and His sweat became like great drops of blood falling down to the ground."*[18] As I mentioned in Chapter Eleven, there is a rare, but well-documented, condition called hematidrosis, or bloody sweat. Under great emotional stress of the kind Jesus suffered, tiny capillaries in the sweat glands break, causing a mixing of blood with sweat. This process produces marked weakness and possible shock.

Dr. James Buswell, professor of Systematic Theology at Covenant Theological Seminary in Saint Louis, Missouri, states:

> I am personally convinced that the "cup" from which Jesus asked to be delivered in Gethsemane was physical collapse and death in the garden before He reached the cross. Luke describes His physical condition, "An angel from heaven appeared to Him and strengthened Him; [for] as He prayed He was in extreme agony, and His sweat was like great drops of blood falling down upon the ground" (see Luke 22:43-44). Matthew and Mark do not describe these particular symptoms, but they record the fact that He said, "My soul is in great pain, to the

point of death" (see Matt. 26:38; Mark 13:34). In this saying the word translated "in great pain," or "exceeding sorrowful," is the word in the LXX which translates "cast down" in the repeated refrain in Psalm 42, "Why art thou cast down, O my soul?" As Jesus used these words in speaking to His disciples, they would undoubtedly recognize that He was referring to this particular refrain in the Psalm. But He added, "To the point of death," indicating that He thought Himself to be in a state of physical collapse.

Extremely profuse perspiration such as Luke described is characteristic of a state of physical shock in which the sufferer is in imminent danger of collapse and even death. My suggestion is that our Lord Jesus Christ, finding Himself in this physical state of extreme shock, prayed for deliverance from death in the garden, in order that He might accomplish His purpose on the cross.[19]

I am not a medical doctor, but I have heard several medical doctors describing this condition. They stated that this represents an aneurism where the main blood vessel going to the brain has burst, which would have meant imminent death. In other words, Dr. Buswell was correct: Jesus was dying in the garden. Jesus was not praying for the cup of the Cross to pass; He was praying that the cup of His dying in the garden before He could get to the Cross would pass.

We can gain further insight into what exactly was going on in the garden from the Book of Hebrews:

*In the days of His flesh, Jesus offered up **prayers and supplications, with loud cries and tears,** to Him who was able to save Him from death, and He was heard because of His reverence.*[20]

JESUS NEVER WAVERED

There is no scriptural evidence in any of the texts related to Jesus' garden experience that would indicate that Jesus wavered in His commitment to go to the Cross. The texts that are used by some to advance this argument are the same ones I am contending mean something else altogether. In order to come to that false conclusion, one has to come to the text with a presupposition and make arguments from silence—that conclusion cannot be reached from the text itself. There is abundant evidence from Jesus' statements throughout His ministry that He knew of the inevitability of the Cross and that He was wholeheartedly committed to that end.

JESUS' WILL WAS THE SAME AS HIS FATHER'S WILL

Throughout the Gospels, we see that from beginning to end, Jesus' entire life and ministry was an unquestionable example of exemplary dependence on the authority, will, power, and agency of the Father.[21] The Gospel of John especially emphasizes this reality. Jesus explained clearly:

Truly, truly, I say to you, the Son can do nothing of His own accord, but only what He sees the Father doing. For whatever the Father does, that the Son does likewise. For the Father loves the Son and shows Him all that He Himself is doing. And greater works than these will He show Him, so that you may marvel. For as the Father raises the dead and gives them life, so also the Son gives life to whom He will.[22]

I can do nothing on My own. As I hear, I judge, and My judgment is just, because I seek not My own will but the will of Him who sent Me.[23]

Notice what Jesus is saying here. What pleases the Father is not contrary to what pleases Jesus. Jesus takes pleasure in the same things that please the Father. Jesus continues, *"the very works that I am doing, bear witness about Me that the Father has sent Me.*"[24]

I often use the analogy that if Jesus is in one room and the Father in another and you ask Them the same question, you will always get the same answer from both of Them. Not an exact reality, but you get the picture.

John is telling us that Jesus' desires and the Father's desires are always the same when he quotes Jesus:

> *So Jesus answered them, "My teaching is not Mine, but His who sent Me. If anyone's will is to do God's will, he will know whether the teaching is from God or whether I am speaking on My own authority.*"[25]

Notice closely the next verse: Jesus tells us directly that He is not only submitted to God's will, but He is also in agreement with God's will: *"The one who speaks on his own authority seeks his own glory; but the One who seeks the glory of Him who sent Him is true, and in Him there is no falsehood.*"[26]

When Jesus uses the phrase *"not My will, but Yours,"* it reminds us of similar statements He made in John 5:30 and 6:38. There is no disharmony between the wills or desires of God the Father and God the Son. They are in full agreement with each other at all times about all things. But what about Jesus in His humanity? In His humanity, Jesus places the priority of the Father's will over His human will. In other words, Jesus is in exact agreement with the Father, but in His humanity, His humanness, He submits all of His words and works to the authority of the Father as a model for the rest of us. In theological circles it is stated this way: we are saved by Christ's active obedience and His passive obedience, not only because of what He did, but under what authority He did what He did.

John gives us more insight into Jesus' like-mindedness with the Father concerning His coming crucifixion:

When you have lifted up the Son of Man, then you will know that I am He, and that I do nothing on My own authority, but speak just as the Father taught Me. And He who sent Me is with Me. He has not left Me alone, for I always do the things that are pleasing to Him.[27]

Although John gives us the clearest picture of Jesus' submission to the Father, it is not limited to John's Gospel. The undercurrent of Jesus' entire ministry is His agreement and submission to the Father. Jesus' delight was not only to die to redeem us, but also to live for us, so that we would see the love the Father had for Him and He for the Father, and that we would desire to enter into that as well. Jesus' whole ministry was an example of the loving Son who came in the name—power and authority—of His Father. The Scriptures admonish us to live lives of humility and self-sacrifice in imitation of Jesus and His relationship to His Father.

Whoever receives this child in My name receives Me, and whoever receives Me receives Him who sent Me. For he who is least among you all is the one who is great.[28]

Jesus was comfortable receiving only what the Father gave Him. *"All things have been handed over to Me by My Father."*[29] Jesus reminds His disciples, *"to sit at My right hand and at My left is not Mine to grant, but it is for those for whom it has been prepared by My Father."*[30] Jesus directly related His role in His humanity as a servant to the Father to His commandments for His disciples, saying:

But I am among you as the One who serves. You are those who have stayed with Me in My trials, and I assign to you, as My Father assigned to Me, a Kingdom.[31]

So, as we have seen, it is overwhelmingly clear that Jesus was submitted to the Father in will, purpose, action, and speech. His will was not contrary to the Father's will, but in submission to the Father's authority or will.

Jesus' Prayer Was Answered

We have seen that in the garden Jesus was in imminent danger of death, that He prayed for the Father to rescue Him, that He was fully cognizant of and committed to the Cross, and that His will was not contrary to the Father but in submission to Him. The only piece of our garden puzzle left to insert is evidence that His prayer was answered affirmatively.

Earlier we looked at Hebrews 5:7 and how it stated that Christ prayed to be delivered from death in the garden. The result?

> *In the days of His flesh, Jesus offered up prayers and supplications, with loud cries and tears, to Him who was able to save Him from death, and He was heard because of His reverence.*[32]

The common biblical idiom is that when one's prayer is "heard," it is answered in the affirmative. This corresponds perfectly with the Gospel account, *"And there appeared to Him an angel from heaven, strengthening Him."*[33] Matthew and Mark note that immediately after His recovery He came to the disciples the third time and said to them, *"Are you still sleeping and taking your rest? It is enough; see, the hour is at hand, and the Son of Man is betrayed into the hands of sinners."*[34]

Conclusion

Our study has proven conclusively that Jesus did not have a last-minute crisis of faith and become fearful of His imminent crucifixion. He did not have to struggle to ignore and overcome His own desires in order to submit and obey His Father's will. Jesus was not guilty of falling into fear as Peter had done when Jesus had rebuked him for trying to stop Him from going to the Cross.

Even in the midst of the most intense circumstances a human being could imagine, conditions critical enough that He would have died without immediate intervention, He proved again that

His life was a life in perfect agreement and submission to His Father. In the garden, as at all other times, He depended on His Father for everything He taught, everything He did, and even for sustaining His life so that He could fulfill the mission determined by God's definite plan and foreknowledge[35]—His death on the Cross for our sins.

Beloved, we can rejoice that we worship the One who lived for us and died for us, who looked forward to His crucifixion with unwavering purpose and commitment, who said:

> *The hour has come for the Son of Man to be glorified. Truly, truly, I say to you, unless a grain of wheat falls into the earth and dies, it remains alone; but if it dies, it bears much fruit. ...Now is My soul troubled. And what shall I say? "Father, save Me from this hour?" But for this purpose I have come to this hour.*[36]

Endnotes

INTRODUCTION

1. 1 Corinthians 15:33; 2 Corinthians 6:14; James 4:4.
2. Ephesians 5:22-24.
3. Ephesians 5:25-31.
4. Ephesians 5:32.

CHAPTER ONE

1. James W. Sheets Jr., "My Sickness." Unpublished poem.
2. Gene Raskin, "Those Were the Days."
3. Revelation 2:2-3.
4. Revelation 2:4-5.
5. Matthew 25:21.
6. Psalm 14:1-3; 53:1-3; Romans 3:10-12.
7. Saint Bernard of Claivaux, *On Loving God* (Createspace, 2009).
8. 1 John 4:10,19.
9. John 3:16; 1 John 4:16.
10. John 3:16; Titus 3:4.
11. John 16:27; 17:23; 2 Thessalonians 2:16; 1 John 4:16.
12. Ephesians 2:2; 5:6.
13. Ephesians 5:1; Colossians 3:12; 2 Thessalonians 2:13.
14. Isaiah 62:4.
15. Isaiah 62:5.

16. Ruth Peters, *Bible Illustrations–Illustrations of Bible Truths* (Chattanooga, TN: AMG Publishers, 1998), WORD*search* CROSS e-book, 142.

17. 1 Corinthians 15:46.

18. Ephesians 5:28.

19. Proverbs 31:10.

20. Ephesians 5:25-30 with author's capitalization changes.

21. Hebrews 12:2.

22. Ronald M. Payne and Ronnie Hinson, "When He Was on the Cross, I Was on His Mind" (Wind in Willow Publishing, 1984).

23. Ephesians 5:29-30.

24. Blaise Pascal, *Pensees* (Hackett Publishing Company, 2005).

25. Ephesians 5:28.

26. Leviticus 19:18; Matthew 22:39.

27. Genesis 2:24; Ephesians 5:31.

28. Ephesians 5:32.

CHAPTER TWO

1. Genesis 1:1–2:3.

2. Genesis 1:3,6,9,11,14,20,24.

3. Genesis 2:7.

4. Genesis 2:8.

5. Genesis 2:15.

6. Genesis 2:6.

7. Genesis 2:9.

8. Genesis 2:15-17.

9. Genesis 3:17-19.

10. Genesis 2:17.

11. John 14:6.

12. 1 Corinthians 2:9.

13. Acts 17:28.

14. Genesis 2:18-20.

15. 1 John 4:8,16

16. Genesis 2:21-22.

17. Genesis 2:23.

18. Genesis 2:23-24.

19. Ephesians 1:23.

20. Galatians 3:28.

21. 2 Corinthians 11:2.

CHAPTER THREE

1. Genesis 1:11-12.

2. 1 John 4:19.

3. Hebrews 7:27.

4. Hebrews 13:8.

5. Bill Johnson, *When Heaven Invades Earth* (Shippensburg, PA: Destiny Image, 2003), 110.

6. John 3:29.

7. Matthew 11:11-13.

8. Abraham J. Heschel, *The Prophets* (New York: Harper and Row, Perennial Classics Edition 2001), 30-31.

9. Numbers 13:8,16.

10. Matthew 1:21.

11. Hosea 1:1.

12. 1 Samuel 10:5-6;10-13; 2 Kings 2–6.

13. Hosea 1:1.

14. Hosea 1:2.

15. Hosea 1:3.

16. Deuteronomy 22:13-30.

17. Hosea 2:4.

18. 2 Kings 10:11.

19. Hosea 1:6.

20. Hosea 1:8-9.

21. Hosea 1:10-11.

22. Hosea 2:1.

23. Hosea 2:2–3, 6, paraphrased.

24. Hosea 2:14.

25. 1 John 4:8,16.

26. Ephesians 5:27.

27. Hosea 2:14-15.

28. Hosea 2:16.

29. *The NET Bible First Edition* (Biblical Studies Press, 2006).

30. Hosea 2:19.

31. 1 Corinthians 15:46.

32. Hosea 2:19-23.

33. Hosea 3:1.

34. *The NET Bible First Edition.*

35. Song of Solomon 2:5.

CHAPTER FOUR

1. J.F. Walvoord, R.B. Zuck, and Dallas Theological Seminary. *The Bible Knowledge Commentary: An Exposition of the Scriptures* (1:1387) (Wheaton, IL: Victor Books, 1983-c1985).

2. Hosea 3:2.

3. Exodus 21:32.

4. John 8:34; Romans 6:16-20; 2 Peter 2:19.

5. Numbers 5:15.

6. Matthew 26:15.

7. Hosea 3:3.

8. Song of Solomon 2:16; 6:3; 7:10.

9. Romans 3:23.

10. Romans 6:23.

11. Romans 5:8.

12. 1 Corinthians 6:20.

13. John 14:1-3.

14. Jeremiah 2:2.

15. Genesis 2:23–3:1.

16. Genesis 3:2-5.

17. Genesis 3:6.

18. 1 Timothy 2:13-14.

19. Genesis 3:7-8.

20. Isaiah 46:10.

21. Genesis 3:9.

22. H.D.M. Spence-Jones, Ed., *The Pulpit Commentary: Genesis* (Bellingham, WA: Logos Research Systems, Inc., 2004), 59.

23. Genesis 3:10-11.

24. Genesis 3:12.

25. Genesis 3:13.

26. Genesis 3:14-15.

27. Genesis 1:26-28.

28. Luke 4:5-7.

29. Galatians 3:16.

30. Genesis 12:1-7.

31. Genesis 11:31.

32. Genesis 15:1,9-18.

33. Psalm 3:3; 18:2; 84:11; 119:114.

34. S.J. Hill, *Burning Desire* (Orlando, FL: Relevant Books, 2005), 29.

35. J. Orr, Ed., *The International Standard Bible Encyclopedia* (Chicago: Howard-Severance Co., 1915).

36. M. Easton, *Easton's Bible Dictionary* (Oak Harbor, WA: Logos Research Systems, Inc., 1996-c1897).

37. Genesis 15:5.

38. Genesis 15:6.

39. Genesis 15:8.

Chapter Five

1. Genesis 15:6.

2. Genesis 15:8.

3. Luke 1:5-10.

4. Leviticus 6:13.

5. Luke 1:11.

6. Luke 1:12.

7. Luke 1:13-17.

8. Luke 1:18.

9. Luke 1:19-20.

10. Luke 1:26-28.

11. Luke 1:29-33.

12. Luke 1:34.

13. Luke 1:35.

14. Genesis 15:9.

15. Genesis 15:10.

16. J.W. Hayford, *Spirit-Filled Life Bible for Students* (Nashville, TN: Thomas Nelson Publisher, 1997, c1995).

17. S.J. Hill, *Burning Desire* (Orlando, FL: Relevant Books, 2005), 31.

18. Genesis 15:12.

19. Genesis 2:21.

20. D.S. Dockery, T.C. Butler, C.L. Church, L.L. Scott, M.A. Ellis Smith, J.E. White, and *Holman Bible Publishers, Holman Bible Handbook* (Nashville, TN: Holman Bible Publishers, 1992).

21. S. Zodhiates, *The Complete Word Study Dictionary: New Testament* (Chattanooga, TN: AMG Publishers, 1993), G1611.

22. Genesis 2:21; Ezekiel 1:1; Acts 10:10; 11:5; 2 Corinthians 12:2.

23. J. Wesley, *Explanatory Notes on the New Testament* (Ada, MI: Baker Pubishing Group, 1983).

24. Psalm 113:4-6; Isaiah 6:3; 40:25.

25. E.D. Radmacher, R.B. Allen, H.W. House, *The Nelson Study Bible: New King James Version* (Nashville, TN: Thomas Nelson Publishers, 1997).

26. John 8:56.

27. James 1:22.

28. John 3:16.

29. Ephesians 2:4.

30. Luke 23:34; 1 John 2:12.

31. Genesis 15:13.

32. Genesis 15:14.

33. Genesis 15:17.

34. Galatians 3:7.

35. John 1:29; Hebrews 9:26.

36. 1 John 4:19.

37. Genesis 2:24; Ephesians 5:28-32.

38. 1 Peter 1:18-19.

39. Hebrews 12:2.

40. Genesis 17:5.

41. Exodus 6:5-8.

42. Ezekiel 16:6-7.

43. Ezekiel 16:6.

44. Exodus 3:14.

45. Psalm 95:10.

46. Exodus 19:4-5.

47. *The NET Bible First Edition* (Biblical Studies Press, 2006).

48. Ezekiel 16:8.

49. Isaiah 54:5-6.

50. Isaiah 62:5.

51. Jeremiah 31:31-32.

CHAPTER SIX

1. Exodus 19:5-6.

2. Exodus 19:7.

3. D.H. Stern, *Jewish New Testament Commentary: A Companion Volume to the Jewish New Testament* (Clarksville, MD: Jewish New Testament Publications, 1996, c1992). Electronic edition.

4. Ibid.

5. Exodus 19:10.

6. Exodus 19:6; 1 Peter 2:9.

7. Matthew 3:1-4.

8. Ephesians 5:26-27.

9. The word *epistle* is just another word for a letter.

10. Titus 3:5.

11. Exodus 19:12-15.

12. Exodus 19:8.

13. Exodus 19:16-18.

14. S.J. Hill, *Burning Desire* (Orlando, FL: Relevant Books, 2005), 45.

15. Exodus 19:16; 20:18.

16. J. Strong, *The Exhaustive Concordance of the Bible* (Ontario: Woodside Bible Fellowship, 1996).

17. Exodus 20:18-19.

18. Exodus 20:20.

19. Job 28:28; Psalm 34:11; 111:10.

20. Proverbs 15:33.

21. James Swanson, *Dictionary of Biblical Languages with Semantic Domains: Hebrew (Old Testament)* (Logos Research Systems, 1997).

22. Exodus 19:21-22.

23. Isaiah 6:2-3; Revelation 4:8.

24. Isaiah 6:1-3.

25. Revelation 4:6b-11.

26. Revelation 4:8.

27. Isaiah 9:6.

28. 1 Corinthians 2:9.

29. Ephesians 5:18, (*Daniel Mace's New Testament*, 1729).

30. 1 Samuel 13:14; Acts 13:22.

31. Psalm 27:4.

32. 1 Corinthians 2:9-12.

33. Proverbs 25:2.

34. Revelation 22:17.

35. 2 Thessalonians 1:3-12.

36. 2 Thessalonians 2:8.

CHAPTER SEVEN

1. The inspiration for this chapter came partially from a training session held by Gary Weins at the International House of Prayer in Kansas City.

2. Charles H. Kraft, *Christianity and Culture* (Maryknoll, NY: Orbis Books, 1979).

3. James Sire, *The Universe Next Door* (Downers Grove, IL: InterVarsity Press, 1976), 17.

4. Kraft, *Christianity and Culture*, 53.

5. 1 Corinthians 12:7.

6. Acts 14:8-18.

7. John MacArthur, *The Charismatics* (Grand Rapids, MI: Zondervan Publishing Company, 1978), 131, 149.

8. James Sire, *Scripture Twisting* (Downers Grove, IL: InterVarsity Press, 1980), 26, emphasis added.

9. Paul Hiebert, "The Flaw of the Excluded Middle" (January 1982), 36. *Missiology: An International Review,* American Society of Missiology (Elkhart). 35-47, Vol. X, no. 1.

10. Ibid., 37-39.

11. Usually referred to as the "Boring figure," it is credited to American psychologist E.G. Boring.

CHAPTER EIGHT

1. C. Brand, C. Draper, A. England, S. Bond, E.R. Clendenen, T.C. Butler, and B. Latta, *Holman Illustrated Bible Dictionary* (Nashville, TN: Holman Bible Publishers, 2003), 432.

2. The gifts (charismata) or gracelets is a term coined by Dr. Russ Spittler, a professor at Fuller Theological Seminary referring to the spiritual gifts or the charismata, the transrational manifestations of God.

3. W.C. Kaiser, *Hard Sayings of the Bible* (Downers Grove, IL: InterVarsity, 1997).

4. Proverbs 8:22-31.

5. John 1:1-3.

6. Colossians 1:15-17.

7. Hebrews 1:2.

8. The word *trinity* is never found in the Bible, though the idea represented by the word is taught in many places. Trinity means tri-unity or three-in-oneness. It is used to summarize the teaching of Scripture that God is three persons yet one God. W.A. Grudem, *Systematic Theology: An Introduction to Biblical Doctrine* (Leicester, England; Grand Rapids, MI: InterVarsity Press, Zondervan, 1994), 226.

9. Jeremiah 30:19.

10. 2 Samuel 6:5,21; Jeremiah 15:17.

11. Psalm 104:26.

12. W. Baker, *The Complete Word Study Dictionary: Old Testament* (Chattanooga, TN: AMG Publishers), 1124.

13. Ephesians 1:4.

14. Genesis 2:18-20.

15. C.S. Lewis, *The Weight of Glory* (San Fransisco, CA: HarperSanFranscico, 2001).

16. Genesis 2:21-23.

17. John 19:34.

18. Genesis 2:24.

19. Ephesians 5:31-32.

20. Genesis 3:1-7; 2 Corinthians 11:3.

21. D.L. Moody, *Notes From My Bible* (Grand Rapids, MI: Baker Book House, 1979).

22. John 17:23.

23. Matthew 22:2.

24. Genesis 24:2-4.

25. S.J. Hill, *Burning Desire* (Orlando, FL: Relevant Books, 2005), 14.

26. Genesis 24:12-14.

27. Genesis 24:15-21.

28. Genesis 24:22-33.

29. Hill, *Burning Desire,* 15; Genesis 24:34-49.

30. Genesis 24:50-58.

31. Genesis 24:59-61.

32. Psalm 45:7.

33. Ephesians 2:12.

34. Genesis 15:1-21.

35. Exodus 20:3; Deuteronomy 5:7.

36. Exodus 20:17; Deuteronomy 5:21.

37. Exodus 20:5; 34:14-15; Numbers 25:11-13; Deuteronomy 4:24; 5:9; 6:15.

38. Ephesians 5:27.

39. Matthew 6:33.

40. 2 Peter 3:14.

41. Revelation 3:18-22.

42. Psalm 23:5.

43. For more insight on bridal intercession, I highly recommend *Bridal Intercession* by my friend, Gary Wiens, available at www.burningheartministries.com.

CHAPTER NINE

1. J.W. Hayford and Thomas Nelson Publishers, *Hayford's Bible Handbook* (Nashville: Thomas Nelson Publishers, 1995).

2. Ibid.

3. Psalm 2, 8, 16, 22, 40, 45, 69, 72, 89, 102, 109, 110, and 132 are just a few examples of recognized Messianic Psalms.

4. Psalm 45:1-9.

5. Psalm 45:10-17.

6. Compare Psalm 45:6-7 to Hebrews 1:8-9.

7. D.S. Dockery, T.C. Butler, C.L. Church, L.L. Scott, M.A. Ellis Smith, J.E. White, and *Holman Bible Publishers, Holman Bible Handbook* (Nashville, TN: Holman Bible Publishers, 1992), 337.

8. Psalm 45:1.

9. W. Baker, *The Complete Word Study Dictionary: Old Testament,* (Chattanooga, TN: AMG Publishers), 223.

10. James Swanson, *Dictionary of Biblical Languages with Semantic Domains,* (Logos Research Systems, 1997), DBLH 3206, #1.

11. Jeremiah 5:13.

12. Baker, *The Complete Word Study Dictionary: Old Testament,* 223.

13. Psalm 45:2.

14. W.D. Mounce, *Mounce's Complete Expository Dictionary of Old & New Testament Words* (Grand Rapids, MI: Zondervan, 2006).

15. 2 Corinthians 3:18 NKJV.

16. Ephesians 6:17.

17. Psalm 45:3-5.

18. 1 Timothy 6:15.

19. Matthew 6:10.

20. Jeremiah 1:12.

21. Psalm 45:6-7.

22. Psalm 45:8.

23. Proverbs 7:17.

24. Exodus 30:23.

25. John 19:39-40.

26. Matthew 2:11.

27. Mark 15:23.

28. Song of Solomon 4:14.

29. Exodus 30:24.

30. C. Brand, C. Draper, A. England, S. Bond, E.R. Clendenen, T.C. Butler, and B. Latta, *Holman Illustrated Bible Dictionary* (Nashville, TN: Holman Bible Publishers, 2003), 271.

31. Psalm 45:9.

32. 1 Kings 9:28; 10:11; 22:48; 2 Chronicles 8:18; 9:10.

33. 1 Chronicles 29:4; Job 22:24; 28:16; Psalm 45:9.

34. Paul E. Billheimer, *Destined for the Throne* (Minneapolis, MN: Christian Literature Crusade, 1975).

35. Ibid., 15-16.

36. Psalm 45:10-11.

37. Psalm 45:10.

38. 1 John 2:15-16.

39. Psalm 45:11.

40. Isaiah 61:3.

41. Song of Solomon 1:5.

42. Psalm 45:13-15.

43. E.D. Radmacher, R.B. Allen, H.W. House, *The Nelson Study Bible: New King James Version* (Nashville, TN: Thomas Nelson Publishers, 1997).

44. R. Ellsworth, *Opening up Psalms* (Leominster, UK: Day One Publications, 2006), 180.

45. Psalm 45:16-17.

46. 1 Timothy 6:15; Revelation 3:21.

47. Revelation 5:9.

48. Isaiah 1:1.

49. Isaiah 49:18.

50. Isaiah 50:1.

51. Isaiah 54:1-8.

52. Isaiah 61:10-11.

53. Isaiah 62:4-5.

54. Jeremiah 2:2.

55. Jeremiah 2:32.

56. Jeremiah 3:6-10.

57. Jeremiah 4:30.

58. Jeremiah 16:1-4.

59. Jeremiah 31:4.

60. Jeremiah 31:31-32 with clarifying comments by the author.

61. Jeremiah 33:10-11 with clarifying comments by the author.

62. Ezekiel 16:1-7.

63. Ezekiel 16:8-14 with clarifying comments by the author.

64. Ezekiel 16:15-23 with clarifying comments by the author.

CHAPTER TEN

1. Song of Solomon 1:2.

2. Song of Solomon 1:4.

3. Song of Solomon 1:8-9a.

4. Song of Solomon 1:5-6b.

5. Song of Solomon l:6.

6. The kisses of God are metaphorical, representing how He touches her heart with His Spirit and His Word.

7. Song of Solomon 1:6.

8. Song of Solomon 1:6b.

9. Song of Solomon 1:6a-7b.

10. Song of Solomon 1:7.

11. Song of Solomon 1:7.

12. Song of Solomon 1:8.

13. Song of Solomon 1:12.

14. Song of Solomon 1:12; 2:3.

15. Song of Solomon 1:12b.

16. Song of Solomon 1:13-14.

17. Song of Solomon 1:15.

18. Song of Solomon 2:1.

19. Song of Solomon 2:2.

20. Song of Solomon 2:3-4.

21. Song of Solomon 2:3-4.

22. Song of Solomon 2:5.

23. Song of Solomon 2:8-9a.

24. Song of Solomon 2:8.

25. Song of Solomon 2:10.

26. Song of Solomon 2:10.

27. Song of Solomon 2:17.

28. Hebrews 12:5-12.

29. A quote from Corrie Ten Boom on the PTL Club.

30. In the Scriptures, God's face often represents His manifest Presence.

31. Song of Solomon 1:3.

32. Jeremiah 20:7.

33. Song of Solomon 3:2.

34. Song of Solomon 3:4.

35. Romans 4:17.

36. Song of Solomon 4:1,7.

37. Song of Solomon 4:6.

38. Song of Solomon 2:9-10.

39. Song of Solomon 4:6.

40. Song of Solomon 4:8a.

41. Song of Solomon 4:8.

42. Song of Solomon 4:9-10.

43. Song of Solomon 4:10d-11.

44. Song of Solomon 4:12-15.

45. Song of Solomon 4:16.

46. Song of Solomon 5:1.

47. Song of Solomon 5:2.

48. Romans 8:18; Philippians 3:10; Colossians 1:24.

49. Song of Solomon 5:3-5.

50. Song of Solomon 5:6.

51. Song of Solomon 3:1-2.

52. Song of Solomon 5:7.

53. Song of Solomon 1:4.

54. Song of Solomon 5:8.

55. Song of Solomon 5:9.

56. Song of Solomon 5:10-16.

57. Song of Solomon 6:1.

58. Song of Solomon 6:4.

59. Song of Solomon 6:5a,b.

60. Song of Solomon 6:5c-7.

61. Song of Solomon 6:8-9.

62. Song of Solomon 6:10.

63. Song of Solomon 6:11.

64. Song of Solomon 6:12.

65. Song of Solomon 6:13a,b.

66. Song of Solomon 6:13c,d.

67. Song of Solomon 7:1-5.

68. Song of Solomon 7:6-9a.

69. Song of Solomon 7:9b-10.

70. Song of Solomon 7:11-13.

71. Song of Solomon 8:1-2.

72. Song of Solomon 8:3-4.

73. Song of Solomon 8:5-7.

74. Song of Solomon 8:8-9.

75. Song of Solomon 8:13.

76. Song of Solomon 8:14.

77. Song of Solomon 2:8.

78. Song of Solomon 8:14.

79. Song of Solomon 1:13.

80. Revelation 22:20.

CHAPTER ELEVEN

1. John 2:1-11.
2. Revelation 19:7.
3. Revelation 22:20.
4. John 3:29a.
5. Hosea 2:16.
6. Matthew 9:15.
7. Revelation 21:9.
8. Matthew 22:2.
9. Matthew 22:3.
10. Revelation 22:17.
11. Hebrews 7:25.
12. Matthew 25:6.
13. John 17:21-26.
14. John 17:24.
15. John 17:26.
16. John 14:9.
17. Hebrews 12:2.
18. Luke 23:39.
19. Psalm 40:6-8; Hebrews 10:7.
20. Matthew 26:39 paraphrased.
21. Luke 22:44.
22. For more on this, see Appendix A.
23. Luke 23:42.
24. Isaiah 52:14, *The NET Bible First Edition* (Biblical Studies Press, 2006).
25. Hebrews 12:2.
26. Luke 23:43.
27. John 14:1-3.
28. John 17:24.

29. John 17:3, *Wuest's New Testament Volume 4* (Rapids/ Cambridge: Wm. B. Eerdmans Publishing Grand, 1961).

30. John 17:3,24.

31. Revelation 2:4, author paraphrase of *Jewish New Testament* (Clarksville, MD: Messianic Jewish Resourses International, 1989).

32. Revelation 1:1.

33. Revelation 3:20.

34. Revelation 19:7.

35. Matthew 11:11.

36. John 3:29.

37. Matthew 6:3.

38. Matthew 9:14-15 NKJV.

39. Matthew 9:16-17; Mark 2:21-22; Luke 5:36-39.

40. Luke 24:52, Dr. Jack Hayford, *Spirit-Filled Life Study Bible* (Nashville, TN: Thomas Nelson Publishers, 2005).Electronic edition.

41. Acts 23:6.

42. Acts 9:1-18.

43. Colossians 1:23.

44. 2 Corinthians 11:2, *New Century Version* (Nashville, TN: Thomas Nelson Publishers, 2005).

45. 2 Corinthians 11:3.

46. 2 Corinthians 11:2-4; Galatians 1:8-9.

47. Ephesians 5:25-32 with author's capitalization changes.

48. Ephesians 1:17-18.

49. The definition of hope is a joyful expectation based on the promises of God contained in His Word.

50. Ephesians 1:22-23.

51. John 3:29.

52. John 5:35.

53. Matthew 11:11.

54. John 3:30.

55. From a Last Days Ministries tract entitled *A Christless Pentecost* by David Wilkerson.

56. 2 Corinthians 3:18.

57. John 17:26.

58. Joel 2:28-29; Acts 2:17-18.

59. Zechariah 12:10.

60. John 14:12; Jude 3.

61. Matthew 16:18; 22:37; Ephesians 3:19; 4:13; 5:26-27; Revelation 7:9; 12:11; 15:2; 19:7-8; 22:17.

62. Matthew 24:14; Revelation 5:9; 7:9,14; 14:6.

63. In the Book of Acts, the Church was in unity with the Spirit, but it was an immature unity and was localized and short-lived.

64. Revelation 22:17.

65. Hosea 2:16.

66. Isaiah 62:4-5.

CHAPTER TWELVE

1. John Piper, *God is the Gospel: Meditations on God's Love as the Gift of Himself* (Wheaton, IL: Crossway Books, 2005).

2. Matthew 22:34-36.

3. Deuteronomy 20:3-17.

4. Exodus 20:3.

5. Exodus 20:12.

6. Exodus 20:15.

7. Deuteronomy 6:4-5.

8. This is a compilation of the synoptic versions of Jesus' reply to the lawyer's question. See Matthew 22:37-40, Mark 12:29-31, and Luke 10:27.

9. Matthew 22:38.

10. Matthew 22:38 NKJV.

11. Matthew 22:38, *Holman Christian Standard Bible* (Nashville, TN: Holman Bible Publisherws, 1999, 2003).

12. Ibid.

13. Psalm 2:8 paraphrased.

14. http://ll.newsforchristians.com/sermons/sermon030.html.

15. Philippians 2:9-11.

16. Isaiah 45:23; Philippians 2:10-11.

17. Psalm 110:3.

18. Ephesians 3:19.

19. Romans 5:5.

20. Matthew 22:39 paraphrased.

21. Amos 3:3 KJV.

22. 1 John 4:19 NKJV.

23. Matthew 3:17; 17:5; John 12:28.

24. John 17:26.

25. Revelation 19:7.

26. John 17:26 paraphrased.

27. Revelation 19:7.

28. Acts 19–20.

29. Revelation 2:4.

30. 2 Corinthians 11:3.

31. Psalm 91:14.

32. Matthew 4:17.

33. 2 Corinthians 13:5.

34. John 14:15.

35. John 14:21.

36. John 14:23.

37. The Sermon on the Mount is recorded in Matthew 5–7.

38. Matthew 11:29-30.

39. Deuteronomy 6:44-45 loosely paraphrased.

40. Luke 10:38-42.

41. James 4:8.

42. 2 Chronicles 16:9, Eugene Peterson, *The Message Bible* (Colorado Springs, CO: NavPress Publishing Group, 1993, 2002).

43. Deuteronomy 6:4-5 paraphrased.

CHAPTER THIRTEEN

1. 1 John 4:19.
2. Ephesians 3:18-19; 1 John 4:19.
3. John 15:9.
4. 1 Corinthians 9:24-27.
5. Hebrews 12:5-11.
6. John Piper, *Future Grace* (New York: Multnomah Publishers, 1995).
7. John 17:26.
8. Romans 5:5.
9. Matthew 11:12; Luke 16:16.
10. Matthew 22:39.
11. 2 Corinthians 5:17; Ephesians 1:18.
12. Psalm 139:13-17.
13. Psalm 139:14 paraphrased.
14. John 13:34-35; 1 John 3:18-19.
15. John 13:35.

CHAPTER FOURTEEN

1. Mark 12:30.
2. John 14:6; Acts 9:2; 19:23.
3. Luke 10:37-42.
4. John 14:15-23.
5. John 14:15-23.
6. Matthew 5–7.
7. Revelation 5:9.
8. Romans 2:4.
9. Psalm 45:1-2.
10. 1 Timothy 4:1-2.
11. John 16:13-14.
12. John 14:6.

13. Song 5:8.

14. Exodus 34:14.

15. Ephesians 5:29-32.

16. John 15:13.

17. Psalm 45:10; Ephesians 5:29.

CHAPTER FIFTEEN

1. John 2:25.

2. Proverbs 4:23.

3. Matthew 6:21.

4. Matthew 6:21; Luke 12:34.

5. Psalm 91:14.

6. 1 John 2:15-16.

7. 1 Samuel 13:14; Acts 13:22.

8. Psalm 18:1 NKJV.

9. Of course, I understand that there might be some exceptions: there are emotional issues that can be related to chemical or physiological reactions, so I am not strictly stating that "all of our emotions" are results of our past focuses; but generally speaking, the emotions we have today are the fruit of the choices we made that acted as the setting we had ten years ago.

10. 2 Corinthians 3:18 NKJV.

11. Psalm 37:3-5.

12. Romans 5:5.

13. Psalm 37:4.

14. 1 Corinthians 2:9.

15. Job 22:24-25.

16. Matthew 6:33.

17. A quality decision is a decision from which there is no retreat.

18. Matthew 5:18.

19. 2 Corinthians 3:18.

20. 2 Thessalonians 3:5.

21. Hebrews 13:15.

22. 1 Corinthians 13:12.
23. A quote from John Wimber.
24. 2 Corinthians 5:12.

CHAPTER SIXTEEN

1. Mark 12:30.
2. Ephesians 4:29-32; 5:4.
3. Matthew 12:34-35.
4. Ephesians 4:29-32; 5:1-6.
5. 1 Corinthians 3:2-3; 16-18; James 3:6-10; 4:10-11; 5:8-9.
6. Proverbs 18:21.
7. Ephesians 4:29-32.
8. Ephesians 5:1-6.
9. James 3:1.
10. James 3:1-2.
11. James 1:4.
12. James 3:6-10.
13. 1 Corinthians 3:2-3;16-18.
14. 1 Corinthians 10:8-13.
15. James 4:10-11; 5:8-9.
16. James 4:6.
17. Philippians 2:12.
18. It takes God to love God.
19. Matthew 11:29; Mark 10:45.
20. John 16:13-14.
21. 1 Corinthians 15:24-28.
22. Psalm 113:4-8.
23. Hebrews 1:3.
24. John 14:9.
25. John 10:30.
26. 1 John 4:8,16.
27. Philippians 2:3-9.

28. Hebrews 1:3, *New American Standard Bible* (La Habra, CA: The Lockman Foundation, 1960, 1995).

29. John 17:5; Colossians 1:15; Hebrews 1:3.

30. 1 Timothy 3:16.

31. Philippians 2:6.

32. Revelation 3:21.

33. Hebrews 2:17.

34. Colossians 1:17; Hebrews 1:3.

35. Philippians 2:7.

36. 2 Corinthians 8:9.

37. James 3:15.

38. Matthew 17:1-17.

39. Mark 10:45.

40. Luke 6:35.

41. Philippians 2:5.

42. 2 Corinthians 8:9; Revelation 5:12.

43. Philippians 2:7.

44. Philippians 2:7 NKJV.

45. Revelation 4:3.

46. Isaiah 53:2.

47. Philippians 2:8.

48. Galatians 3:10,13.

49. 1 John 3:16; 4:16-21.

50. John 13:3-17.

51. Luke 12:37.

52. John 17:26.

53. John 14:7-9; 17:26.

54. Ephesians 2:4-7.

55. Philippians 2:3-5.

56. Philippians 2:12-16.

57. James 1:19-21.

58. Ephesians 4:29-32; 5:1-6.
59. Matthew 12:34; James 3:6-8.
60. 1 Peter 2:21-23.
61. Psalm 31:5; Romans 12:19; 1 Peter 2:23.
62. Ephesians 2:1-12.
63. Luke 17:7-10.

CHAPTER SEVENTEEN

1. Mark 12:30.
2. 1 Corinthians 4:20.
3. James 2:17, J.B. Phillips, *New Testament in Modern English* (New York: Touchstone, Simon & Schuster Inc., 1972, 1995).
4. Joshua 1:8.
5. Joshua 1:1-2.
6. Joshua 1:3-7.
7. Joshua 1:7.
8. Joshua 1:8-9.
9. Hebrews 10:16 commentary added.
10. 2 Corinthians 3:3.
11. Exodus 31:18.
12. Luke 24:32.
13. Luke 24:45.
14. Matthew 4:4.
15. Romans 10:8.
16. Hosea 2:16.
17. John 5:39-40.
18. 2 Corinthians 3:6.
19. Romans 5:8.
20. Luke 6:38.
21. Ephesians 1:17.
22. Matthew 22:37.
23. James 3:2

24. Matthew 6:13.
25. John 17:15.
26. Genesis 1:2-3.
27. Colossians 1:17; Hebrews 1:3.
28. Genesis 1:3,6,9,11,14,20,24,26,28-29.
29. Genesis 1:3,6,9,11,14,20,24,26.
30. Genesis 1:3,7,9,11,15,24,30.
31. Genesis 1:4,7,12,16,21,25,27.
32. Matthew 4:3-11.
33. Ephesians 6:13-17.

CHAPTER EIGHTEEN

1. John 14:15.
2. S. Zodhiates, *The Complete Word Study Dictionary New Testament* (Chattanooga, TN: AMG Publisher, 1993). Electronic edition.
3. Matthew 6:1-4; 19-21.
4. Matthew 6:5-13.
5. Matthew 5:44; 6:14-15.
6. Matthew 6:16-18.
7. 2 Corinthians 12:9.
8. Romans 5:5.
9. Matthew 5:6.
10. 1 Corinthians 15:28.
11. Revelation 4:10.
12. Matthew 6:1-23.
13. 2 Corinthians 12:7-9.
14. 1 Corinthians 1:27-29.
15. Matthew 6:3-4.
16. Matthew 6:19-20,24.
17. Matthew 6:19-20.
18. Matthew 6:21-22.

19. Luke. 21:1-4.

20. 2 Samuel 24:24; 1 Chronicles 22:14; 29:3.

21. Malachi 3:7b, 10.

22. Malachi 1:6-10.

23. Exodus 25:1-8.

24. Hebrews 6:10.

25. Matthew 6:6.

26. Matthew 6:5-13.

27. Matthew 24:36,42-44,50; 25:13; Mark 13:33-38; Luke 21:36; Revelation 3:3; 16:15.

28. Matthew 24:42; 25:13.

29. Matthew 5:44; 6:14

30. 1 Peter 2:23.

31. Matthew 6:17-18.

32. Psalm 109:24.

33. Matthew 11:11.

34. John 10:41.

35. 2 Corinthians 10:4-5.

36. Isaiah 58:6.

37. Ephesians 3:16-19.

38. Ephesians 1:17-18.

Chapter Nineteen

1. John 13:34-35; 1 John 4:20-21.

2. Matthew 5:17.

3. Ephesians 3:18-19.

4. 1 John 4:19.

5. John 17:26; Romans 5:5.

6. 2 Corinthians 5:17.

7. Psalm 139:13-17.

8. John 13:34-35; 1 John 3:18-19.

9. Matthew 22:39.

10. 1 John 4:19.

11. Romans 5:5.

12. Matthew 22:40.

13. Romans 13:8-10.

14. Romans 8:1.

15. 1 Timothy 1:5.

16. Matthew 7:12; Romans 13:8-10.

17. Matthew 7:7-12.

18. John 3:16-17.

19. John 3:18.

20. Romans 14:10-12; 2 Corinthians 5:10.

21. 1 Corinthians 3:10-15; 13:1-3.

22. 1 Corinthians 13:4-7.

23. 1 Corinthians 13:4a.

24. 1 Corinthians 13:4b-6b.

25. 1 Corinthians 13:6-7.

26. 1 Corinthians 13:8.

27. Hebrews 6:10.

28. 1 John 4:8,16.

29. C. Brand, C. Draper, A. England, S. Bond, E.R. Clendenen, T.C. Butler, and B. Latta, *Holman Illustrated Bible Dictionary* (Nashville, TN: Holman Bible Publishers, 2003), 780.

30. 1 Corinthians 13:13.

CHAPTER TWENTY

1. Romans 5:5.

2. John 15:4-5.

3. Psalm 91:14.

4. Luke 10:38-42.

5. Psalm 42:7.

6. Luke 10:42.

7. Psalm 18:1 NKJV; John 21:20 NKJV.

8. James 4:8.

9. 1 John 4:19.

10. Hebrews 4:12.

11. 1 John 3:1.

12. James 4:2.

13. Ephesians 3:18-19; Philippians 1:9.

14. Dr. Deere taught at Dallas Theological Seminary for 11 years. He is presently the senior pastor of Wellspring Church in North Richland Hills, Texas; http://wellspringdfw.org/.

15. *The Last Days* newsletter is published by Last Days Ministries; http://www.lastdaysministries.org/.

16. Dr. Jack Deere "Last Days Ministries"; http://www.lastdaysministries.com/mobile/default.aspx?group_id=1000068847&article_id=1000008597; accessed 12/16/10.

17. Psalm 18:19; John 21:7.

18. James 5:16; 1 John 1:7.

19. 2 Corinthians 6:14.

20. Matthew 16:13-17.

21. Matthew 16:21.

22. Matthew 16:23.

23. Matthew 16:23, *The Amplified Bible* (La Habra, CA: The Lockman Foundation and Grand Rapids, MI: Zondervan Publishing, 1987).

24. James 3:15.

25. James 3:15, *The Amplified Bible*.

26. James 3:15, *New International Readers Version* (Colorado Springs, CO: Biblica, 1996, 1998).

27. 1 John 2:15-16.

28. Acts 2:42.

29. 1 Corinthians 10:16.

30. 2 Corinthians 6:14.

31. 1 John 1:3.

32. 3 John 2 NKJV.

33. Proverbs 29:18.

34. 2 Corinthians 11:3.

35. Psalm 27:4.

36. 605–539 B.C. or 66 years.

37. Daniel 6:10 NKJV.

38. Zechariah 4:10 NKJV.

39. Mark 4:26-27.

CHAPTER TWENTY-ONE

1. Matthew 5:20.

2. John 14:15-23.

3. 1 John 5:3.

4. Matthew 5:48.

5. 1 John 1:7.

6. 1 John 2:1.

7. Psalm 36:9.

8. Hebrews 11:5.

9. Ronnie Hinson, of the Original Singing Hinsons.

10. Romans 14:10.

11. Matthew 25:21; Hebrews 11:5.

12. Psalm 19:12-13; 139:23-24; James 1:3-5.

13. 1 Corinthians 9:24-27.

14. Philippians 3:12.

15. Philippians 3:12-14.

16. 2 Timothy 4:8.

17. James 3:2.

18. Job 31:1.

19. Psalm 101:2-3.

20. 2 Corinthians 10:5-6.

21. Romans 5:3-5.

22. Colossians 2:10 NKJV.

23. Philippians 1:6; Colossians 4:12; 2 Timothy 3:17; James 2:22; Revelation 3:2.

24. Matthew 5:48; 19:21; John 17:23; Galatians 3:3; James 3:2; 1 Peter 5:10.

25. Ephesians 4:13; Philippians 3:15; 4:12; Colossians 1:28; 4:12.

26. Luke 1:6; Philippians 2:15; 1 Thessalonians 3:13; 5:23; 1 Timothy 3:10; 2 Peter 3:14.

27. Ephesians 5:27.

28. Matthew 10:37-38; 22:8; Luke 20:35; Ephesians 4:1; Philippians 1:27; Colossians 1:9-10; 1 Thessalonians 2:12; 2 Thessalonians 1:5,11; Revelation 3:4-5.

29. Luke 21:36; 1 Corinthians 16:13; Ephesians 6:10-14; Philippians 4:1; 1 Thessalonians 3:8; Revelation 6:17.

30. James 1:4.

31. Hebrews 13:20-21.

32. 1 Corinthians 1:6-8.

33. 1 Timothy 3:2; 5:5-7; 6:14.

34. 2 Corinthians 13:9-11; Colossians 1:28-29.

35. Philippians 1:6-10; 1 Thessalonians 3:10-13.

36. Colossians 4:12; Jude 24.

37. Matthew 19:20-21.

38. 1 John 4:12-18.

39. Matthew 5:3-4.

40. Exodus 34:14.

41. 1 Corinthians 3:12-15.

42. 2 John 8.

43. Hebrews 9:27.

44. 1 Corinthians 3:12-15.

45. Hebrews 2:1-3.

CHAPTER TWENTY-TWO

1. Luke 1:80.

2. Luke 3:2.

3. Mark 1:4.

4. Joel 2:8-29; Malachi 3:1-4; 4:5-6; Matthew 11:7-15.

5. Luke 3:16.

6. Mark 1:11.

7. Luke 3:21-22.

8. Mark 1:7.

9. John 3:28-31.

10. John 1:29,35-36.

11. John 1:34 H. Knowles, ed., *New English Bible* (Bible Society, 1990).

12. John 3:30.

13. Matthew 14:2-4.

14. Luke 7:20.

15. Luke 7:21-23.

16. Matthew 11:2-6.

17. Matthew 11:7-12.

18. John 2:14-20.

19. John 20:29.

20. 1 Chronicles 16:34.

21. 1 Chronicles 16:34,41; 2 Chronicles 5:13; 7:3,6; 20:21.

22. 2 Chronicles 20:20-22.

23. 1 Chronicles 16:34,41; 2 Chronicles 5:13; 7:3,6; 20:21; Ezra 3:11; Jeremiah 33:11; Psalm 52:1; 100:5; 106:1; 107:1; 117:2; 118:1-4,29; 138:8; 136:1-26.

24. Revelation 5:12.

25. Matthew 6:33.

26. Song 2:4; Romans 8:28.

27. Revelation 15:2-4.

28. Revelation 12:11; 13:6-7.

29. Genesis 3:1-5.

30. Luke 7:47.

31. Luke 17:7-10 NKJV.

32. Philippians 1:9-10.

33. Psalm 19:12-14.

34. Romans 11:32-34.

35. Matthew 24:10 NKJV and *Holman Christian Standard Bible* (Nashville, TN: Holman Bible Publishers, 1999, 2003).

36. Matthew 24:10-12.

37. Revelation 11:18.

38. Psalm 110:3.

39. FEAR—False Evidence Appearing Real

40. 2 Thessalonians 2:7.

41. Ephesians 2:4-7.

42. Revelation 22:11.

43. Revelation 15:2-4.

APPENDIX A: NOT MY WILL, BUT YOURS BE DONE

1. Luke 22:41-42.

2. Matthew 26:39.

3. Matthew 26:42.

4. Mark 14:36.

5. Hebrews 2:18.

6. Hebrews 4:15.

7. Colossians 2:9.

8. John 10:11,15.

9. John 15:13.

10. Matthew 16:21-23; Mark's account in Mark 8:31-33 adds that Jesus *"said this plainly."*

11. Luke 13:32-33.

12. Luke 24:25-26.

13. 1 Corinthians 15:1-4.

14. 1 Corinthians 2:2.

15. Luke 24:46-47.

16. Hebrews 7:26.

17. Matthew 26:37-38; Mark 14:33-34 combined.

18. Luke 22:44.

19. J.O. Buswell, *A Systematic Theology of the Christian Religion* (Grand Rapids, MI: Zondervan Publishing House, 1962 (vol. 1), 1963 (vol. 2) (bound together), II, 62-65.

20. Hebrews 5:7.

21. John 6:29.

22. John 5:19-21.

23. John 5:30.

24. John 5:36.

25. John 7:16-17.

26. John 7:18.

27. John 8:28-29.

28. Luke 9:48.

29. Matthew 11:27; Luke 10:22.

30. Matthew 20:23.

31. Luke 22:27b-29.

32. Hebrews 5:7.

33. Luke 22:43.

34. Matthew 26:45; Mark 14:41 combined.

35. Acts 2:23.

36. John 12:23-24,27.

In the right hands, This Book will Change Lives!

Most of the people who need this message will not be looking for this book. To change their lives, you need to put a copy of this book in their hands.

> But others (seeds) fell into good ground, and brought forth fruit, some a hundred-fold, some sixty-fold, some thirty-fold (Matthew 13:8).

Our ministry is constantly seeking methods to find the good ground, the people who need this anointed message to change their lives. Will you help us reach these people?

> Remember this—a farmer who plants only a few seeds will get a small crop. But the one who plants generously will get a generous crop (2 Corinthians 9:6).

EXTEND THIS MINISTRY BY SOWING
3 BOOKS, 5 BOOKS, 10 BOOKS, OR MORE TODAY,
AND BECOME A LIFE CHANGER!

Thank you,

Don Nori Sr., Publisher
Destiny Image
Since 1982

Endnotes